IT'S GAME TIME
SOMEWHERE

IT'S GAME TIME SOMEWHERE

How One Year, 100 Events, and 50 Different Sports Changed My Life

TIM FORBES

BASCOM HILL PUBLISHING GROUP

Bascom Hill Publishing Group
212 3rd Avenue North, Suite 290
Minneapolis, MN 55401
612.455.2293
www.bascomhillbooks.com

ISBN-13: 978-1-938008-12-2
LCCN: 2012948931

Distributed by Itasca Books

Book Design by Kristeen Ott

Printed in the United States of America

IN APPRECIATION

It would not have been possible to bring this book to you were it not for the generous backing of the project by the following people. I'd like to recognize and thank the members of my Kickstarter "coaching staff"…

Don Bortniak

Donald Chase III (Chamonix 2012)

Ken Fisher

Martha "Mae" Fox

Chris Kelly & Tamar Vezirian

Ken Kottke

Danette Kelley Smith

Joe & Evelyn Wieszbicki

CONTENTS

INTRODUCTION

AS MANY FAMOUS PEOPLE WILL TELL YOU, it's life *after* life in the wake of a major fork in the road that makes all the difference. OK, I just made that up. I don't, in fact, know any famous people, let alone much about their lives after major forks in their roads. We have *People* magazine for that sort of thing. But I do know me.

Let me begin by telling you that I've seen a ton of movies in my life, and I remember a lot of great scenes. Without question, though, the one that stands out as my all-time favorite is the one in which we meet Ray Kinsella, working in his cornfield in the opening moments of *Field of Dreams*. I dust off my VHS copy of that movie from time to time, just to hear Kevin Costner's voiceover of that scene: *I'm 36 years old, I love my family, I love baseball, and I'm about to become a farmer. But until I heard the voice, I'd never done a crazy thing in my whole life.*

I could relate—aside from the whole "become a farmer" thing, that is. I was just shy of Ray Kinsella's age when I first saw *Field of Dreams*, and I recall idly thinking, *I wonder if any crazy thing awaits me?* Little did I know at the time that *crazy thing* can turn out to be plural.

The story I'm about to tell you is actually two stories—both true, one of which would not have happened without the other. The first is about a guy who was just plain stuck, flailing around in his day-to-day life, all the while knowing that there was something else he was destined to do, someplace else he was meant to be. Getting from here to there, however, necessitated doing a *crazy thing*. So he did.

The second story begins as a cautionary tale, reminiscent of that dream that all kids have, in which they're accidentally locked in a candy factory overnight—only to discover that yes, there *is* such a thing as too much chocolate. Or at the very least, that it doesn't taste very good after a while. And consequently it turns out that the very same guy who had already done one *crazy thing* would feel he had no choice but to do another.

Being the clever reader that you are, you've no doubt figured out that chocolate is just a metaphor—in this case, for sports—and that "the guy" in this story-within-a-story happens to be yours truly. It's just quite possible, though, that you may see a bit of yourself in the following pages...

ONE

The Deal

I NOTICED IT WAS GETTING LATE, so I considered going outside to turn 40. Technically speaking, I wouldn't reach that age for another 10½ hours—I was a morning baby—but we always mark momentous days by the stroke of midnight, and I was not going to make an exception of this one.

More to the point, I also wanted to lock up the feeling that I had right then and there, because I knew I needed to harness the misery for future consideration and motivation.

Everyone imagines that their milestone birthdays will be memorable, spent with those they care most about. But as I glanced around the dimly lit room, all I saw were people I barely knew. And what I knew about them I didn't like. We were all in the employ of a prestigious consulting firm, to whom we had sold our souls for six-figure salaries and an attention-grabbing line on a résumé. It had seemed like such a good idea at the time.

But here we were on-site, in a cramped conference room that looked out on miles of aisles of cubicles. Dark cubicles, because every last one of our client's employees had long ago packed up and headed home. We were still grinding away, though, trying desperately to come up with a way to help our client improve profits and productivity, which is consultant-speak for trying to justify our humongous fee and score a renewal engagement in the bargain.

At 9:00, the fluorescent lights had dimmed automatically to save on energy. To my mind, it was a logical time to wrap things up; we could start fresh the next day. But I had clearly underestimated the sadistic tendencies of our team lead, whose name I vaguely remember as Attila the Hun—or something like that. I had only met him the previous day when we had assembled at the airport, and the word that had jumped immediately to mind was "zealot." He was not only drinking the firm's Kool-Aid, he was doing the backstroke in endless pools of it.

The thought of quitting "early," merely because it was too dark to see, was clearly a sign of weakness in Attila's mind. Instead he had us ransack cubicles in search of desk lamps that could be brought in to illuminate the conference room. The truly alarming thing was that I seemed to be the only one who thought that this was a little…umm…nonstandard. I didn't belong there. I hadn't belonged there in my thirties, and I *certainly* wouldn't belong there in another few hours when I entered my forties.

At 11:50, I got up to "stretch my legs" and headed out to the sterile chrome and glass lobby. Propping the door open behind me, I slipped into the crystal-clear darkness of the courtyard. It was February in the Northeast—cold and dry—and I looked up at an endless sky full of stars. I took a deep breath and muttered aloud, "What the hell am I doing here?" Had anyone been there to hear me, I'm pretty sure they would have figured out that by "here" I meant "in my life" and not "in a business park in suburban Philadelphia."

I pushed the button to light up my watch and saw the second hand making its final swing through the age of 39. At precisely midnight, I looked back up at the stars and said, "Happy freakin' birthday, Tim." More quietly, I added, "Only six more months until The Deal kicks in. I hope I can last."

* * *

The Deal was simple, and the day that my wife Cheryl, aka "The Bird" (don't ask—it involves a younger brother, the Boston Celtics, and too much alcohol one Christmas night), and I came up with it, it seemed like the most natural thing in the world. The cocktails at the pool might have had something to do with that.

At the time we were both "doing well" in career vernacular. As in, "They've both got nice cars, and I hear they just came back from ten days in Hawaii—they must be doing well." Truth be told, we were miserable. A life that consists mostly of trading lots of time for lots of money will do that to you.

Our circumstances were certainly not unique and probably not even unusual. Life up until that point had been about pursuing the opportunities that seemed the most economically promising at the time. We'd figure out the rest after we'd made our first million. Most everyone we knew had the same game plan. The economy was roaring, and as long as you didn't get too picky about whom you worked for or what you did on a daily basis, money pretty much *did* grow on trees.

The tragic flaw in the whole thing, though, was that we actually did care what we did on a daily basis. We'd simply stifled that nagging line of thought, although we both knew there was a reckoning coming. So I guess I shouldn't have been surprised when, right around that time, I found myself asking the same question almost every day: *How exactly did I get here?*

As Bill Cosby once said, I started out as a child. And in my case, a child inexorably drawn to sports. It is debated within my family whether or not I actually emerged from the womb with a copy of *Sports Illustrated* tucked under my arm, but what's certain is that I grew up chasing a ball.

It didn't matter what size or shape the ball was—I chased them all. I was fortunate enough to have come of age in a time when *kids themselves* scheduled their own games and "officiated" them via the kids' code of sports ethics—an arcane collection of arguments, declarations, and insults that inevitably led to the do-over. Or somebody taking their ball and going home.

On those occasions when a quorum wasn't available for even the most streamlined of games, I played them solo. Not only did I play them, I announced them. Each game was what ESPN would now call an "Instant Classic," always coming down to a single shot, throw, swing, etc., with yours truly providing the heroics on an eerily consistent basis. And a funny thing happened on the way to winning all of those backyard and driveway epics. I got pretty skilled, especially at basketball. Hey, after you've won countless imaginary world championships single-handedly, the real thing is cake.

And so it came to be that I went to college on a basketball scholarship. Annoyingly enough, they don't let you just major in Basketball—well, not in 1977, anyway. So I chose to pursue a degree in Psychology...for no particular reason. And when my undergraduate days ended, I decided to obtain an MBA, because...well...because.

Master's degree in hand, for no particularly compelling reason, I became a grown-up. I was never really good at it, though. My heart just wasn't in it.

Fortunately, my employers never caught on to this, and slowly but surely I climbed the corporate ladder. What is it they say about a rising tide and all boats? I got up every morning and went to work, where I arrived early and stayed late. I traveled heavily and never complained about it—well, not in the office, anyway. I kept up with industry trends, used the right buzzwords, and did my best to avoid entrapment in office politics. But after many years of this charade, my greatest career achievement wasn't one that appeared anywhere on my résumé. I speak, of course, of mastering the art of stretching six disinterested hours of work into nine each day.

And on top of it all, I struggled continually to protect a dirty little secret: I am a Game Junkie.

You kindred spirits need no additional explanation, but please bear with me while I explain myself to others. In a nutshell, Game Junkies are those who, from birth, love athleticism and competition and the vague euphoria of kinesthetic movement so much that they make almost *everything* into a game or contest. It is our destiny. Our lot in life. Consider the following:

Several years back, The Bird and I were on vacation with another couple. We had rented a house near the beach on Nantucket and had fallen into a nice pattern of lazy mornings, afternoons along the shoreline, and extended cocktailing at night. I had brought along on the trip a small football that almost *anyone* could immediately grip and throw with an Elway-esque spiral. It absolutely begged to be tossed back and forth.

On one particularly sun-drenched morning, the girls volunteered to go into town to pick up groceries and other liquid necessities. Assuring us they'd be back in time for the daily beach ritual, they assigned us the mundane tasks of packing the cooler and then the car. Simple stuff. Wouldn't take but 20 minutes. So of course we procrastinated. Out came the football, and the tossing began. Leisurely at first, separated by maybe 20 feet in the backyard. Just talking and tossing, tossing and talking—getting into a nice languid rhythm. Then gradually backing up. Then running mock pass routes. Working on a sweat. And by the time the girls returned home to a still unpacked cooler and car, we were throwing high, arching passes blindly over the house to each other, in search of the highlight-reel reception. I still have a small scar on my leg from diving (OK, falling) into the rose bushes.

The girls were not amused.

If that story makes perfect sense to you, then (with apologies to Jeff Foxworthy) you might just be a Game Junkie. And just to be sure, take this little test. Ask yourself, "Why have people for centuries done things like throw a football over a house to a friend?" If the obvious answer that comes to mind is, "Because he'll throw it back!" you, my friend, are certifiably a Game Junkie. We share the same DNA.

The tragic thing is that, while Game Junkies grow older, we never fully grow *up*. The whole "make a living and become a contributing member of society" thing really cuts into the time available to chase a ball ourselves, so we live vicariously through others who have perfected the art of doing so. We morph into Sports Fans.

In my case, as I fraudulently stumbled through my workaday life, televised sports provided the soundtrack of my existence. A movie of my life would have to include subtitles for the never-ending stream of assorted sports frames of reference. I still can, on demand, tell you who won every single Super Bowl ever played. I can tell you the winner of the last 37 (and counting) NCAA Final Fours. Name a year since 1967, and I can tell you the winners and losers of that year's World Series. I've occasionally considered renting myself out for parties.

As far as I know, I'm not a savant. Quite simply, these events were a huge part of the fabric of my life. I marked the passage of time—where I was living, what job I was working, and who I was with—by recalling those games. In contrast, during my years of wandering through Corporate America, recalling the name of my current company's CEO was a brainteaser requiring some considerable effort.

I tried. I really, *really* tried to compartmentalize, as I saw so many of my coworkers do. They kept their job in an "8 AM to 6 PM, Monday through Friday" box and focused on their real interests in the remaining hours. I was envious of that skill and longed to replicate it. But I just…couldn't. And it became increasingly difficult to block out the siren song: "Perhaps there's a way to merge my job with my personal interests…?"

About the time that I joined the soul-crushing consulting company that would eventually send me—and Attila the Hun—to Philadelphia on my 40th birthday, I became vaguely aware that folks were beginning to attend college to earn a degree in something called Sports Management. And evidently upon graduation they were—get this—*getting paid to work in sports!* This represented a cruel irony to me, for neither Psychology nor Business Administration would have entered the matriculation conversation had Sports Management been an academic option when I entered college.

Having discovered the existence of what was rightfully *my* chosen field of work, I spent the next several months alternating between a state of agitation over having been born a decade too early and thoughtful rumination on how I could still pull off a second-half rally and transition to my natural calling.

Which brings me back to The Deal.

I was not the only member of the household who was flopping around professionally. Although The Bird came of age before Title IX and the subsequent explosion of opportunities for girls to play organized sports, she has the soul of a Game Junkie, nonetheless. It simply manifests itself in a different way. She is a purposeful striver, with a goal assigned to everything she does—even if she has to make up that goal. In the world of The Bird, there is a scoreboard to which only she is privy, and as spring turned to summer in the year of The Deal, as far as she was concerned, she was losing more often than not. It was her considered opinion that she was wasting her time running the back-office operations of a financial-services company. She wasn't challenged. And that would never do.

It was a lazy Sunday morning, and I was slowly working my way through the newspaper in the usual manner: sports section…everything else. And cleverly positioned within that sports section was an ad for an open house at Wake Forest University's Babcock School of Management. They had recently opened a satellite campus near our home in Charlotte and were unveiling a new MBA program. If it was a challenge she wanted, a graduate degree from a Southern Ivy school would certainly fit the bill.

I presented the concept. The Bird was intrigued. We went to the open house, just a few blocks away. The Bird was hooked. So we did what we normally did when we had something momentous to discuss: we filled a cooler and went to the pool.

It was never a question of whether she would do it—it was more a matter of logistics. The program was of the evenings-and-weekends variety, set up to enable students to work full-time and progress toward their degrees simultaneously. Masochistic students, that is. The difficulty in pulling this off had been somewhat soft-sold during the open house, but I knew the real story.

Prior to meeting The Bird, I had done the second half of my own MBA at night. In a word, it was brutal. Life had been limited strictly to work, school, and sleep, with the last coming solely on a best-efforts basis. Even with that level of sacrifice, the program took years, because I was only able to schedule two or three classes per semester. This would be no way to live for either of us, no matter how many Bird points for stamina were on the table.

We talked about it. We had another cocktail. We went for a swim. We talked some more. We had another cocktail. And as everyone else at the pool began to pack up and head home, a plan started to emerge. "What if you quit your job, worked just part-time, and took a full load of classes every semester?" I ventured.

A long silence. This was a revolutionary idea for someone whose work ethic made James Brown on stage look like a slacker. Finally, "Can we afford that?"

The fact of the matter was that we could, but it wouldn't be without some sacrifice. We talked through some of the specifics, and each scenario that emerged did indeed include some significant forfeiture of lifestyle— mostly for me. And being the "what's fair is fair" type that she is, The Bird wasn't buying any of it. "Why should you suffer for the next two years while I enjoy a life-changing experience?" she said.

More silence. "How about this," I said. "Once you have your MBA and are all set up in a good job, it will be my turn. I want to work in the sports business. I don't exactly know how I'm going to make that happen, but I'm pretty sure it'll involve a huge step backward financially. Then the sacrificing will be yours."

And as the last bit of sunshine retreated from the pool deck and twilight announced itself with a chilly breeze, The Bird turned to me and smiled. "It's a deal."

As the great philosopher Tom Petty once said, "The waiting is the hardest part."

The Deal was in place. In the days that followed our poolside summit, The Bird and I had fleshed out the concept and test-marketed it with some close friends. Thumbs-up all around. Evidently, we hadn't been doing as well as we had thought in concealing our general dissatisfaction with our vocational lives. "You two have been like fish flopping around on the end of a dock," was one particularly evocative comment.

Normally I might compare my life over the following two years to that of a seven-year-old awaiting Christmas. But that would be unfair to seven-year-olds, who, in comparison to yours truly at that time, display the patience of Job.

Batting leadoff in this grand experiment, The Bird had the easy part. At least it seemed that way to me. Only a short period of time elapsed between the birth of The Deal and her activation of it. In fairly rapid order, she took her GMAT, applied for admission and was accepted, and told her employers exactly what they could do with their job. In the nicest possible way, of course. She started school in the fall and never looked back. I doubt that Wake Forest University will ever be the same.

As for me, in addition to the two-year waiting period, I had to wrestle with the tiny detail of figuring out exactly how I was going to execute my part of The Deal when the time came. I knew I'd be ready to charge out of the gate, but to where? This may come as a shock to you, but there's no blueprint for exactly how to walk away from Corporate America and into the sports business. I didn't have anyone to consult. And if I had, how would I have phrased the opening question? "Excuse me, but I'm looking to throw sanity and financial security out the window so that I can follow a passion and go to work in sports. Can you suggest some logical first steps?"

So I did what I would normally do when looking for a new job. I inventoried my skills, identified organizations that might benefit from my transferring these skills (plus more than ten years of work experience) into their line of business, and went about contacting them to see if they might be hiring. Ask any career counselor, and they'll frame out a career-change strategy that looks more or less like mine.

As it turns out, though, the whole conversation lies much more within the domain of an economist, what with their expertise in the area of supply and demand. I learned pretty quickly that, at any given time, the number of interested candidates for each decent-paying job in the sports world hovers somewhere between 1,459,239 and infinity. Evidently, people don't just "transfer over" into the sports industry. In fact, regardless of your title and status in the "real world," you have three available options: (1) Become a world-class athlete; (2) Marry into a family that owns a sports franchise; or (3) Start at the bottom, put your ego in long-term storage, and be prepared to work your tail off.

It was a tad too late for me to pull off option #1, and The Bird would undoubtedly have quibbled over the use of option #2, so for me it boiled down to option #3. I wasn't averse to paying my dues with hard work, but I was more or less clueless about identifying which entry-level jobs would lead to a career and which would lead to a dead end.

As the months went by and The Bird immersed herself in her schooling, I mulled this over on a more or less continual basis. And as I think I may have mentioned previously, I turned 40. The whole concept started receding like the tide back into the ocean, slowly taking my enthusiasm with it. In fact, I might have bagged it entirely if I weren't haunted by the specter of what life would be like at 50…or 60…if I were still trading time for money and watching the world that I ached to be a part of pass by me every time I went to a game or turned on the television.

Then one day, I turned a page—quite literally—and the answer was right there.

One of my clients had taken out an ad in the hyperglossy *PGA Tour Yearbook* that was published annually in the predigital days. Knowing that I was a sports fan, she passed along a complimentary copy to me. I was in the process of devouring it when I came across an advertisement for the Professional Golfers Career College. Its message was simple and direct: "How would you like to earn a living in the golf industry?"

Well, now that you ask, I'd like that quite a bit.

You see, golf and I had a history. At the age of 13 I had taken my first job—as a caddie at Ellington Ridge Country Club. My friend Chris Benincasa had heard one day that they were hiring. So I went with him to check it out, because it was a fairly short bike ride away and…well…because I had nothing better to do that day. Truth be told, I had no interest in golf at the time. In fact, up to that point my only connection to the game was when somebody, for reasons unknown, left a sizable box full of golf balls in my driveway one day. I had been absolutely thrilled to come home from school and discover this, for golf balls travel a long distance when struck with a baseball bat. And this particular box of golf balls provided several afternoons full of amusement as I walloped one prodigious blast after another into the woods. But to actually take up the game of golf? The thought had never occurred to me. Until I started caddying.

At first I was simply enthralled with the concept that, at the end of four or five hours of walking around a park with a bag on my back, somebody would hand me a wad of cash. After a while, though, I actually started to pay attention to the game that was being played. And when the school year ended, my friends and I decided to take advantage of the mother of all fringe benefits—Monday Play Day. Like most private clubs, the golf course at Ellington Ridge was closed to members on Mondays. But any caddie who had looped the previous weekend was "welcome" to play. Until noon, anyway.

I don't remember how I got my hands on the set of golf clubs that I used on that first Monday of my golf career, but I do recall wishing I hadn't hit those 2,569 free golf balls into the woods with a 31-inch Louisville Slugger. In just one round I became hooked, despite shooting somewhere north of 150 for 18 holes. It was the beginning of a beautiful relationship.

I was naturally blessed with good hand-eye coordination, and as a kid I considered spending hours and hours practicing a sport to be the very embodiment of fun. So proficiency at sports came pretty easily to me at that age. With golf, though…not so much. As Jim Nantz tells us in a syrupy voice every April, golf is a challenge "unlike any other." I became enthralled by that challenge.

There was also the scent of golf. To this day, I can smell healthy, freshly watered sod a mile away. That's what morning and evening smell like on a golf course. The afternoon smells like cut grass, with hints of suntan lotion and the soft leather of a new golf glove. And don't even get me *started* on the serenity of a golf course.

I caddied at Ellington Ridge for several years, and throughout that time, it never occurred to me that people were actually employed there on a full-time basis. Yes, I saw people actively engaged in maintaining the paradise and managing the activity that took place there, but I guess I thought they did it in their spare time. As a hobby, perhaps. With the help of elves.

But years later, here was this educational institution that paired the word *golf* with the word *career*. The ad for the Professional Golfers Career College plainly stated that it was possible to work in golf and that they would be thrilled to show me exactly how this could be achieved. This was a revelation. I felt like Alexander Graham Bell during that first phone call: "Tom Watson, come here, I need you," so to speak.

There was a hitch, though. This school was located in Southern California. The Bird and I were comfortably located in North Carolina. Commuting to class was probably out of the question. Now, as much as I loved Charlotte, I would've moved to Sri Lanka to pursue what looked to be a dream career-change scenario. It occurred to me, however, that The Bird might feel differently.

Only partially deterred, I contacted the college for an information package, which I subsequently read from cover to cover. Three times. It looked like the real deal, and my pulse began to quicken every time I envisioned myself on campus. But there was no getting around the fact that I would eventually have to introduce to The Bird the concept of relocation. She would probably take notice if I just suddenly began to pack up the house, and there would undoubtedly be problems with luring her into the car for a six-day drive under the guise of "Let's go get some ice cream." I was going to have to take the much more traditional route of calmly presenting the concept to her and asking for her thoughts on the matter. After all, I reasoned, we had The Deal. It was just a matter of finding the right time to remind her of this.

I wrote a script and incorporated it into a PowerPoint presentation. I role-played, using Betty the Cat as my test audience. I made a list of concessions to toss on the negotiating table at the appropriate point. I practiced falling to my knees and begging. You know, all of the basics. And on a sultry June evening at the end of The Bird's final semester of school, I made my initial pitch.

Her reply? "OK, let's do it."

"Excuse me?" I had barely finished my presentation. My list of concessions was untouched. The begging hadn't begun.

"Let's go out there and check it out. You can visit the school, and I can line up some job interviews while we're there." She walked over to the computer, sat down, and started to search job boards for listings in Southern California. I, in turn, retrieved my jaw from where it lay on the floor.

Three weeks later we were checking in to the Hyatt Hotel in La Jolla—just down the road from Torrey Pines Golf Course, for those interested in that kind of thing. We'd arrived in Los Angeles late the night before and then made the long drive to our hotel in Temecula, the home of the Professional Golfers Career College. I was just starting to come down from the adrenaline high that had been the result of my meeting at the college that morning, and The Bird was burnt out from researching and preparing for the three interviews she'd lined up over the next two days.

We were exhausted. Fortunately, all of the travel that I'd done for the benefit of Attila the Hun and his colleagues had given me something like Beluga Caviar status with Hyatt, and we had been upgraded to a suite that looked out over a stunning vista.

"How can we *not* do this?" I asked quietly as we stood and stared out the window.

"We did make a deal, after all," came the reply.

And so began my career in sports.

TWO

Pro Golf's Oldest Living Intern

IT WAS PARADISE FOUND.

Those who have ever stopped to look around themselves and been motivated to say out loud, "Life couldn't possibly get any better than this," shared at that moment what I experienced over the next 16 months.

You know that awkward transitional stage you go through when you relocate to a place about which you know nothing? The uncomfortable feeling you get when you confront the notion that you've uprooted yourself and moved thousands of miles to somewhere where you know not a soul? If you do, you'll have to describe it to me someday—because it took just about eight and a half minutes for The Bird and me to fall in love with our new life.

This was the middle of the dot-com boom days, and San Diego had acquired a reputation as "Silicon Beach." There were scores of smart people who had acquired start-up funding on a good idea but knew nothing about how to create and run an actual company. Enter The Bird, with her ten years of operational expertise and her brand-new MBA. Her job search didn't last long, and before we had even arrived in California, her new employer was clamoring for her to start work ASAP. Which, having found her niche, she was more than happy to do.

My own state of mind couldn't quite accurately be described as "happy." It was more like "consumed with spasmodic episodes of ecstasy, separated by lengthy periods of quiet bliss." Things were pretty good, in other words.

California agreed with us, to put it mildly. We set up housekeeping in Carlsbad, a coastal town roughly 35 miles north of downtown San Diego. The Bird's office was less than two miles away, as was the beach. We made new friends quickly and took full advantage of the fact that the Golden State is basically one big outdoor playground to romp around in. And every weekday morning, I arose and made the 40-minute drive to Temecula, with a smile plastered on my face the entire time.

The Professional Golfers Career College was everything that I thought it would be—and then some. I was pursuing a somewhat nonstandard educational path, which had started with a bachelor's degree, progressed through a master's degree, and was now culminating in…an associate's degree. An associate's degree in Professional Golf Management, to be precise. I bet you didn't know that existed—or that thousands of people roaming the very same planet that you do carry that credential.

I expected two things: First, that I would be one of the oldest students at the school. Second, that much of the academic material would be a little pedestrian. I was more or less on target with that first assumption, but I was pleasantly surprised to find at least a handful of similarly "mature" (chronologically, anyway) students who, like me, were in search of a meaningful career change.

It was on that second assumption that I missed the mark wildly. To be blunt about it, going into the experience I viewed PGCC enrollment as a more or less financial transaction. In exchange for tuition, I would gain access to a giant rolodex—and thus a way to circumvent the process of breaking into and quickly moving up the ranks of the golf industry. The teachers and administrators at the school were all industry veterans, many with connections throughout the world of golf. My thinking went along these lines: *Shut up about having to attend entry-level business classes again, do the work without getting cocky, pull straight A's, and invest time getting to know those who possess the widest network of industry associates.* Frankly, I didn't anticipate learning anything new.

To my unexpected delight, I was wrong.

Yes, some of the prerequisite classes were tough to sit through. But the specialized classes that followed were eye-opening. The material was very specific to the golf industry, about which my lack of knowledge was humbling. Rather than coasting through to get a ticket punched on the Rolodex Express, I found myself challenged by the material and the coursework. And somewhere along the line it struck me that all I'd done in my previous career was talk a good ballgame about running a business. I'd never actually gotten my hands dirty. Part of that was due to the nature of Corporate America, where a nice suit and a vocabulary full of the latest buzzwords often substitute for actual productivity. But most of it was due to the fact that my heart was never fully into anything I had done previously. With golf, not only did I *want* to get my hands dirty, I couldn't wait to start rolling around in huge, hulking *piles* of dirt.

And as if that weren't enough, we got to play golf! Every day, if we wanted to! In fact, for the first three semesters, we were *required* to play in a schoolwide tournament each week, ostensibly to bond with our classmates and future industry colleagues. Professional instruction was free for the asking. As were all the range balls we could possibly want to hit. For the first time in my golf-playing life I was taught the proper mechanics of the golf swing, a process that revealed to me exactly *why* my game was so crappy. When I began the PGCC program, I was the worst golfer in the school. But by the time I graduated…well, I was still the worst golfer in the school—let's not get ridiculous here. You can't get blood from a stone.

It was late in my first semester that I got the opportunity to work my first professional event. Kent Brown, one of the deans of the college came into class one morning and announced that the organizers of the Inland Empire Classic, a stop on the Buy.com (now Nationwide) Tour, had approached the college about recruiting volunteers to help stage the tournament. Intrigued, I stopped by Kent's office after class to learn more. That conversation turned out to be life-changing.

It turned out that, in addition to the standard volunteer roles that need to be filled by every tournament organizing committee (marshals, scorers, etc.), there was one opening for a far meatier role. The tournament's director of operations needed an assistant for the week. It entailed a good bit of grunt work, to be sure, and it would require a long drive and an even longer workday. But for one full week I would be exposed to nearly every aspect of staging a professional golf tournament. I was granted excused absences from all of my classes that week, even the required golf tournament—for once, somebody else would have to finish last.

I don't recall the name of the director of operations of the Buy.com Inland Empire Classic. Or of the tournament's director, for that matter. But I remember everything else about the experience as if it were yesterday: The manicured beauty of Empire Lakes Golf Course. The magnificence of Mt. Baldy as it stared down at me from the nearby San Gabriel Mountains. The breathtaking clarity of the blue sky, under which I worked like a joyful stevedore—assuming such a thing exists, that is.

One of the first things we did was "rope and stake" the course. Anyone who has ever been to a golf tournament recognizes the ubiquitous yellow ropes that frame the course and separate the galleries from the golfers. I'd hazard a guess, however, that few people ever wonder about the process by which those ropes come to occupy the space that they do—or how many stakes are required to keep those ropes taut and looking sharp. I'm here to tell you that it takes 4,786,239,010 individual stakes—give or take—each of which has to be pounded into the ground to just the right depth.

At most PGA Tour events, an entire crew of people well versed in doing so will stake and string rope around a course in no time at all. At this particular Buy.com Tour event, though, the "crew" consisted of me and a couple of retirees who lasted a few hours on the first day before remembering precisely why they enjoyed being retired. The problem was this: Empire Lakes Golf Course was built upon arid ground that had been baked hard by years of plentiful sunshine and little rain. During construction of the course, the fairways, greens, and other playing areas had been cultivated and covered with several inches of pristine turf. It was easy to drive stakes into these areas. A few decent taps with a small sledgehammer would do the trick. But most of the ropes we were installing were set up to keep people *off* of the playing areas, and thus the vast majority of stakes had to be driven into ground that more closely resembled concrete. This required three or four full wind-ups and blows with a full-sized sledge. For each stake.

After the second day of roping and staking, I awoke in the middle of the night vaguely aware of the fact that my hands had fallen off of my arms. At least that was what it felt like. The repeated impact of sledgehammer on stake had jangled the muscles and nerve endings in my hands to such an extent that I had no feeling from my elbows down. This concerned me.

By the time I got to the course that morning, the forces of gravity and Motrin had combined to restore some measure of circulation to my hands, but I mentioned my predicament to my boss nonetheless. "Oh yeah, that's why I have work gloves with special cushioning," he said. Thanks for the heads-up.

One might imagine that, at this point, the bloom would have been off the rose—that the novelty of working behind the scenes at a professional golf tournament would have worn off and that I would have been looking forward to getting back onto the less painful side of those yellow ropes. One would have been wrong.

I reveled in that week, and despite having to rise at 4:00 AM to get to the course on time each morning, I was always awake before the alarm clock sounded. The long hours of working side-by-side with my boss gave me the opportunity to ask tons of questions, and he was more than willing to answer each and every one of them. It was a one-week crash course in tournament operations, and by the time it was over, I was hooked. When I returned to the college the next week, the first thing I did was visit Kent Brown. "I want very badly to work on the tour side of the business," I said. "Anything that you can do to help would be greatly appreciated."

"I can't promise anything, but I'll see what I can do," he replied.

A few weeks later, Kent caught me in the hallway between classes.

"There's somebody I think you should meet," he began. "Last year we had some students volunteer at the Match Play. I've heard that, since that time, they've revamped the management staff of the event, and there may be an opportunity for some longer-term work. If you're interested, I could make a call."

The "Match Play" was the WGC-Accenture Match Play Championship, which was not only a PGA Tour event but one of the four tournaments that at the time made up the uber-exclusive World Golf Championships. Outside of professional golf's "majors," no other tournament drew a better field of players or got higher television ratings than the Match Play. And it's probably worth mentioning that it was played at La Costa Resort & Spa—a mere driver and a solid four-iron from my Carlsbad home.

Yes, Kent. I am, in fact, interested.

Mike Garten was the Executive Director of the WGC-Accenture Match Play Championship. But more important, he was, in a nutshell… me—but with one major differentiating characteristic. He had possessed the sense to realize at a young age that one could actually make a living working in sports, and he had gone about doing so right out of the gate. He was years younger than me, but by the time we met, he had already done a stint in the athletic department at USC before being recruited by the NBA to head up their fledgling special events department. After several successful years in New York, the opportunity arose for Mike to return to his native California to run the Match Play. Let's just say he didn't need to be asked twice.

The interview that Kent had set up for me was actually with Jeannette Crobarger, Mike's right arm and a World Golf Championships veteran. Jeannette was crisp and businesslike, yet friendly and patient with what probably seemed to be an exorbitant number of questions.

During the course of our conversation, I learned that the PGA Tour had recently decided to streamline the operations of the WGC division by creating a SWAT team that would manage the early build-out stages of each

WGC tournament from a centralized office at Tour headquarters in Florida. Then, several weeks prior to the beginning of each event, this group would gradually, person by person, take up full-time residence on-site and remain throughout tournament week, before heading off to the next event.

Since the four WGC tournaments were sufficiently spaced apart in the Tour schedule, it was possible to pull off this rotating dynamic, assuming that there was some modicum of assistance at each tournament site to help the full-time dedicated staff keep things rolling during the months in which the operations SWAT team was otherwise occupied elsewhere.

I was interviewing for the role of "modicum of assistance"—otherwise known as "intern." The oldest intern in the storied history of the PGA Tour, I'm guessing.

Prior to this reorganization, the Match Play had employed a full-time operations director based in the La Costa office. That was no longer the case. In essence, the challenge handed down to Mike Garten by the Tour had been to find a way to replace an experienced full-time employee with someone to fill in the gaps until the folks from Florida rotated into the picture. Without spending any money.

It was just about this time that Kent Brown called the Match Play office to talk about somebody at the college who was interested in the professional tour side of the golf industry. It was a match made in heaven. Jeannette, being the consummate professional that she was, though, wasn't tipping her hand during our meeting. "I'll talk with Mr. Garten and get back to you," she said. At which point, almost on cue, he arrived in the office.

An hour later we were still at it. Two sports fans having discovered a kindred spirit. We talked about golf, basketball, baseball, the experience of playing a college sport. We even touched briefly on the topic at hand, i.e. me coming to work for him. Mike's last words to me as I was leaving were, "I'm sure we'll be talking again soon." I'm pretty sure that as I was getting in my car, Jeannette was giving him a good-natured chiding for being such a transparent pushover.

The financial package offered to me was fairly straightforward: the lack of a salary of any kind would be supplemented by a nonexistent collection of benefits. Mike gave it to me straight, as he would do for the entire time that I worked for him. "We're going to get far more from you than you'll get from us," he told me matter-of-factly. He was an honorable guy, and he felt that he owed it to me to at least put it on the table that the golf tour business in general, and the PGA Tour specifically, was the home office of exploitation.

But while there was nothing like remuneration or health-care coverage or a 401(k) in the offing, there were two much more important benefits: experience and exposure.

While I had received a fire-hose education about tournament-week operations during my time at the Buy.com Inland Empire Classic, over the course of the next year I gained valuable know-how in almost every aspect of creating the foundation upon which a professional golf tournament is based. Supporting the efforts of the tournament staff, I was involved in membership ticket sales, sponsorship prospecting, budgeting, special-events management, procurement—you name it. All while cranking through my degree program at PGCC. I was getting about a decade's worth of knowledge and experience in the course of just one year. It was exactly what I needed to make up for the time that I'd lost while wandering through fluorescent-lit corridors and conference rooms.

Shortly before graduation, Mike called me into his office. "You're getting a raise," he smiled. The WGC operations staff had begun their rotation into La Costa, and with them came additional budget, which just happened to include a stipend for a full-time event-staff member. I was to become a PGA Tour employee. Of sorts.

The job was to last only through the end of the tournament's breakdown and cleanup period, and there was no guarantee that I would be offered continued employment by the Tour after that—my job title, after all, would still be *Intern*. But I would be paid, albeit an amount that, if broken down into an hourly equivalent, would have worked out to about $0.09 per hour. But I would meet at least some of the movers and shakers from Tour HQ.

In the weeks that followed, I witnessed nothing less than a small town being built on the grounds of the La Costa Resort & Spa. The space that I had occupied in the condominium housing the tournament's office was given over to the advancing staff from Florida, and I moved to a desk in the tournament operations trailer, where I was to support the build-out efforts of the WGC operations staff. And I became much more of what typically comes to mind when one hears the word "intern": a gofer. Yes, that's *gofer*—not *golfer.*

It was ironic that during the time that I was *not* being paid, I had been entrusted with responsibilities of some substance, but once I was on the payroll, I became simply a manual laborer awaiting instruction. But I had been bitten badly by the bug, and I was up for pretty much anything I was asked to do. After all, word was that the PGA Tour had a habit of drawing largely from its pool of interns when the need arose to add to full-time staff.

In fact, the whole intern-to-employee system worked like a charm for all concerned, unless the rare eventuality of a hiring freeze or the *really* unlikely scenario of an actual downsizing cropped up. But the PGA Tour was growing rapidly at that point in time, and it would take something truly unforeseeable—something completely out of the blue—to trigger either of those staffing scenarios.

The world's best golfers were on the driving range at Bellerive Country Club in St. Louis when the planes flew into the Twin Towers on September 11, 2001. It was the week of the WGC-American Express Championship, which had brought big-time tournament golf back to a golf-starved market. It had cost a fortune to build out the Amex Championship, but that was OK with the PGA Tour, because the event had been sold out to the hilt months before the first tee shot was to be struck. Every ticket, every corporate tent, every pro-am spot had gone for top dollar.

A significant number of those top dollars were refunded when the tournament was cancelled at literally the last minute. As for the expenses incurred in creating the tournament site, many of those bills had already been paid, and the Tour wound up honoring almost all of those that had yet to be submitted. And in a show of patriotism, the Tour kicked in a seven-figure donation to the recovery effort.

I wasn't privy to the actual number-crunching, but my razor-sharp mind for accounting told me that the PGA Tour had taken a financial bath. So it was little wonder that, not too long after that, a hiring freeze was put in place. Then, several existing positions were selectively evaluated and ultimately eliminated. Like that, for example, of Kathy Anderson, the Director of Sales and Marketing for the Match Play Championship—one of my mentors and advocates.

Suffice to say, the timing wasn't exactly optimal for yours truly to strike up a meaningful conversation about a budding career with the PGA Tour. To their credit, they did put me through the interview process at Tour headquarters and had nothing but nice things to say about the work that I had done. But when those proceedings concluded with an "of course we'll be happy to provide you with glowing references," the writing on the wall appeared in indelible ink.

After having spent almost a year and a half living and breathing tour golf, it was hard for me to conceive of doing anything else. And I'd be lying if I said that I didn't spend many a sleepless night ruminating about the injustice of the whole situation—trying desperately to rationalize it. But in the grand scheme of things, my lost opportunity to work full-time for the PGA Tour was a flyspeck compared to the loss suffered by so many others as a result of the 9/11 attacks. For me it was simply one of those times in life that you have to suck it up and move on.

Corporate refugee-turned-world's oldest intern, I was faced with reinventing myself once again. Fortunately for me, the old saying about one door closing and another one opening turned out to be more than a cliché. The financial circumstances that had brought an end to my time at the Match Play Championship, and which so negatively impacted the economy in general in the post-9/11 days, served to create opportunities in a roundabout way.

Two months prior to working out the string on my final PGA Tour event, I had proudly delivered the valedictorian address at my graduation from PGCC. At the time, I had said to my classmates that their degrees in Professional Golf Management would eventually take them to places they probably hadn't yet considered. Little did I know at the time that I was also addressing myself. For while I was busy scheming like a madman on a strategy for staying within the tour side of the industry, the facility-management side of the golf world came calling.

These were the post-boom days in the golf course business. A now-infamous study commissioned in the late 1980s by the National Golf Foundation had declared that, "There are not enough golf courses in the country, and you could build a golf course a day through 2000 and still not have enough for supply and demand." Not so much, it turned out.

The supply of new golf courses exploded over the next decade. Demand for the use of those golf courses…did not. So simply mowing the fairways, opening the pro shop doors, and rolling out the range balls no longer qualified as a growth strategy. While the industry still struggled with the idea of interlopers, grudging acceptance had begun to emerge of the need for people with both the proper perspective about the unique business of golf *and* objective business acumen acquired in the "outside world." My prior years of corporate experience, coupled with my newly minted degree, had put me in a unique position.

And meanwhile, back at the ranch, other winds of change were blowing.

If there is such a thing as a *fortunate* stroke of bad luck, The Bird and I experienced it in the spring of 2002. The continued economic fallout from the 9/11 attacks had merged with the swelling dot-com bubble at just about the same time that opportunities unraveled for me at the PGA Tour—consequently leaving The Bird's job fortunes as imperiled as mine. Being the accomplished reader of tea leaves that she is, however, The Bird saw what was coming and created an opportunity to engineer her own tidy exit strategy before the walls came crashing down upon her Internet-based company.

On top of that, we were in the right place at the right time, real-estate-wise, and found ourselves in position to receive a nice windfall on the sale of our Carlsbad condo. *Poof*—we were both unencumbered *and* possessed of a comfortable rainy day fund.

Just as I'd told my fellow graduates, my PGCC credentials were about to take me to places I hadn't yet considered—namely Tennessee and then Florida, where I would become perhaps the golf industry's least likely general manager. My diabolical plan for infiltrating the golf business, while slightly diverted, was officially back on track.

My subsequent years as a golf course GM were among the most challenging, stressful…and rewarding of my life. I was finally able to put to work the abstract principles of business that I'd learned but never had the opportunity to practice during my previous career. And to do so each day surrounded by the physical beauty of a golf course and the high spirits of people who had left their worries elsewhere in the pursuit of play was life-affirming. It was also humbling and a bit overwhelming at times, when I stopped to think about the level of responsibility that I carried. For the first time in my life, I was the boss, a concept that I sometimes found unsettling. In my private thoughts I preferred to consider my role as that of "sports host," charged with creating the best possible experience at all times for my guests.

But throughout those years I still had the itch for tournament golf. And I knew that the itch could only be scratched by returning to a life of event production. It's a lifestyle for which people are either ideally suited…or suited not at all. Long hours. Tons of pressure. Lots of travel. And although you are intimately involved in creating a compelling entertainment environment, you rarely see much of the event that you are there to produce. There is virtually no public recognition of your work, and very little glamour.

Ah, but the people you get to work with…

Smart, creative, dedicated people. Fun people who can see the humor in almost any situation, no matter how challenging. People who you can count on to deliver—no questions asked, no matter what. The resulting sense of teamwork and camaraderie that pervades each venue makes for deeply satisfying work.

When you get right down to it, staging a competition is very much like being *part of* a competition in and of itself. Getting everything done just right and on time—versus immovable deadlines and often within a rapidly changing operating environment—is the equivalent of winning the actual game you're there to stage! Is it any wonder that a confessed Game Junkie like me is drawn preternaturally to this line of work?

As much as I tried to substitute hosting charity fundraisers and member-guest tournaments at the golf clubs I managed, it was never quite the same. My pulse never quickened with anticipation as the first tee time drew near. The air was never thick with the possibility of seeing something truly remarkable that day. So when the opportunity arose to take a humble position in tournament operations for a women's professional golf tour, the deliberation process didn't take all that long. I could always return to facility management. The job with the Futures Tour offered something else entirely: crappy pay, 12-hour workdays, and weeks at a time on the road. I couldn't wait to start.

THREE

The Question—
The Walkabout's First Step

MY FIRST DECADE in the sports business flew by like the simple turning of a page (which, through the miracle of literary device, is exactly what it was for you as well). I had found a home in sports-event production, which challenged both of my brain hemispheres. The creative, the strategic, and the tactical were always in play, and rarely were there two similar days in a row. I honestly couldn't remember anything about my vocational life before sports.

After a lengthy tour of duty in the Southeast, The Bird and I returned to the West Coast. During the many years that had intervened between our California addresses, she had built a thriving career composed of successively higher-profile jobs that involved telling ever-larger groups of people what to do—while making them think it was their own idea. Kind of like how she handles me, come to think of it.

The Deal had been done. We had pulled it off. Everything was just like I had imagined. Fade to black…roll credits…cue the inspirational music. Happy ending, right? *Welllll…*

I was embarrassed by it, and I never said it out loud, but in moments of quiet honesty I had to admit—life actually *wasn't* just like I'd imagined. But I could never put my finger on exactly why. It wasn't the work itself. It wasn't the travel. And it wasn't a case of disillusionment with the broad gap between the perceived glamour and the very real lack thereof in the day-to-day sports business. I had been well prepared for all of that.

Whenever those nagging doubts cropped up, the best rationale that I could conjure for them was that my world had grown small. Tour seasons had started to merge into one another until all frames of previous reference about one event or another had coagulated into one big blob. It was imperceptible at first, but somewhere along the way, the word "grind" started to show up in a lot of conversations with colleagues—which, not surprisingly, were pretty much the only people with whom I was having conversations. A spaceship full of aliens could have landed on my lawn, and I wouldn't have noticed. Unless they were either carrying golf clubs or expressed interest in a sponsorship investment.

Reading, for example, was a lifelong hobby that had just melted away. Who had the time? Actually that is not 100 percent accurate. I read a lot about the business of sports—go figure. Stockbrokers read the *Wall St. Journal*, show biz types read *Variety*, and IT professionals read *InfoWorld*. I devoured *Sports Business Journal* each week, and it was a small item in *SBJ* that caught my eye one day.

The Conference Board had just released a study indicating that only 45 percent of Americans were currently satisfied with their work—the lowest number in the 22 years that they'd been conducting the annual survey. And it wasn't just because of the general gloom brought on by the Great Recession. In fact, that number had been dropping steadily since the survey debuted in 1987 with a 61 percent satisfaction rate. To my mind, though, the story's lead was buried in the text of the release: "One clue that may explain workers' growing dissatisfaction: Only 51% now find their jobs interesting, another low in the survey's 22 years."

Despite its merits, *Sports Business Journal* can sometimes venture into the realm of being a self-congratulatory cheerleader for the industry, and so it struck me that the tone that permeated this blurb was one of, "Aren't we, the happy campers of the sports biz, all that and a bag of chips?" So it didn't strike me as that compelling a news item. But it got me to thinking.

As I had learned years before, jobs are certainly not immune to the laws of supply-and-demand pricing. It stands to reason that jobs that are "interesting" come at a premium, which typically takes the form of reduced financial compensation. Of course, "interesting" is in the eye of the beholder, and remuneration comes in many forms other than simply salary, with the ideal being that the work itself serves as compensation. That would be the case with me.

Wouldn't it?

At that point in my sports career, my job responsibilities had become more focused upon the decidedly challenging work of "paying the bills." It may go without saying, but just because games are games doesn't mean they're free. Every match, every race, every tournament costs something, even if the participating athletes are amateurs. Some cost a little, and some cost a lot. And since ticket sales and entry fees don't feed the bulldog by themselves, God created sponsors, the delicate care and feeding of whom is a cottage industry all by itself. An insanely competitive cottage industry. So I was once or twice removed from the "fun" stuff by then.

But hey—over the course of ten years in the sports industry, I had acquired the kind of perspective that can only be gained through experience on both sides of the ropes, so to speak. I had grown thoroughly familiar with all of the main character roles in the parallel universe called sports: the executives, the marketers, the operations folks, and the athletes. I had successfully found a way to merge my vocation and avocation. I had beaten the system! I had won!

Hadn't I?

As I sat there contemplating that *Sports Business Journal* piece, the following phrases came to mind: (a) "Do what you love, and you'll never work a day in your life;" and (b) "Pursue your passion, and the money will follow." I don't know who initially uttered these pearls of wisdom, but at that moment I suddenly desired a word with them.

Don't get me wrong. I loved my chosen career. I loved the work. I loved the energy and passion of the people that I'd worked with. I loved spending a big chunk of my time outdoors. And much more often than not, it had been very gratifying. But…the alarmingly low wages…the exceedingly long hours…the severely limited upward mobility. Sinclair Lewis would have had a field day with my industry. Norma Rae would *still* be standing there with a UNION placard held overhead. I didn't know anyone in the sports business who would classify their work as uninteresting. Then again, I also didn't know too many people in the industry with a lot of disposable cash.

But I did know a lot of Lost Innocents.

My chosen field was littered with Lost Innocents—the Game Junkies who parachuted out of the role of sensible human being and managed to secure employment within the wild, wonderful world of sports—only to discover that the childlike purity of athletic endeavors tends to ebb. They don't even notice at first, and even when they do, it's relatively easy for them to summon back the energy and raw enthusiasm they felt on day one of their first job in sports. The "I'm getting *paid* to be immersed in *games!*" high. But time marches on, and after a while, even the most dedicated Game Junkies find themselves *not even watching* the contests that were once the center of their universe. There are clients to entertain, operational snafus to attend to, and athletes to coddle.

Let me be crystal clear here. I personally couldn't imagine working in another industry. But as I sat there ruminating, I had to admit…over the past ten years, I'd missed out on the purity of sports. I'd missed out on being able to watch an event without obsessing over the quality of the sponsorship activation. I had missed out on going home right after an event, blissfully oblivious to who would clean up the mess—or how things were progressing on the setup of the next one. I had missed out on experiencing the drama that unfolds uniquely in every competition ever conducted. I'd missed out on the heart and soul of being a plain old sports fan.

I stared out the window for a long time as the late afternoon coastal marine layer settled like a huge grey cotton ball over my home and my mood. And for the very first time I found myself wondering if I too had become a Lost Innocent.

Of course, none of this schizophrenic stock-taking would have occurred if it hadn't been for the Question.

It was during a casual telephone conversation with an old friend a couple of weeks prior. Just catching up…the typical "How's the wife?" and "What have you been up to lately?" chat. I'm not even sure of the exact topic we were kicking around when he came out with an offhand remark: "Sometimes it seems like you care a lot less about sports now than you did before you went to work in the business." And then the Question: "Do you still love sports?"

In a moment of blinding clarity I realized that I honestly didn't know the answer.

I don't remember what pat reply I undoubtedly mumbled, but the moment stuck with me long after hanging up. And now *Sports Business Journal* and the Conference Board had conspired to bring the matter to the forefront once again.

This was serious. No, this was *beyond* serious. Let's recap. Ten years prior, I had willingly traded financial security and a stable existence to pursue a passion—walked away from a cushy life full of corporate perks to start all over again at the bottom. And over time perhaps that unequivocal love of sports that started it all in motion had turned into something more akin to…"deep like"?

Houston, we have a problem.

I began to have trouble sleeping. And I wasn't doing so well with the waking hours either. I couldn't shake it—had it all been just a waste? What would life be like in two years? Five? Would I be completely jaded and disinterested in sports? Would I bail out at some point and return to the life that I'd been so apprehensive about—that of a cubicle dweller trading time for money for things? Or even worse—a cubicle dweller now devoid of any weekend passions?

Distressing as this was to confront, I had no choice but to do something. I *had* to find out if the sports career I had painstakingly built had been worth what I'd sacrificed—or if all I had succeeded in doing was torching both my bank account *and* my cherished lifelong relationship with sports. But how in the world was I going to do that?

Where would I even begin?

* * *

It had happened gradually and insidiously over ten years of work in the sports industry. I stopped going to games. My intake of sports had become limited to that which was fed to me on highlight shows—and more often than not, even that was on as sort of background music in my house. My appreciation for sports had become the equivalent of ambient noise. Some sort of a reverse intervention was clearly needed if I was to become rapturously addicted once again, assuming that was even possible anymore.

Baby steps. I decided to go to a game—off the clock, so to speak. I wanted not to work the game; not to analyze, strategize or otherwise view it from the critical eye of a sports management professional. I just wanted to watch and listen to my thoughts. Then, of course, after committing to doing this, I procrastinated, no doubt anxious about what I might discover. Weeks went by, and then…

Put up or shut up. Instead of just musing about the state of live sports beyond the filter of the major media, I decided it was high time to check out the games people play firsthand. No comfy couch. No clicker. No instant replay. Cold turkey. Truth be told, the decision pretty much made itself when the perfect storm of opportunity developed.

Of all sports, college basketball has a special place in both my heart and the creases of the brain where life's experiences are preserved long after you've started forgetting what you had for breakfast this morning. Sometime in between the reigns of King Tut and Alexander the Great, I actually played college basketball, albeit not very well. The Bird, in fact, thinks that the cause of my chronically sore knees is the pounding that they took from repeated trips up and down the court. I don't have the heart to tell her that more likely it was the wear and tear from repeatedly rising from the bench and then sitting back down at the conclusion of each timeout. But I digress.

In scanning the *L.A. Times* sports section one morning, I noted with interest that Gonzaga, the #9 team in the country at the time, would soon be heading down the coast to play the southern swing of its West Coast Conference road schedule. Which meant that they would be visiting Loyola Marymount. Imagine that—a Top 10 team coming to my backyard. I wouldn't even have to get on a freeway to see them. In fact, I could be on the LMU campus in just three turns once I pulled out of my garage. I had no earthly reason *not* to go.

And so it was that I wandered into the 4,156-seat Gersten Pavilion and found a comfortable vantage point in the wooden bleachers, well in advance of tip-off. I hadn't been in a campus gym in a long, long time (Syracuse's Carrier Dome doesn't really count, because its cavernous size enables it to routinely house most of central New York). But I was struck by how wonderfully familiar it seemed. All of the pregame sights, sounds, and smells were no different than they had been back in the day. I even started to feel pregame butterflies as a purely reflexive reaction.

As I looked around, it reminded me that this Loyola Marymount program had some memorable history of its own. Back in the late '80s, this small-school team rose to national prominence with a run-and-gun style that virtually ignored the concept of playing traditional defense. Yes, *even more so* than is currently the case in the NBA. At the height of this era, coach Paul Westhead enticed star USC players Bo Kimble and Hank Gathers into transferring across town, and tiny Gersten Pavilion became *the* hot sports place to be in Los Angeles. For a time, even the mighty UCLA took a backseat to LMU in SoCal college hoops. And then tragedy struck.

Well on their way to a third straight NCAA tournament appearance, LMU was comfortably leading a West Coast Conference tournament game when Gathers scored on an alley-oop dunk, turned to head up court...and suddenly fell to the ground. Dead of a massive heart attack.

In one of the most stirring two-week spans of college basketball history, LMU dedicated its NCAA tournament to their fallen star and proceeded to knock off New Mexico State, defending national champion Michigan (by *34 points*, no less), and Alabama before falling to eventual tournament champion UNLV. Gathers' costar of that team, Bo Kimble, honored his best friend in each of those games by shooting his first foul shot left-handed, as Gathers had done once while trying to break out of a foul-shooting slump. Kimble made each of those three shots in the team's run to the Elite Eight. It was the farthest that Loyola Marymount would ever advance in the Madness of March.

My visit to Gersten took place almost 20 years to the day after Hank Gathers died, and his presence could still be felt everywhere—from the large HANK'S HOUSE sign on the wall to the replica #44 jerseys that the cheerleaders, band, and pep squad wore. In one of the on-court contests that ran during a timeout, the winning fan was genuinely thrilled to receive a piece of twine from the net cut down after one of those historic NCAA wins in 1990.

But here's the thing—in spite of all of that history and all of those big wins, Loyola Marymount had *never* beaten a ranked team in the 29 years since Gersten Pavilion first opened its doors. And the odds were pretty good that this game against Gonzaga would add to that string. In preparation for this excursion I had watched on television the week before as the Zags rolled up 19 points before a pretty decent University of San Diego team could even get on the board. Now, as I watched both teams take the floor for warm-ups, I couldn't help noticing how small the LMU Lions looked in comparison to Gonzaga.

It was then that a flurry of activity across the way caught my eye. When I focused on its source, the first word that popped into my head was "contrived." Followed by the word "depressing." I had journeyed (if ten minutes in moderate traffic qualifies as a "journey") this night to watch mighty Gonzaga University unleash the attack that had propelled them to Top 10 national status. But I'd also come to see how the live college basketball experience had changed from that which had been part of my romance with sports in the first place. Based on what I was viewing at that moment, things had indeed changed, and not for the better.

Still 20 minutes prior to tip-off, across the court the first fans in the student section milled around near the railing that separated the stands from media row. Most of the two dozen or so students were dressed in LMU regalia, some outrageously so, as has been de rigueur since Dick Vitale first body-surfed through the Cameron Crazies prior to a Duke-Carolina game. It was well beyond old but pretty benign stuff. And then the handheld TV camera appeared, accompanied by a producer who beseeched the students to go nuts as the camera rolled. Which they did through repeated takes, flip-flopping on command between idle conversation and full "Times Square at midnight" mode. This was part of the television introduction to the game, and while the viewer at home saw a rabid group of fans hungry for a big game to start, I saw 30 people in an otherwise empty section of stands going gaga on cue, hungry to get their faces on television. Staged fanaticism. Sigh.

The charade ended soon enough, though, and I refocused on the pregame rituals that were unfolding: the players gliding through warm-up drills, the fans filling up the stands and greeting each other enthusiastically, the band and the cheerleaders starting to hit their stride. It was nice. It was comfortable. It was vaguely hypnotic, and I found myself smiling. This feel, this rhythm, hadn't changed since the days when I had been an active part of it. And I had the notion that long ago, when the rhythm was still new to me, it was familiar to a previous generation that sat in the bleachers on those nights taking it all in.

The game began, and as expected, Gonzaga jumped out to an early lead. They were big, they were fast, and they could all shoot three-pointers like they were layups. Conversely, Loyola Marymount had been out of synch since they stumbled through player introductions prior to the game. Gonzaga by three, Gonzaga by five, by seven, by ten. It was a mesmerizing display, as wave after wave of fresh bodies came off the Gonzaga bench with no discern-able drop-off in talent. In fact, their substitution pattern struck me as a little *too* brisk. Players were in and right back out, having spent only a minute or two on the court. So it shouldn't have been that surprising that, as time went by, their cadence started to get a little sluggish. Their shots started hitting rim instead of net. And LMU sensed opportunity.

A hustle basket here, a circus shot there, a tightening of the screws on defense, and the Lions began to claw back into the game. By halftime they were down by just three points. As the teams exited the floor for the break, an idea began to swell in the minds of the faithful. Perhaps on this night Gonzaga could be beaten? And if there was any doubt whatsoever that something unusual was afoot, it was countered during the halftime festivities.

I'm sure you know the drill. A fan is chosen at random from the crowd to take part in a contest on the court—something ostensibly achievable. The combination of nerves and lack of skill, however, typically results in a sympathetic, "Ooohhh, nice try! Let's give our contestant a nice big round of applause." On this night the fan had to make four shots from progressively greater distances. His layup was solid, but his foul shot *banked* in. Never a good sign. Then his top-of-the-key shot also banked in. What were the odds? So I guess I shouldn't have been surprised when his half-court heave hit nothing but net. What the hell was going on here?!

LMU came out of the locker room like men possessed. They got every defensive rebound, every loose ball. They got confident. And Gonzaga started to clang shots with increasing regularity. The tide had turned, and when a driving layup put LMU ahead by five with 13:20 remaining, Gonzaga called timeout to try and squelch the upset fever now coursing throughout the gym. It didn't work.

With 4:23 left in the game, LMU had extended their lead to ten and had reached that point in an athletic contest when a huge upset is right there for the taking—as long as the underdog continues playing to win instead of playing *not to lose*. It was painful to watch. LMU became tentative, and Gonzaga got aggressive. In little more than a minute, the ten-point lead was down to four. On its next possession LMU found themselves scrambling just to get a shot off before the 35-second clock expired, and with just one tick left Gonzaga deflected the ball out of bounds. The Lions had one second to get the ball in, hoist up some kind of shot that would draw iron, and jockey for position to snare the rebound. Pretty long odds, given the circumstances.

So it was understandable that the place went absolutely bonkers when an acrobatic shot off the inbounds pass…*actually went in the hoop.*

After that it came down to foul shots, and bless their hearts, LMU made each and every one of them down the stretch. As the last few seconds ticked off the clock, delirium reigned. And when the final horn sounded on a 74–66 Lion's win, there was nothing but pure, unabashed joy. The stands emptied in a torrent onto the floor. I could see people hugging and mouthing "Can you believe this?" to each other amidst the pandemonium. Others were taking cell-phone pictures of the scoreboard to send to friends and to preserve for posterity. For the first time in the 29-year history of Gersten Pavilion, the LMU Lions had beaten a nationally ranked team at home—*a Top 10 team, no less!*

The irony did not escape me. Only two hours before I had witnessed completely staged fanaticism that made a sleepy environment seem frenzied for the benefit of television. Now, as I watched the celebration on the court continue, I knew that there was no way that television could effectively be capturing the actual *genuine* euphoria that spread itself out before me. It was real, it was authentic, and it was just what I had been searching for.

I lingered in the stands much longer than I normally would have, not wanting to pull the plug on the jubilant sensation. I'm sure the grin on my face was in place all the way home. On its surface, the game meant nothing to me; I entered the gym as a fan of neither team. But the jolt of energy was certainly meaningful. When I awoke the next morning still feeling vaguely euphoric, I began to think seriously about taking a sabbatical from hunting down the next event-management contract, the next sponsorship deal, the next piece of sports *business*. There would be plenty of time for that later. More urgent was the need to reconnect with sports—and hopefully to save myself from my career.

But how exactly would I do that?

Ten years is a long time.

It had taken me that long to merely make *inroads* on fully understanding the good, the bad, and the ugly about pursuing a second career within the sports industry. And now there was no escaping it. I was confronted with a crisis of confidence.

Did I still love sports?

The more I thought about it, the more I realized that the topic had surfaced on a more-or-less recurring basis for some time. I've often been asked for my perspective when friends, friends of friends, and assorted stray individuals learn of my story and are considering replicating my path into the sports business. And in fact, the most common line of questioning that I receive is some variant of the basic question, "Do you still love sports?" I had always just laughed it off, though. *Of course* I still loved sports! You'd have to be out of your mind to do what I did if you didn't deeply and passionately love sports.

Wouldn't you?

The experience at Gersten Pavilion had verified one thing for sure. I still loved getting lost in the games—becoming mesmerized by the rhythm and energized by the drama. So I started to entertain the idea of going to more games as just a pure spectator. And not just the premier, highly visible games, but all kinds of games played at all kinds of levels. I would do this, in essence, to regain my "amateur status" as a fan.

"Yeah, that's the ticket. I could just go to a lot of games in my spare time. That will fix everything." Saying it out loud made the concept seem even sketchier. If I were being at all truthful with myself, I could easily envision a scenario in which I charged into being a born-again sports fan with a full head of steam—and then rapidly tapered off. Instead of an affirmation, the idea of faithfully attending more games started to feel more like a New Year's resolution. And we all know the life span of those.

Then again, I couldn't just blow off the whole thing. I couldn't just ignore the tightness in my throat or the churning in my stomach every time I thought about it. This truly was a moment of truth for me, for if I had indeed lost the spark, I was staring at the career equivalent of a loveless marriage—one that I'd ditched an heiress for, so to speak.

I needed to find a way to legitimize the exercise, to elevate it above the status of a whim and hold my feet to the fire. I obviously needed to talk to Da Guy.

Da Guy is Jerry, my dear friend and cofounder of the Mutual Bemusement Society (which, astonishingly enough, still consists of only two members). I explained my quandary while Da Guy listened patiently. "Tell me a story," he said, when I had finished rambling. "Tell me a *lot* of stories. Tell *us* a lot of stories." This is the way Da Guy talks, which is why I love Da Guy. And, per usual, he was on to something big.

I have been many things over the course of my lifetime: An enthusiastic sports participant at the collegiate, amateur, and recreational level. A marketer and sponsor of sporting events, with an appreciation for the unique power of sports to reach people like no other vehicle. A ten-year veteran of the sports business, from the trenches to the boardroom. An admirer of those who seek to compete at the highest levels of their respective sports. And an unabashed fan of the games people play.

This is what I have learned from the combination of the above: for every story that unfolds on the field, court, pitch, or track, there are dozens more that live on the sidelines, in the stands, and even in the inner sanctum of stadiums and arenas. Every sports event that I could possibly conceive of holds a host of stories just waiting to be captured and shared. So with an "I second" contributed by Da Guy, I nominated myself to capture and share them. I would set up a blog, on which I would commit to providing stories to anyone who wanted to read them. Structure would be added to an otherwise quixotic quest. I would be on the hook.

And thus began germinating the idea of a "sports walkabout"—an effort to reconnect with my ball-chasing, sports-loving roots and infuse that effervescence into a career that had lately gone wanting in the passion department.

It would work this way: Over the course of one year I would single-mindedly immerse myself in the landscape of sports at all competitive levels and in as many corners of America as possible. I would visit sports meccas and distant outposts, armed only with a notebook, a camera, a Flip video cam, and one burning question: "How can I rekindle my romance with sports and ensure that it's sustainable when it's time to go back to the business of play?" OK, technically that's two questions, but you get the idea.

I resolved that my walkabout would take me to 100 events and would encompass 50 distinctly different sports and the various genres of competition within them. Amateur badminton, high school volleyball, college lacrosse, professional polo. I'd see big games and little games. Games that I knew intimately and games whose rules were a mystery to me. There was just one hard and fast maxim: Each game had to have something at stake—something on the line to draw out the best in the competitors. Wandering over to my local park to watch T-ball wasn't going to qualify.

Why 100 events? Why 50 sports? I couldn't exactly tell you—I just knew it felt dead, solid, perfectly right. That is, until I started doing the research and found that, umm…50 is a *lot* of different sports. Many of which have an annoying habit of being played at the same time in widely varying localities. Crafting the logistics of the project became a daunting exercise in and of itself, and on more than one occasion a moment of weakness would leave me thinking, *Really, Tim—let it go. Just let sleeping dogs lie.* After all, there was no guarantee that I would come away with the answers that I sought. There was also the distinctly sobering possibility that I might wind up *more* disillusioned rather than less so. It was textbook approach-avoidance stuff.

Somewhere around this time I also addressed the distinct possibility that not everyone in the household would be enthralled by my new brainchild.

"Precisely how would this work?" asked The Bird after listening to my light-on-specifics description of my plan. I explained that I was pretty sure that I could get a sponsor for the blog that I would write—heck, I had been "offering unique sponsorship investment opportunities" for years. Travel expenses would be heavily mitigated by the stockpile of airline and hotel points that we'd accumulated over the years. Tickets and other admission fees would be the easiest part—sports industry folks legendarily take care of each other. So out-of-pocket costs weren't really the issue.

But there *was* that little revenue-interruption thing.

When we had moved back to California I had been able to seamlessly move into the role of independent contractor, handling on an outsourced basis a lot of the work that I had done previously as an employee. It had worked well to that point—but the ripple effects of the financial sector melt-down were certainly lapping at my door, and a downturn in business was almost inevitable. In other words, the concept of "sabbatical" had been all but *invented* for my use in presenting the idea to The Bird.

She was quiet. Which is never a good thing. She arched an eyebrow. I had no choice but to wait her out.

"So what I'm hearing," she began, "is that, one way or another, you're looking at some potential down time in the near future, and you might as well spend it productively."

"Of course! That's *exactly* what I'm trying to say," I lied enthusiastically, for her explanation was a whole lot more concise and salable than my own.

The Bird held my gaze for what seemed an eternity, and then in a case of déjà vu for the ages said, "Well, I don't see how you can *not* do this. Just don't bankrupt us. And don't make a fool of yourself."

I wasn't positive that I could deliver on that last requirement, but the train was pulling out of the station on this project, and I wanted to make sure I was on board. Truth be told, I don't even remember what else I specifically agreed to during this green-lighting session. I just knew it needed to be done. And if I had any additional reservations whatsoever, they were laid to rest a short time later, when I stumbled across a compelling literary fact during a research session: the home that Odysseus, the mythological protagonist of Homer's *Odyssey*, struggled mightily to return to was named Ithaca. My love of sports had at one time drawn me to the southern tip of central New York's Lake Cayuga—where I spent four years at Ithaca College. Coincidence?

The concept had been validated. I was going to do this. But what would I call the endeavor? Every odyssey has to have a name.

A few days later, it came to me. It was a spectacular Friday afternoon, and The Bird arrived home early. It's a momentous occasion when even *she* decides that it's far too nice to be working—and especially working indoors. "Cocktails on the deck?" she invited.

She knew what my answer would be. This running joke had been the product of a vacation spent years ago with a group of friends. It had been day four or day five, and everyone had lost all track of both stress and time. The noon hour was still just a speck on the horizon when somebody first suggested, "Beer?" Without missing a beat, somebody else mused, "Well, it's 5:00 somewhere." A few years after that, Alan Jackson and Jimmy Buffett either egregiously infringed upon our intellectual property or made us legends in our own minds, depending on your point of view. But that's not important right now.

This is what is: just as the cocktail hour can commence at pretty much any time for a vacationer, for a sports fan it's undoubtedly game time somewhere at any given moment. And so it was only fitting that for the next year of my life, I would become the self-appointed commissioner of the It's Game Time Somewhere Tour.

God help me.

FOUR

Low-Hanging Fruit

To enjoy golf in the desert during the winter months, you have to acquire a taste for sunshine, zero humidity, and temperatures in the upper 70s. It's not too bad, if you like that sort of thing. As luck would have it, I do. So starting my walkabout in a familiar place with a familiar sport seemed like a natural. But that was not the only motivating factor in including the Bob Hope Classic on the It's Game Time Somewhere Tour schedule. I was actually there to see a celebrity.

The Hope Classic is one of just two PGA Tour events in which celebrities and amateurs play alongside Tour pros in multiple rounds of tournament play. This isn't the standard Wednesday Pro-Am Hit & Giggle. This is 72 holes with something on the line. And there was one particular luminary in the field that I felt *compelled* to follow.

Not Kurt Russell. Or Sugar Ray Leonard. Or even Alice Cooper. No, I was there to see Feesh tee it up.

I'll save you a quick check of the PGA Tour's website, because you won't find the name "Feesh" anywhere on the player roster. A former college roommate, Feesh happens to be one of my oldest friends. And he is an amateur golfer, in the purest, truest sense of the word: he plays golf for fun. Don't get me wrong—he takes his game deadly seriously. But five minutes after his round is over, any bad shots he's hit have already faded from memory. I can tell you this because I've borne witness to both the bad shots and the forgetting of same.

Every year Feesh ponies up the money to take his place alongside four different Tour pros over four days of tournament competition. Every year Feesh is absolutely, rock-solid *certain* that this is the year that his amateur team will walk away with the crystal. Every year he is stunned and amazed that this does not indeed happen.

This was the ideal way to begin my quest. If I couldn't reconnect with the soul of sports while watching Feesh undergo this annual drama, there was no hope for me. In fact, the IGTS Tour had been front-end loaded with golf events of all types. "Might as well get a running head start with the low-hanging fruit," I reasoned. Truth be told, a part of me felt that if the walkabout wound up floundering at some point down the road, I at least wanted to have some good memories to show for it. And I knew that golf—and Feesh—would fill the bill reliably.

Contradictory as it may sound, the atmosphere was both sleepy and electric when I arrived at PGA West. It was the first day of tournament action, and while attendance was modest, aspirations were anything but. From my first step onto the Nicklaus Course—one of the four tracks that host play during the first four days of the tournament—I was dialed in to the underlying adrenaline buzz. It was easy to recognize, for this undercurrent had been a staple of my existence during the years in which I had worked in tournament operations. When the sun rose on the first day of competition each week, I could feel it in the marrow of my bones. I had often wondered if it was the same way for everybody. Strange that I never got around to asking anyone.

Purely by the luck of the draw, the Feesh-some Foursome was the last group of the day off the tee. The 10th tee. Which happened to be located a fair distance from the clubhouse. Casual walk-up fans were in short supply out there. So by the time my favorite group was introduced, the gallery consisted primary of me and the Lovely Lisa—the wife and biggest fan of Feesh's teammate Craig. OK, I exaggerated. The gallery consisted *solely* of Lisa and me.

Michael Putnam, the Tour pro paired with the group for this day's round, appeared to be a refugee from some NFL team's roster of linebackers. I would normally say that he hits the ball a mile, except that I could never actually see far enough to witness one of his tee shots land—so I can't say with confidence that its flight didn't actually *exceed* a mile.

After launching his inaugural shot, Putnam wandered over to the tee box from which his amateur partners would each put their chest-restricting, knee-knocking first shot into play. Afterward, he strolled side by side with them up the first fairway, conversing jovially. Because usually, in a pro-am situation, the PGA Tour pro tends to resemble a random single who's trying to play through without being noticed, I guessed Putnam might be a rookie.

It turned out, though, that the affable Putnam had actually turned pro a few years prior, after an amateur career that included four years at Pepperdine and invitations to play on the 2005 Palmer Cup and Walker Cup teams. And while he hadn't yet made a major impact on the PGA Tour, you wouldn't have known it on this day. He birdied the first two holes, on his way to shooting 30 on the front side. Since the Tour pro's results count as part of the amateur team's score at the Hope Classic, this was very helpful to the cause.

As for Feesh, he struggled over the first few holes, shaking off the rust that accumulates pretty quickly on a Northeastern golfer during the winter. But like most feel players, he just needed that first good swing in order to get rolling. In his case, it was an eight-iron approach on the fourth hole, and while he didn't convert the putt, that shot opened the door to pars on four of the next five holes. "This is as good as I can play," he confided to a certain pseudo-journalist at the turn.

Any of Feesh's earthly troubles were clearly light years away from consciousness at that point. He was grinning broadly. He was competing. He was competing *successfully*. He was a poster boy for the allure of golf. And although I didn't have a club in my hands, I was right there with him vicariously, having a ball and soaking in the atmosphere.

It was inevitable that Putnam would cool off after his scorching start, but almost as soon as he did, his amateur partners took turns picking up the slack. It was what any $10 Nassau fourball golfer would recognize instantly as consummate "hamming & egging." And with three relatively short, straightforward holes left to play, our heroes stood within reach of the tournament's leading amateur teams. Spirits were high. We had even picked up another spectator, thus increasing our gallery size by 50 percent.

Sadly, the prized appearance on the leaderboard was not to be. Three straight finishing pars relegated Team Feesh to middle-of-the-pack status after day one. But the next day would bring another round, as would the day after that and the day after that. So as the sun slowly melted away behind the stark desert mountains, my favorite amateur combatants crafted their plans for dinner and some spirited…*strategery,* I guess you could call it.

Now that's *the way to start a walkabout!* I thought as I waited in line for the bus that would take me from the Nicklaus Course back to the parking lot. Yes, beginning with golf was probably cheating, but I didn't care. As the desert's evening chill descended and the first stars blazed, I was most definitely loving sports.

The Stanford University Golf Course is a rare gem, providing truly memorable vistas—especially from the back nine—when, on a clear day, San Francisco and its surrounding bay reveal themselves to those who make the hike up to the 18th tee box. The day that I attended the Western Regional of the NCAA Women's Golf Championships was one of those clear days.

Just getting out of the car evoked exhilaration for me. Again the first round of a tournament, again the surge of adrenaline. And while I had gone to the Bob Hope Classic with a laser-like focus on one particular team, these regionals provided a host of rooting interests for me.

For several years it had been my calling to market women's golf in general and the Futures Tour specifically. The Futures Tour is the "feeder" tour for the LPGA Tour, much as the Nationwide Tour serves that purpose for the PGA Tour. Or if you prefer your analogies to be of a baseball variety, the Futures Tour is the Triple-A minor league of women's golf.

Naturally, not everyone who makes it to the Futures Tour level manages to make the next leap into the LPGA Tour ranks, and inevitably the time comes when players make the decision to pursue other opportunities—one of which is coaching golf at the elite amateur level, helping to prepare the next generation for their own assault on the pro ranks. In fact, at this particular tournament, there were no fewer than six former Futures Tour players now coaching collegiate teams that they'd led into this NCAA regional level of competition. And, *of course*, I had no favorites; I wanted badly for each of them to finish among the eight teams that would qualify for the following week's NCAA Championship.

With an entire day of golf laid out for me to sample, I decided to spend some time focusing on contrasts. Twenty-four teams had been invited to play in this regional, with UCLA at the top of the heap based on its national #1 ranking. Team #24 in the draw was Portland State, with a national ranking of #125. While pulling for my Super Six coaches throughout, this was also the perfect opportunity for me to ascertain exactly how big a gulf there was between college golf's elite and...not so elite.

I started by following a morning pairing that consisted of the lead players from each of the three top-ranked schools in the draw. In a nutshell, had I not known that this was a collegiate event, I could have easily been convinced that I was watching any random pairing on the professional level—the Futures Tour certainly, and perhaps even the LPGA. Each player had long, beautifully flowing swings devoid of fear. They carried themselves with confidence and dressed like they'd stepped right off the pages of a golf-fashion magazine.

There was also one other thing that brought to mind the women's professional game: Each of these players had long ago been schooled to... ummm...shall we say, "take their time." Their pace of play was just like the pros, and by that I mean that glaciers could form, melt, and form again in the time it took to line up and execute a putt. I wondered when exactly in the development of their game it was that these golfers first received the advice to sloooooowwwww down.

When I played high school golf, if you took more than ten seconds to play a shot, you risked having loose change thrown at you by your own teammates. I distinctly remember Dean Palozej emptying the contents of my golf bag on Ellington Ridge Country Club's par-three 17th hole when I changed clubs for the third time prior to my tee shot. This was during a match, no less. I learned to pick up the pace. And you know what? It made me a better golfer. As I watched these future tour players labor through their rounds, it occurred to me that Dean Palozej could single-handedly improve the professional golf viewing experience. But I digress.

The afternoon wave of tee times brought with it the second half of my "field test," which had me following players from the three teams that occupied the final three spots in the draw: Texas State, Pennsylvania, and Portland State. These players had swings that were a little less perfect, dress that was a little more casual, and—God bless them—a pace of play that was decidedly *less* casual than that of those in the upper echelons of the field.

But the one thing that made all of the athletes that I saw throughout the day indistinguishable from one another was their grace. Good shots or bad, I saw not a single display of negative emotion. No outbursts, profane or otherwise. No slamming of clubs into bags. I saw class from one end of the draw to the other.

Even though this wasn't "big-time" golf, I certainly had a lot of company in roaming the course. For I had entered the realm of the golf parent. Nurturing the career of an aspiring elite athlete takes true sacrifice and devotion, and nowhere is that on better display than in the galleries of collegiate golfers. At tournaments across the country, hopeful parents trudge around the golf course watching their kids play from a respectful distance. Hanging on every swing, they quietly suffer with every pulled drive or three-putt—all while rarely setting foot themselves on the luxurious short grass of the tees, fairways, and greens. They don't even have the opportunity for the occasional cathartic release of yelling at a referee or umpire.

I had the pleasure that day of spending time "in the rough" with a full spectrum of personalities that shared a common bond of fierce pride in their daughters' accomplishments. But of all the delightful people I encountered, two vastly different personalities stuck out in my mind in particular—and coincidentally I encountered them at opposite ends of the field's draw.

While following a marquee threesome of players from the tournament's highest-seeded teams, I was approached by a woman with a dazzling smile and effervescent personality. "Hi, I'm Margarita's mom," she said, extending her hand in greeting and referring to her namesake, the University of Arizona's Margarita Ramos. We walked the next few holes together as she shared proud stories of her daughter's golfing career to that point—those great parental stories that, had her daughter been with us, would have caused her to blush and beg her mom to stop.

At the time, Margarita was the top-rated amateur in all of Mexico and one of those natural-born talents who picks up a club at an early age and inherently knows just how to make it work. Before she had hit her teens, mother and daughter moved to Florida, where Margarita enrolled in that most prestigious of junior golf institutions, the David Leadbetter Academy. From there it was on to Xavier College Prep in Phoenix, a high school renowned for turning out well-rounded students who just happen to receive college golf scholarship offers by the truckload. The one from the Arizona Wildcats was particularly well received by the Ramos family.

It's at this point in this type of story that the young phenom typically eschews the remainder of her amateur eligibility and attempts to make the jump directly to the LPGA Tour. When I delicately posed the question of Margarita's intentions at the end of her sophomore year, her mom looked as if I had just suggested that her daughter was thinking about becoming a longshoreman.

"Why would she want to leave Arizona before she graduates?" she asked, appearing to be sincerely baffled by the concept. "She loves it there." And indeed she was getting the full collegiate experience. Majoring in Business, with a minor in Communications, Ramos had already been honored with inclusion on the NGCA All-America Scholar Team and received Honorable Mention status on the Pac-10 All-Academic Team.

In other words, Margarita had a life—one not defined solely by how well she struck a golf ball on any particular day. I found that to be wonderfully refreshing in an age where athletically gifted kids are societally programmed to cash in shortly after progressing beyond embryo status.

Equally refreshing was the persona of Stephanie Johns, who was there with Portland State, the final team to be invited to play in the West Regional. She caught my eye as being a tad unconventional right from her first tee shot. Dressed as if she was channeling her inner Shawn White, you'd never know whether she was an X Games athlete or a golfer—until she wound up and belted her drive. She wore knee-length shorts, a simple white polo shirt (sans designer logo), large dangling earrings…and sneakers.

Early in her round, Johns had the misfortune of landing her drive in a spot that by all rights should have been a free-drop area but which may have been overlooked by those marking the course. A lot of players would've panicked, but Stephanie had the presence of mind to invoke her right to play the rest of the hole with two separate golf balls, thus enabling her to plead her case in the scorer's tent after the round. As I was watching this unfold, I got to talking with a gentleman named Brian about the situation and about golf in general. I commented that this Johns girl was handling a potential round-derailing situation with a lot of poise, and he silently nodded his agreement. Three holes later, I discovered almost by accident that Stephanie was Brian's daughter.

A case study for the PGA's grow-the-game efforts, Stephanie first picked up a club at the age of six, when Brian took her to a driving range. Hooked from the start, she developed a more-or-less self-taught swing that, while not classic, allowed her to clear her hips and launch the ball impressively. On several holes, she outdrove her playing partners by more than 30 yards. And apparently she had a reputation for being quite the scrambler; Brian smiled at one point and said that he wouldn't mind spending just one round without his heart in his throat while watching her play.

When I asked him about her unique sartorial style, he laughed and said "You know, I'm not sure she even *owns* a pair of golf shoes."

This was great stuff, and just what I had hoped to discover on my journey. I *knew* I could count on golf to surround me with the essence of sports all day. Drawing upon deep memories of my own days of competitive golf, I could palpably relate to the experiences of these golfers as they stood over difficult recovery shots or knee-knocking putts. It was exhilarating, inspirational. And by the way…it was doing wonders for the resurrection of my sports fandom.

I began to doubt whether I would even need to complete the entire walkabout. If I only knew then…

FIVE

Drop the Camera and Back Away Slowly

WHEN YOU'VE COMMITTED to spending a year speed-dating with the entire sporting world, you should expect the unexpected. But this?

I was 20 yards behind the 6th tee at Pebble Beach Golf Links, and I had been there for a while. There was no way I was going anywhere—quite literally, in fact. For at the time I was enmeshed in human gridlock.

A pilgrimage had brought me to this point. Actually a pilgrimage within a pilgrimage; for out of the 100 events that made up my IGTS Tour schedule, this one stood head and shoulders above the others in terms of anticipation. Because I'm a golf guy. And this was the U.S. Open! At *Pebble freakin' Beach!!* This would be special. This was going to be epic.

Unfortunately, the U.S. Golf Association, which owns and operates the Open, was at the moment engaged in conducting a clinic on how to scare people away from the sport of golf. It's a fairly reliable format: take a golf course capable of comfortably accommodating *X* number of spectators, then sell one and a half times that number of tickets. This would, of course, be impossible at an arena or a stadium, but with a large expanse of land to work with...*voila!* All maximum-capacity constraints become, shall we say, subject to interpretation. Which brings me to the dilemma at hand.

The course routing at Pebble Beach is more or less a figure-eight, with a natural bottleneck where the inner and outer loops intersect. That spot lies about halfway down the 13th fairway, at which point the 6th hole lays out perpendicularly, heading away toward the ocean. The cart path there is about ten feet wide, with another few feet of grass on either side before you are reined in by the "impenetrable" borders of the gallery ropes. When I crossed that point on my way to the outer loop that morning, things were already congested, despite it being early in the day. I made a mental note to find a different return route. Imagine my surprise when a couple of hours later I realized there *was* no alternate route.

So there I stood, in close quarters with roughly 500 other people. The crowd behind the 6th tee had swelled in size as the day had worn on, and it now bulged out well onto the rapidly shrinking pedestrian pathway. With equal numbers of people trying to head opposite ways through this mosh pit, we were all at a standstill. The standoff dragged on for ten minutes…then 15…increasing in scope as more and more unsuspecting people wandered into the fray.

Equal parts intrigued and annoyed, I reversed course and spawned back upstream to higher ground to watch the scene unfold. After a time, a golf cart carrying tournament officials pulled up and inched its way into the crowd, eventually becoming as stuck as everyone else. A larger cart carrying uniformed security personnel followed shortly thereafter. They too became engulfed.

The whole thing would've been funny if it weren't for the tension that started to emanate from deep within the scrum. Disabled people in small motorized carts and parents pushing baby strollers were all in there some-where, along with the requisite number of people in any crowd who are some-what claustrophobic by nature. Folks were getting panicky.

Finally the inevitable happened. People started to realize that those yellow ropes weren't actually electrified invisible fences. Fans started ducking under them, spilling out onto the 13th hole. Mass hysteria! Dogs and cats living together! Volunteer marshals yelling out to nobody in particular, "You can't do that! Please return behind the ropes!" It was the golf equivalent of the obligatory Los Angeles riot to celebrate a Lakers win in the NBA Finals.

I'm sure that this scene repeated itself throughout the day. In fact, after I had cleared the area via that very same ethically and morally questionable route down the 13th fairway, it dawned on me that the Tiger Woods gallery would be returning from the outer loop at just about the same time that the Phil Mickelson crowd was entering it. If Pebble Beach had been a building, fire marshals would've been lined up three-deep awaiting their turn to shut it down.

This gnawed at me. On a couple of fronts.

First, the event producer in me recoiled at the scope of this snafu— the fact that one of the preeminent golf organizations in the world had fumbled so badly on fan comfort and safety in their premier tournament. The *Mona Lisa* had suddenly frowned. The Hope Diamond was found to have a small chip in it. Carrot Top inexplicably failed to be hilarious. Street mimes ceased being delightful. OK, maybe I'm getting carried away here.

Most important, this was supposed to be a layup in my quest for primal reconnection with sports. Did I mention that this was the U.S. Open? At *Pebble freakin' Beach?!* It was a bucket-list event for golf fans of every stripe. I was supposed to be reveling in this experience, but at almost every turn throughout the day, disappointment and irritation had taken the place of exultation.

Maybe I'd have felt differently if the process of getting to the course hadn't felt like a Monterey Peninsula version of the Bataan Death March.

Google Maps had told me that it was 82 miles from my hotel to Pebble Beach Golf Links, and that it should take 1 hour and 31 minutes. Obviously, Google Maps did not know or care that my destination was the U.S. Open, so their estimate of time was predictably well understated. That said, I left my hotel at 6:30…and I saw my first golf shot at 10:15. For those of you scoring at home, that's an additional *135 minutes of time* beyond what Google reported I should expect. I've had dental surgery that took less time and involved less pain.

By far the largest chunk of my morning was spent at the General Spectator Parking Lot, negotiating the process of getting through security and loaded onto shuttle buses, each of which could hold 50 people. Throughout my time in line, there were consistently 1,500 or more people awaiting screening and subsequent boarding. You do the math.

Annoyingly akin to sitting through the same stoplight for about… ohhhh…30 full cycles, it was the only thing I've ever done that made me long for the comparatively "brisk" pace of LAX airport security screening on a Monday morning. At around the 11th or 12th light cycle I began to count among my blessings the fact that The Bird was not with me. She's not one for "process," and the pesky details of her inevitable assault arraignment and bail-posting would have *really* cut into my time on the golf course.

This is not to say that the entire ordeal was disorganized or planned haphazardly—for it was about as efficient as it could have possibly been. No, this was clearly a volume thing, a by-product of the event being wildly over-sold and the hallmark of virtually everything about the day's experience.

But the *real* culprit responsible for this endless queuing? The search for cameras. Or anything that could substitute for same. Like virtually *any* personal communication device, for example.

According to various myths and legends, there are tribes of indigenous people scattered throughout the world who believe that to have their picture taken is to have their souls stolen. While I haven't been able to verify the exact genealogy of these people, I'm pretty certain there's a connection to the U.S. Golf Association. There's really no other rational way to explain the USGA's relentless assault on the harmless pastime of recreational photography.

Picture this (so to speak)—you're with friends, enjoying a once-in-a-lifetime trip to a sporting event…let's say the U.S. Open, for example. You'd love to have a nice little souvenir of your visit to Pebble Beach to email to friends and family. Maybe something to frame and put on your desk. A little insert for the annual Christmas card: "Here we are at Pebble Beach—it was awesome!" Don't even think about it. Why not? Because the USGA says so, that's why not. You will steal the soul of golf.

The USGA's policy regarding cameras at the Open states—I'm paraphrasing here—"If you attempt to enter the course with a camera you will die a slow and horrific death, and any life insurance policies you may hold will immediately be rendered null and void."

I understand the basic concept. The clicking of camera shutters at close range in the middle of a golfer's swing can do damage to the trajectory of that shot. I get it. But given the gallery setup at Pebble Beach, where an "up-close" look at a golfer in midswing is measured in tens of yards and not feet, you could hook up the average handheld digital camera to a *bullhorn* and snap away to your heart's content without remotely disturbing that golfer you see off in the distance. Stevie Williams couldn't find you with a Garmin, let alone be motivated to throw your Canon Sure Shot into the ocean.

So imagine my sheer horror later in the day, when waaaaayyyy out near the 10th green, on the farthest reaches of Pebble Beach Golf Links, I stumbled across a scenario that froze me in my tracks—too stunned to even think about making the requisite citizen's arrest. A smiling young couple was brazenly posing for another young girl holding a...*palm-sized pink camera*. I braced myself and waited for the lightning bolt that would strike the young couple dead on the spot. As for the picture taker herself, I'm a little fuzzy on the particulars, but I'm pretty certain that under USGA regulations, she has since gone directly to hell. Or at least purgatory.

So yes, the lengthy postponement of my blessed arrival upon the sod of a magnum opus of the golf world had set my blood to boiling. It was decidedly *not* how I had envisioned my big day beginning. I shook it off, though. I was still prepared to be mesmerized.

And once I had finally navigated my way onto the golf course, there was no question about it—Pebble Beach was every bit as beautiful as I had anticipated. Shortly after I arrived, a clearing pattern replaced morning fog with brilliant sunshine that rendered the ocean a trademarkable brand of blue. I started at the 18th green and worked my way backward along the course, pausing several times to drink it all in. It was my first time on-site at one of the few true meccas of golf, and I was reflexively attempting to see everything all at once. Which isn't very easy.

See, the very thing that makes Pebble Beach a spectacular location for viewing golf also makes it a very challenging place to view golf. The eight holes that run directly along the ocean are, by definition, "one-sided" holes, by which I mean that only one side of the fairway can accommodate a gallery—well a *dry* gallery, anyway. In addition, most of the tees and greens are located in close proximity to each other on these holes, thus eliminating the possibility of creating viewing areas in between. Consequently, entire swaths of the golf course are roped off and inaccessible. Last, because it is a links course, there is precious little terrain that provides a natural amphitheatre. And that terrain is fully occupied by corporate hospitality tents. Or grandstands—a seat in which requires the kind of advance camp-out strategy I had once reserved solely for Bruce Springsteen or Tom Petty tickets.

In other words, this is the *last* place you want to go if your heart is set on roaming the course and seeing a lot of golf.

While this setup played havoc with my desire to watch golf along the ocean holes, I did eventually discover that there were opportunities to get a clear view of play at several of the inland holes—especially if you were patient enough to take advantage of the turnover of people along the ropes. It was this exact scenario that allowed me to be front and center to see 60-year-old Tom Watson, playing in what was likely to be his final U.S. Open, arrive at the tee on the 12th hole, a par three.

As Watson's group waited for the green to clear, I had the chance to make the acquaintance of a fellow strategic golf-watcher, Don Bortniak. As golf guys are inclined to do, we quickly traded particulars, and I learned that Don and I shared a common bond. Born in Little Falls, New York, and raised in the adjacent village of Herkimer, Don is a walking ambassador for Upstate's Mohawk Valley—a place not terribly far away from where I had spent four years staving off frostbite at Ithaca College. And like me, he'd long ago had his fill of watching perfectly good golf courses lie unused under months-long blankets of snow. His migration to warmer climes saw him eventually settling in Lake Worth, Florida.

Unlike yours truly, this was not Don's first trip to Pebble Beach. He had in fact played the course himself and mentioned with a bit of shy pride that he had hit the shot of his life on that very hole, coming within inches of a hole-in-one. Moments later, in almost eerie fashion, Tom Watson did the exact same thing.

As the ball was in the air and tracking for the pin, escalating murmurs turned to loud exhortations, and when the ball skipped, checked up, and trickled toward the hole, a full-throated roar rumbled toward us from the gallery surrounding the green. When the shot came to rest less than a foot from the hole, I quickly turned to look at Watson and noticed that Don had already done the same. I expected to see arms upraised to the heavens—maybe even a fist pump. Instead, the golf legend stood with glance cast modestly downward as he busied himself with tapping down displaced turf.

Don looked at me and summed it up in two words: "Old school," he said, and I knew exactly what he meant. Watson acted like he'd been there before, which quite obviously was the case. There were no histrionics—not a trace of "Hey, everybody, look at me!" behavior. He simply hit the shot and then focused immediately upon the next one.

Equally old school, to use Don's phrase, was Watson's reaction to the crowd. The wild ovation that exploded as a result of his shot lasted the entire time it took for Watson and his playing partner to walk from tee to green and mark their balls. When he tapped in his birdie putt, another long, warm ovation ensued. And as much as the crowd embraced him, he embraced them right back throughout, with heartfelt smiles and waves of appreciation. Like everyone who witnessed Watson play that hole, Don and I became ardent fans of his, and he made us feel as though the feeling was mutual.

As for the rest of the field...not so much. The only other golfer I saw acknowledge the cheers of the crowd with anything other than a drive-by half-wave was the comebacking David Duval. Otherwise, I was amazed on several occasions by how hard players worked at *not* making eye contact with the fans along the ropes who offered words of congratulations or encouragement. These guys made Garbo seem downright effusive by comparison.

Try as I might, I couldn't remember if things had been that way back when I was a bright-eyed "young" PGA Tour intern. All that I could conjure up was the indelible image of Tiger Woods working as hard as he could to be invisible.

Over the years, when it has come up at cocktail parties or on long plane rides that I left a six-figure corporate job to start over at the bottom of the golf business, the questioning has usually gone something like this:

My new friend: "Are you crazy?"

Me: "Apparently."

My new friend: "No, seriously, what were you thinking?"

Me: "Evidently I wasn't."

My new friend: "Do you know Tiger Woods?"

Me: "Nobody knows Tiger."

My response was based on the fact that, while I had been around Tiger on several occasions, I had never heard him utter a word outside of an obligatory interview—or even acknowledge anyone outside the ropes, for that matter. On practice days, his rounds almost always began at the first hint of daylight, and he was typically long gone from the course by the time most spectators arrived. But there was more to it than that.

Tiger Woods carefully cultivated a brand of ultimate integrity and, to a lesser extent, arrogance well earned through hard work, grit, and determination. We in the golf trade all took his lead. We built upon the brand with complete confidence in its authenticity.

One of my responsibilities at the Match Play Championship had been to solicit local in-kind sponsorships, i.e. "trade-outs" of goods and services for tournament tickets and hospitality-related perks. In one instance I dealt with the CEO of a regional restaurant chain, who turned out to be *quite* interested in providing gobs and gobs of food for the tournament's volunteers in exchange for some up-close and personal Tiger time. As we went back and forth on finalizing this arrangement, I had absolute, total access to this corporate titan. He would excuse himself from meetings to take my calls. He loved the Tiger brand, and by extension I was empowered by the brand.

And as everything began to unravel in late 2009, we learned that it was all a lie. A well-crafted lie, supported by an ongoing tag-team cover-up that would have given Woodward and Bernstein pause.

But there at Pebble Beach I was amazed at the public reaction to Tiger. Everywhere on the property, if you stood and just listened, you never had to wait more than a minute or two before you would hear the word "Tiger." And not once did I hear it spoken in a negative or mocking tone— even from a female voice. It was as if his entire character meltdown had never happened. *There were no discernible consequences of his behavior at all.*

It staggered me. *What does this guy have to do to alienate people?* I wondered. He could popularize cannibalism. At the time, the massive Gulf of Mexico oil spill was dominating the headlines, and it occurred to me that BP could get out ahead of the story by simply replacing CEO Tony Hayward with Tiger Woods. *Poof!* No more public-relations nightmare! Oil spill? Billions of dollars in economic impact? Dead pelicans? Oh, that's just Tiger—he's a fiery competitor and he wins a lot, so it's OK.

So much for the purity of golf.

I'm not saying that I would have liked hearing him booed or heckled, but the adulation heaped upon him was hard to stomach. And the indigestion was only made worse by my anticipation of an indelibly remarkable day. I stayed at Pebble Beach until the bitter end that day, unable to pull myself away. But if I were completely honest with myself, it wasn't because I desperately *wanted* to. It was more like I felt obliged to. Like the experience that I was seeking would suddenly kick in, and I'd hate myself for leaving and missing out on it.

Despite the endless competition for space, everywhere I turned that day I saw smiling fans. They happily stood in long lines for concessions, joined serpentine queues for the port-o-johns, and waited patiently for their turn to buy merchandise that had been marked up beyond all reasonable price points.

For this was an official Scene. As time went by, it became obvious that a significant portion of the multitudes there had really come because… well…because it was the U.S. Open at Pebble Beach. They came for a few beers with friends, some laughs, some spectacular scenery (of both the human and landscape varieties), and the opportunity to buy a souvenir to remember the day by. In fact, if somehow all of the golfers had been secretly air-lifted off the course in the middle of the day, I have no doubt it would have taken more than an hour for everyone on the property to realize it. And all in all, this was, to them, worth the price of a ticket that averaged higher than $100 a pop.

To me the scenario was like staging a potluck barbeque in the Sistine Chapel, but hey—who was I to judge? It quite obviously fit the bill for the average attendee. But was it good enough for a true golf fan? Was it good enough for me? I thought about that long and hard on my drive back to my hotel. I went through each microexperience and impression about the day in turn. I eventually decided that having seen the legendary golf course up close in its most pristine condition was…well, I guess it was better than a sharp stick in the eye. But intoxicating? As euphoria-inducing as I had expected? I hated to admit it, but no. And it bothered me to a degree that was completely out of proportion.

I told myself that this had been just one single event. I'd caught golf on an off day. Hadn't I already accumulated positive experiences while sampling the low-hanging fruit of my quest? Everything golf-related had started out so well. But now, way, way, wayyyy back in my brain a small voice began asking, "Hey, Tim—if this was a premier event in your favorite sport…" Knowing where he was going with that, I tuned him out before he finished the question. It had been a long day.

SIX

The Tour de Golf Tours

THERE'S NO DOUBT ABOUT IT. I had been cocky. Having drawn on golf, a sport that had been the catalyst for my career change, everything had initially come up roses. Removed from the workaday world, I had found the whole "falling back in love with sports" thing to be a cakewalk. Granted, that conclusion had been drawn largely from attending events that featured friends and former colleagues of mine, but I viewed that factor as simply a nice light dessert on top of a hearty, fulfilling meal.

Then came Pebble Beach, an experience that had decidedly produced emotions other than an unbridled love of sports. Had that been a blip? An aberration?

I mulled that possibility over for way too many hours in the days following my return home from the Monterey Peninsula. Finally tired of hearing myself think on that topic, I took action. If I wanted to find out which of my golf-fan experiences was reality, there was one way to ferret out the answer for sure: a golf-tour immersion program. I figured, why visit one pro golf tour when I could see two...or three...or four. In the same week. Seriously—the opportunity was just sitting there for the taking. In fact, it would be logistical child's play:

On Wednesday, the Futures Tour City of Hammond Classic pro-am, just outside of Chicago. On Friday, second-round action at the LPGA Championship in Rochester, New York. On Saturday, the Champions Tour—specifically, day two of the Dick's Sporting Goods Open in Endicott, New York. And to wrap it up, Sunday's final round of the PGA Tour Travelers Championship in Hartford, Connecticut. What could be easier? I would finish the week with a flourish, with my worldview of golf—and by extension, sports—reaffirmed. Buoyed by the thought, I threw myself into travel planning.

Beginning this four-tours-in-five-days adventure with a Futures Tour pro-am was a no-brainer. In addition to furnishing me with the opportunity to actually *take part* in an event I was covering, the City of Hammond Classic would enable me to debunk the age-old saying, "You can't go home again." Sure enough, not only was visiting the Futures Tour like going home, it was like going home on Thanksgiving weekend, playing backyard touch football with all your cousins, and pulling the lucky end of the wishbone from the turkey. It was that comfortable.

Blessed with the most approachable pro athletes on the planet, this tour is the launching pad for a career on women's golf's biggest stage. Scan the final results of virtually any LPGA tournament, and you will find dozens of players who have previously graced the fairways of the Futures Tour. And "grace" is the operative word here.

The purse money is not great. Travel is almost exclusively by car—often hundreds of miles at a time between Tour stops. Sponsorships and endorsement deals are hard to come by. And just five players each year earn the ultimate reward, the right to graduate to the LPGA Tour with fully unrestricted playing privileges. But despite all of that, these young women approach every tournament as simply another opportunity to succeed. And they get it, with "it" being the dynamics of professional sports in the new millennium.

Ask pretty much any Futures Tour player to define her job, and she'll tell you: (a) Play great golf; and (b) Entertain fans and sponsors. They take both responsibilities equally seriously, which is why playing in a Futures Tour pro-am is just about the most fun you can possibly have while losing a dozen golf balls and most of your athletic self-esteem.

I arrived at Lost Marsh Golf Club anticipating that I would be recognized by some, but I never anticipated how warm would be my reception. From tournament director Carole Jo Fremouw to my former colleagues on the Tour's staff to many of the talented and charismatic pros, everyone made a point of stopping by to say hello and check up on me. It was like having about 100 additional sisters for the day, without the requisite battle for time in the family bathroom.

I'm not the most talented golfer in the world, but what I lack in natural skill I make up for with a practice regimen that includes…OK, well it includes next to nothing. Or at least nothing that anyone else would identify as "practice." Take my warm-up routine for that day's tournament:

- 11:15 AM: Arrive at course, turn bag over to course staff to whisk away
- 11:20 AM: Change into golf shoes
- 11:22 AM: Begin socializing
- 12:38 PM: Locate putter, head to practice green to putt
- 12:41 PM: Resume socializing
- 12:56 PM: Remember that I have yet to officially register for play, and sprint to do so
- 12:59 PM: Begin stretching regimen
- 1:00 PM: Hit first tee shot into lake

We started on the back nine of the tournament course, which brought water into play on the first six holes. I lost eight balls in that stretch. Fortunately, the team-based scramble tournament format allowed me to shamelessly piggyback on the contributions of my amateur teammates, Bill Sokolis and Aaron Moore, the owner and GM, respectively, of the Chicago Bandits, a mainstay of the women's National Pro Fastpitch softball league.

And then, of course, we had Futures Tour pro Melissa "Mo" Martin, for whom a "miss" consisted of a ball that varied 0.673 degrees off of its intended line. I'm pretty sure I shielded this from her, but I did feel badly for Mo. I mean, how much adventure is involved in a golf game that involves only fairways and greens? Doesn't it get old when almost every putt you look at is for birdie? I was hopeful that the poor kid could take some solace in her two previous tournament championships and current rank inside the top ten on the Tour's money list.

I'm frankly stumped as to why I can't get any better at this game, but I'm always open to suggestion. And bless her heart, Mo took it upon herself to suggest. After yet another tee shot of mine adopted the problematic left-to-left ball flight and landed deep in the marsh, she called timeout to show me that I had been lining up with my feet aimed significantly right of where I thought I was aiming. This forced me to swing across my body, causing all kinds of problems. Curiously enough, right after Mo realigned me, I hit a straight, solid tee shot. Coincidence?

I happily told Mo that it was worth losing eight balls in six holes to earn free professional instruction. And if I had it to do over, I would've just thrown eight balls into the water on the first tee and moved directly into the lesson.

The weather, as it can do in Midwest summers, took a quick turn for the worse, and we were unfortunately summoned back to the clubhouse having completed only 14 holes. At the time, we were seven shots south of par, prompting us to declare ourselves the pro-am champions. And who could dispute it? Our group included a two-time tournament champion, both the owner and GM of a professional sports franchise, and the commissioner of the marginally renowned It's Game Time Somewhere Tour. Collectively, it was clear we knew how to spot a winner.

The violent thunderstorms that rolled through the area for the next several hours did nothing to dampen my giddy enthusiasm about the start of this golf-immersion program. But how was I to know that they would serve as a metaphor for the rest of the week?

* * *

Thirty-six hours later I had a date with another of professional golf's "major" tournaments. Just two weeks removed from the Men's U.S. Open, I was now navigating my way toward Rochester's Locust Hill Country Club, site of the LPGA Championship and the second stop on my Tour de Golf Tours. I had company for this major, in the form of old friend J.C., who had graciously agreed to serve as a sounding board and adjunct perspective provider. All for the low, low fee of…well, actually there was no fee. And to sweeten the deal, he and his wife Phyllis agreed to house me during the Upstate New York leg of this sojourn. I didn't share this with him at the time, but I think J.C. really needs to brush up on negotiation tactics for pricing his forecaddie services.

Right from our arrival, it was obvious that having a sidekick was not to be the only thing that made this experience different from that of Pebble Beach. For starters there was plenty of available parking—and all within a ZIP code shared by the course. A short stroll brought us to the front gate, where the entry and security-screening process was in marked contrast to the U.S. Open protocol. It basically consisted of friendly senior citizens glancing at our tickets and saying, "Nice to see you today. You don't have a cell phone or camera with you, now, do you?"

That was unfair. It's one thing to lie to a beefy security guard; it's another to fib to somebody who looks like they're just about to offer you home-baked cookies. I crumbled and gave up on any thought of trying to smuggle in a camera.

It quickly became obvious that most in attendance came exclusively to absorb as much tournament golf as possible. The entrenched, oblivious social klatches that marked the U.S. Open scene were replaced here by far more focused golf enthusiasts. Upstate New York golf fans have a reputation for following play instead of camping out and waiting for it to come to them, and that was certainly the case on this day. Despite fairly steamy weather, almost every group on the course had a gallery of some size trailing them around the hilly layout.

The fans were knowledgeable and appreciative, and the environment all day was pleasant and agreeable—much like Upstate New Yorkers themselves.

And this just in: women are different from men. It was not unusual to see the LPGA pros converse with fans as they made their way from one green to the next tee. In fact, in some of the more far-flung areas of the course, the alleys roped off to ensure that this short trip would be unimpeded were not even used by the golfers. Apparently women have the unique ability to give the steely hyperfocus thing a rest long enough to say hello to an old friend.

At this point I must come clean. Remember when I mentioned that I had acceded to the "no camera" policy when entering the gate? Well, I have to admit that I was a little less forthcoming about my BlackBerry. I absolutely needed it, though—I had to track down the highly mobile force of nature known as Cindy Miller.

Cindy is one half of Cindy and Allen Miller, the First Couple of tour golf. In the way that some people collect stamps or trading cards, the Millers have spent their lives collecting tour memberships: the PGA Tour, the LPGA Tour, the Senior PGA Tour, the Futures Tour, and the Legends Tour. Both are now accomplished teaching pros—Allen a member of the PGA of America and Cindy the 2010 LPGA National Teacher of the Year. Daughter Kelly is a producer with Golf Channel, and son Jamie is an aspiring pro currently paying his dues on the mini-tour circuit. This is the Miller Golf Group, operating out of the golfing mecca of...Buffalo? Weird, I know.

I had worked with Cindy and Allen one summer on a series of high-end clinics that we hosted for a preeminent tour sponsor, but I hadn't seen them in a while. So it was wonderful to catch up and spend some time explaining this...this *thing* that I was wrestling with. In retrospect, I shouldn't have been so taken aback when they reacted to my do-I-still-love-sports dilemma with such little surprise. It was almost as if they expected it.

It took much of the day for me to fully grasp this, but the four of us attending the event—J.C., Cindy, Allen, and me—were having entirely different experiences.

What started me thinking this way was J.C.'s commentary as we toured the course. He noticed all of the subtleties about the play in front of us well before I did. He could identify a player's club selection by observing the loft of the clubface as it lay on the ground behind the ball at address. He picked right up on the fact that the tournament was being played under "lift, clean, and place" rules as a result of soggy early morning playing conditions. He loved to read the greens and predict in advance which way putts would break. And he wanted to see as much of the course and as many different players as possible. In short, J.C. is a Golf Fan—pure and unadulterated.

Truth be told, I couldn't make the same claim. I was there partly for walkabout purposes, partly for journalistic pursuits, and partly to root on the players who I had gotten to know while working for the LPGA and Futures Tours. My attention was fragmented at best. Yes, I was interested in seeing golf shots—but only those of the pros who I knew. Nothing that anyone else did was of major interest to me, and I found my attention otherwise drifting toward evaluating the tournament's production.

Vaguely troubled by this realization, I asked Cindy and Allen separately about what they were paying attention to. Allen said without hesitation, "I'm watching golf swings," and he could do it all day long. The pure analytics of the golf swing are not only his business but also a sort of art form to him. He remembers promising players by their swing, and when he is intrigued by their mechanics, he considers them a kindred spirit with whom he would like to work. But Allen, like me on that day, is generally oblivious to trifling things like who's on the leaderboard.

Cindy said equally as immediately that she was there to check up on the players whom she'd played with or worked with—especially on the mental side of the game. She sought their answers to the questions "How are you doing as a person?" and "How is this game treating your life?" She was on wounded-soul patrol.

And there were a lot of souls that needed attending to, for these were challenging times for women's golf. For better or worse, the LPGA Tour had chased hot money during the boom times of the prior decade and wound up with a handful of defunct tournaments when the real-estate speculators and shell-game investment tycoons went bust. At the same time, some of the long-tenured smaller-market tournaments that had struggled to keep up with rising purses and other costs during this bubble wound up stretched too thin to continue.

It was the perfect storm of negative variables, and a tour that as recently as 2006 had a schedule featuring 33 tournaments had shrunk considerably. Incredible as it would have been to conceive of in 2007, only 13 times in 2011 would the LPGA play a tournament on American soil.

The impact on LPGA Tour pros was nothing short of immense, as many went from inserting breaks in their schedules in order to avoid burnout to having to cobble together play on multiple tours around the world in order to make a living. Now players "have to" make the cut, and "have to" finish high enough to earn a certain payout each time they have the opportunity to play. And the pressure grows with each missed cut. Cindy said she could see that financial pressure in their eyes when she spoke with them. She worried that several might crack before the year was out.

Once she had mentioned it, it became obvious to me as well. When you don't see someone whose game you know pretty well for a while, small changes in their mannerisms stand out. And what jumped out at me on this day was that many of the players whom I'd had the pleasure of working with and getting to know were struggling—with their swing and otherwise. One player whom I had looked forward to catching up with in particular looked so forlorn coming up the 18th fairway, I abandoned plans to try and see her after her round. She no doubt would have battled to put on a good front, when what I knew she really needed was a good cry.

None of this was remotely evident to the thousands of fans who had turned out and enjoyed themselves immensely. But I couldn't shake the sobering realization that for me the day had been almost completely about the business of golf and not the game. It was amazing how quickly it served to undermine the deeply satisfying experience I'd had at the Futures Tour event.

More disconcerting still—I had yet to leave the confines of a protective bubble. Every golf event I'd been to other than the U.S. Open at Pebble

Beach had come prepackaged as part of a personal visit with old friends, as opposed to a completely independent sporting event I'd objectively attended. It was as if I had sought to store up a large surplus of positive emotion before actually beginning to contemplate the burning question that motivated this walkabout. Like I was playing a game in which I needed to build up a big early lead in order to withstand an anticipated late-game surge by my opponent. Only, this time, the opponent was me.

I was up early the next morning, even earlier than J.C.'s wake-up knock on the door of my well-appointed guest suite. I was trying to recall whether I had been either delighted or amazed by a single golf shot during the previous day's visit to the LPGA Championship. There had certainly been occasion to be so—J.C. had reflected on several memorable shots during our drive home. But lying there staring at the ceiling as the sun started to filter in the window, I couldn't remember any on my own.

Contemplation on that topic would have to wait, though, because 66 miles of open road lie between us and En-Joie Golf Club. En-Joie is French for "in-joy," which is close enough to "enjoy" for me to co-opt the term. Because that's what I had my heart set on doing that day at the Champions Tour tournament in Endicott, New York.

Endicott was for 35 years the home of the PGA Tour's B.C. Open, and for decades the tournament was *the* social event of the season for Endicott and the environs. It survived from one year to the next, despite both the lack of a corporate title sponsor *and* a slot in the PGA Tour schedule that saw it played during the same week as the British Open—thus guaranteeing that almost all of the Tour's big names would be absent.

Finally, the tournament organizers found themselves no longer able to raise the money that the Tour mandated for status as a sanctioned event, and, in 2006, the last B.C. Open was played—ironically enough, more than 100 miles away at Turning Stone Resort, due to severe flooding at En-Joie. I hadn't been surprised when I heard of the demise of the B.C. Open, and in fact I remember thinking, *What took them so long to pull the plug?*

While the PGA Tour couldn't save the B.C. Open, it did reward the good people of Endicott with a lower-profile Champions (aka Senior) Tour event and even brokered the deal that brought Dick's Sporting Goods on as a title sponsor. And shortly after J.C. and I set foot on En-Joie soil, I discovered why people had been jumping through hoops for so long to keep this humble location on the big-time golf landscape. I've rarely—if ever—been on a golf course that was so perfectly suited to host a professional golf tournament. Granted, En-Joie long ago became outmoded in terms of its distance and challenge for PGA Tour players. But from a fan's standpoint, the course is golf-watching heaven. Let me give you an example.

As I stood next to the 1st tee gathering my bearings upon our arrival, it began to dawn on me that the player groups were being introduced and teeing off at an exceptionally brisk clip. It was then that, in his customary role as Golf Fan and forecaddie, J.C. pointed out that this particular golf course had a humongous tee box that accommodated both the 1st *and* 10th tees. And instead of the normal ten-minute interval between tee times, tournament officials were alternating groups off of #1 and #10, spacing apart their send-offs by just five minutes. This enabled fans to see the entire field get introduced and hit their first tee shot—all in one spot, and at an accelerated pace, no less. Brilliant.

Another characteristic of the course that makes it too small for a PGA Tour event but just right for a Champions Tour event is an old-style routing that "pinwheels" the back nine circularly around the outside of a similarly circular front nine. Thus, just as this creates the opportunity for the dual 1st and 10th tee, it also results in many, many multi-hole vantage points that are scattered throughout the course. Want to tour both the entire course *and* see as many golfers in the field as possible? No problem. Not only can you bounce back and forth from fairway to fairway—you can effortlessly switch your viewing preference from front nine to back nine, depending on who you want to watch play for a while.

If your fondest spectating desires involve picking a comfortable spot for watching a constant stream of players coming and going off of adjoining greens and tees, this is also the perfect place. With very little footwork, for example, J.C. and I were able to watch play on the 3rd, 4th, 7th, and 14th greens, as well as the 8th and 15th tees. You just don't find that kind of fan experience at very many tour venues.

The combination of hospitable environment, rapid-fire action, and J.C.'s enthusiasm served to counteract the pensive, unsettled mood that I had awoken with, and I wholeheartedly began to "in-joy" myself. And I'm neither French nor Upstate New Yorker.

We spent some time early in the day following a pairing that featured Argentinean golfer Eduardo Romero, who goes by the nickname El Gato (the Cat). Romero is an imposing figure who plays fast and hits the ball a ton. But it was his mode of dress that caught my attention, for he was wearing the nicest-looking pair of silk pants that I'd seen in quite a while. I quickly contracted a case of wardrobe envy and, in my mind, "El Gato" quickly morphed into "Los Pantalones."

Curiously enough, despite following this group for several holes, the appropriate time to inquire as to where Romero shopped for his pants never quite seemed to materialize. At one point, however, his caddie did reach into the player-only cooler on the tee box and toss me a bottle of water. *Viva Los Pantalones!*

If the most memorable catch phrase for the PGA Tour is "These Guys are Good," for the Champions Tour it should be "These Guys are Fast." In sharp contrast to the glacial pace of play that we had witnessed the day before, Los Pantalones' group completed their round in just a shade longer than four hours. And there was nothing unusual about that particular pairing—the entire course was moving at that speed. Without, to the best of my knowledge, my bag-emptying high school teammate Dean Palozej even being in the vicinity! None of the golfers looked particularly rushed. They simply didn't waste time second-guessing their own decisions about club selection or putting line. This was golf the way it was meant to be played—and watched!

As I mused more about the comparisons with the LPGA Champion-ship and the LPGA in general, I began to wonder why this venue thrived, while its unofficial "sister" LPGA tournament location a short distance away in Corning was defunct after a 30-year run. The characteristics of each tour-nament were strikingly similar—both were played on classic course layouts, and both were the social event of the summer for small Upstate New York towns passionate about golf. After giving it some thought, I came to the hypothesis that the LPGA tried to force-fit a nice compact tournament into a business model that strives mightily to be a PGA Tour equivalent, while the Champions Tour recognizes the limitations of its model and seeks to create the best possible tournament it can within those limitations.

Realizing that my brain had once again lured me back into thinking about the business of golf when I had up to that point been following my heart and happily taking the day at face value, I became seriously annoyed with myself. My slowly resurging Golf Fan had once again been kicked to the curb—this time by its evil twin, the Golf Marketer. I simply couldn't keep my focus on appreciating the play. My self-annoyance grew a little edgier. But it was too late to stop the floodgates.

As my mind wandered, I recalled that back when the PGA Tour rebranded its Senior Tour to create the Champions Tour, I thought it was simply marketing puffery, designed to con the public into thinking that the Senior Tour was less dusty than it had gotten to be. Roaming the course at En-Joie, I recognized that the Champions Tour was not simply a renamed Senior Tour. It was the PGA Tour "of a certain age." Which was not neces-sarily a wonderful thing.

The field of players at En-Joie included a healthy dose of guys who were on the back nine of their PGA Tour careers when Tiger Woods came along and almost single-handedly made millionaires of the mediocre. They say that absolute power corrupts absolutely. I offer a corollary: absolute purse size dehumanizes absolutely. In 2010, as the country struggled to recover from the worst economy since the Great Depression, the 90th-ranked player on the PGA Tour money list made more than a million dollars. You had to go down the list to #158 to reach someone who struggled by with less than a half-million dollars. And that's just the money earned playing in tournaments. It doesn't include unofficial prize money, endorsements, sponsorships, corporate outings, public appearance fees, etc., etc., etc.

As time has gone by, fans have grudgingly come to expect that PGA Tour players would have the wagons circled tightly around themselves. You hear the mantra repeated over and over—"These guys can't goof around like they used to. There's too much money at stake now." But the Senior Tour? The province of uber-accessible chatterboxes like Lee Trevino, Chi Chi Rodriguez, and Fuzzy Zoeller?

Well those guys are largely gone now, as are the Larry Leorettis and the Tom Wargos of the world—the "Everygolfers" who never made the Big Tour but somehow managed to play their way onto the Senior Tour and have a ball with the fans once they got there. Slowly filling their affable places are the guys who have been ignoring fans and patronizing pro-am partners for the past decade on the PGA Tour and who are now drawn by the allure of the guaranteed paychecks and the less-demanding course layouts of the Champions Tour.

I was already a little peeved by this uninvited thought process, when we stumbled upon its personification in the case of Linda, a sincere and pleasant woman who had volunteered her services at En-Joie as marshal and spotter. The hole on which we encountered her station was bordered on the far side of the fairway by water that was very much in play. And given that it was difficult for golfers to determine from the tee box if their shot had entered the pond, Linda was often called upon to be the bearer of bad news.

In fact, that was exactly the situation that played out shortly after our arrival, as we watched a player patrol the pond's edge in search of his tee shot. Despite possessing precisely the information that the golfer was seeking, Linda appeared uneasy about sharing it.

After that particular golfer had sorted things out and his group had played on, we got to chatting with Linda. She told us that the previous day she had watched a player hit into the water and then play a second, provisional ball that wound up behind a tree near the pond's shore. Not knowing if the player was aware of the exact whereabouts of his two tee shots, Linda was there to meet him when he came up the fairway. "I told him that his first shot went into the water and his second was right behind that tree over there," she told us. "He gave me a nasty look and said, 'Lady, don't you think I know where my balls are?'"

Clearly oblivious to the humorous double entendre, Linda divulged meekly, "Now I don't say a thing unless somebody asks me a specific question." Just that quickly, one pro had turned an eager volunteer into someone who was too intimidated to help. Linda shared with us that this had been her first tournament volunteer experience. I'm guessing it was probably her last. I'm also willing to lay odds that the tour pro in question never gave his rudeness a second thought.

This time it wasn't just me. I could tell that our encounter with Linda had even given pause to J.C., the consummate Golf Fan. He recovered his enthusiasm quickly, though. I, on the other hand, simmered. My supposedly deep-rooted love affair with golf was under siege, and I was rapidly becoming powerless to defend it.

SEVEN
An Old Friend Lost

I WENT TO HARTFORD for the final round of the PGA Tour's Travelers Championship for much the same reason that I began my Tour de Golf Tours at the Futures Tour's City of Hammond Classic. It gave me an opportunity to go home. And while the latter event involved a golfer going home professionally, the former embodied a golfer going home personally. For Ellington Ridge Country Club, the very place where golf had first invaded my soul, was just a niblick or two outside of Hartford.

On one particularly fine summer day of my youth, I had been granted the opportunity to caddie during the Monday qualifier for the Greater Hartford Open—the predecessor of the Travelers Championship to which I was now making a pilgrimage. The golfer for whom I caddied didn't make the field for that year's tournament—I don't even remember his name—but it didn't matter. I was hooked on pro golf and rarely missed an annual trip to the GHO, right up until the time I headed out of New England for warmer pastures.

In the days before UConn became a national men's and women's college basketball power, the GHO was *the* sporting event of the year in northern Connecticut, and everyone from corporate chieftains to...well, to lowly country club caddies, sat side-by-side in the grandstands or stood on the hills overlooking the 18th green, straining to get a better look at the who's who of past GHO champions: Rik Massengale…Rod Funseth…Mac O'Grady…Phil Blackmar. OK, not necessarily a parade of golf legends, but they were plenty good enough for us.

Fast-forward to an unseasonably hot and humid Sunday in present-day Hartford, and you would find yours truly arriving at TPC River Highlands in suburban Cromwell. My brother-in-law Rick was with me, seamlessly picking up the role of forecaddie that had been so capably handled by J.C. during the previous two days. Rick and J.C. shared what was rapidly becoming an enviable trait—they cared nothing about the business of golf and firmly believed that the grass was *always* greener on a golf course, whether they were there as players or spectators.

Despite having worked in the business for a decade, I had learned quite a bit about golf in the previous few days. And at the front gate of the Travelers Championship I added something else to my body of knowledge. Apparently male tour pros under the age of 50 are the only group of golfers whose game will completely fall to pieces in the presence of an iPhone or similar device. Every other golfing demographic miraculously manages to tough it out.

The LPGA Tour puts up a good front about the whole thing, but when push comes to shove, they don't really seem to be *that* concerned about rogue communication devices equipped with the dreaded photographic capabilities. The Champions Tour doesn't even bother to talk about it. And if you bring anything resembling a camera into a Futures Tour event, any given player may just pose for a picture and ask you to email a copy to her mom—who may then invite you over for supper.

But the PGA Tour…not so much. Rick and I got the full TSA wannabe security shakedown. I had foolishly ventured onto the property with a money clip in my pocket, setting off the metal-detector wand. Quite understandably, I was hustled immediately into a small, dark tent with a single naked light bulb swaying overhead. I'm embarrassed to admit it now, but I cracked immediately, coughing up the smartphone, money clip, loose change, and single shiny gum wrapper that I had been trying to smuggle in.

OK, perhaps that's an overdramatization, but I wasn't exactly wild about being forced to choose between hoofing it all the way back to my car or surrendering my BlackBerry to a valet phone check "service" staffed by unpaid volunteers. I chose the latter and received a claim check receipt whose printed disclaimers rendered it the size of a small paperback.

Once Rick and I were re-dressed and inside the gates, the practice complex beckoned. We decided to check out the swings of the tournament leaders, who had just begun their pre-round practice routines. As we sat in the bleachers at the range, I thumbed through the impressive program and pairings list that we had been given. I was curious to know exactly how big the purse had gotten to be since the long-ago days of the Greater Hartford Open. Strangely, nowhere in a publication chock full of detailed information was the purse size listed. This seemed odd to me, because most tournaments across all tours have traditionally trumpeted purse size as evidence of their success in growing their event. Later on, I looked it up on the PGA Tour's website, and the tournament organizer's reticence in listing it in the program made sense to me—at $6 million, the purse had grown to such a size as to be obscene.

I shared with Rick a story from my days as a golf course GM. One facility that I managed happened to have spawned a few individuals who went on to enjoy some significant success in the game. As it was told to me, one of these players had apparently stopped by the course shortly after qualifying to play on the PGA Tour and, in conversing with the staff, volunteered that his current biggest concern in life was avoiding an injury sustained from "falling off my wallet." That was almost ten years ago. I would imagine that things have advanced to the stage that this player is now concerned about potential injury that would arise from his wallet falling on small children.

Rick listened with a bemused smiled and then summed up the PGA Tour mentality very succinctly: "These guys are all untouchable." But he laughed when he said it and didn't appear to be disturbed in the least. "Let's go watch some golf," he ventured. A good idea, for the slow boil of resentment that had started to simmer the previous day at En-Joie was beginning to heat up my brain again.

As we clambered down off of the grandstand, I noticed a colorful sign advertising an AUTOGRAPH ZONE near the practice putting green. This intrigued me, for I had not seen anything like that at a PGA Tour event before. Ordinary, run-of-the-mill fans are a necessary evil to these guys—not somebody you actually interact with. For God's sake, you could *catch something!* But there it was. I went over for a closer look at the sign and immediately found the catch. In much smaller print size was the qualifying legend, RESERVED FOR KIDS 15 AND UNDER. If you can drive, you can't get a PGA Tour autograph. Sorry. I wondered how one obtains an ID that proves they are *not* yet 16…

What the PGA Tour lacks in warmth and approachability, it makes up for in technology. Years ago the Tour began to invest heavily in developing a program called ShotLink, with the goal of collecting, analyzing, and packaging statistical information on virtually every golf shot hit at every tournament on the Tour schedule. Initially the output was popular only among golf media types and assorted stat wonks, who pored through this information on the Tour's website. With the advent of higher-definition scoreboards, however, ShotLink really hit its stride.

Attend any PGA Tour event and position yourself within view of one of their huge ShotLink-fueled video boards, and you will be the beneficiary of a rudimentary "broadcast" that supplements the tournament that you are watching live. As each group passes through the hole on which you sit, key stats about each player appear on screen, updated in real time. During the time between groups, relevant scores and data from elsewhere on the course are presented.

The evolution of ShotLink has truly reinvented the way that live golf can be consumed on-site, and it will no doubt enable the PGA Tour to extend its dominance over other golf tours with which it competes for fans. It's highly unlikely that any other tour or tournament venue will ever be able to afford the expense inherent in developing and delivering what golf fans who have attended a PGA Tour event have now come to expect. You could make the argument that the PGA Tour is offering a completely different product than are other golf tours.

The true beauty of ShotLink, though, is that it costs the Tour a relative pittance to operate on-site. For, at each tournament venue, volunteers do the grunt work needed to collect the vast array of raw data. In fact, people line up for the right to operate the ShotLink equipment. This, after paying a "volunteer registration fee" to acquire the requisite uniform and tournament credentials. That's right—people *pay* a good bit of money for the right to work at a PGA Tour event. Somewhere Tom Sawyer is grinning broadly.

As Rick and I wandered down the 10th hole, we came upon one such gentleman who was operating a ShotLink laser that tracked driving distance. Within seconds after the tee shots of the group that we were following came to rest, the exact distance of each was projected on the fairway video board, along with pictures and information about the pros who had struck them. Our man on the job beamed as he pointed this out. He was living the PGA Tour dream for the day and spoke wistfully of wanting to be able to travel with the Tour and do this on a regular basis. "If I wasn't married…" he said.

The words were barely out of his mouth when out of the blue I was struck by the memory of a random event that had occurred during my "world's oldest intern" days at the Match Play Championship.

We were finishing up work in the operations compound one evening prior to the tournament, when a pickup truck pulled in and an earnest-looking guy hopped out. He was clearly nervous and stammered a bit getting his story out, but in a nutshell, he was an experienced local carpenter who was an avid golfer. He had obviously screwed up his courage for a cold call on the PGA Tour, offering his services at what he indicated would be a deeply discounted rate. As someone who happened to be doing that very thing at the time, I could almost read his mind—*Hell, I'll even do some work for* free *if it will get me a foot in the door with the PGA Tour.* Birds of a feather.

He chatted amiably with the two operations managers in charge for a bit and then, with a noticeable spring in his step, climbed into his truck and drove away across the brown dirt parking lot. The dust cloud had barely settled when one of my two bosses turned to the other and chuckled, "Looks like we'll be able to get a bunch of free work from *him*."

Guys...hello...I'm standing right here. I can hear you, had passed quickly through my brain. But then it was gone, and I hadn't given it another thought. Until this steamy Sunday afternoon in Hartford, when it returned to me with crystal clarity.

It stayed with me throughout the afternoon, piling on top of all the annoyances and irritations that had accumulated over the past several days. And try as I might, I could not come to terms with all of these vexations and simply lose myself in the sport that I was seeing played at world-class levels in front of me.

Regular tournament play ended in a three-way tie, and as fans scurried to position themselves for the playoff to come, I asked Rick if he wanted to head out and beat the traffic. "Leave early?" he double-taked. He recovered quickly, though. When you're related to me, you become accustomed to eccentric behavior.

It took 15 minutes to walk to the car, and with each step I could feel the pressure building. I was angry with the Travelers Championship, angry with the PGA Tour...angry with pro golf. I found myself wanting to lash out—demand retribution for...for what?

To be honest, I didn't really know. I knew I was overreacting, but I didn't know why. Where was this coming from? I had never cared how much money pro golfers made before. Never gave much thought to whether they were nice to fans and marshals. Why did I care so fervently now? As for belatedly becoming offended about having been exploited as an indentured servant at the Match Play...well, hadn't I knowingly and willingly signed up for that? Although a job with the PGA Tour turned out not to be in the cards, things worked out fine for me career-wise, and the lost gamble had never bothered me in the past. And the BlackBerry shakedown...well, OK, the aggravation about that ridiculous policy will always be legitimate.

For everything else, though, I was beginning to grudgingly recognize that there was really no other explanation: the feeling of discomfort and disillusionment that had crept up so often during this Tour de Golf Tours was really a smokescreen I had created to avoid a realization that I had been repressing for a long time.

If you'll pardon the mixed sports metaphor, golf should have been a layup. Surely the sport that had intoxicated me for decades, the one whose vocational siren song I had succumbed to, could make things right with my sports fandom. Much to my horror, though, the first lesson that I was learning from my sports walkabout was that I honestly didn't love golf anymore. In fact, I didn't even *like* the sport much.

Not only had golf failed to dispel what I had come to fear, it had verified it.

I wondered if just maybe I should have continued to trade time for corporate-world money and pursued the weekend-warrior route to embracing sports. Would that have been worse than the ongoing scramble to make a living chasing something it turned out may simply be ethereal? *Perhaps,* I thought, *you* can't *mix business and pleasure after all. What now?*

EIGHT

The Cartoon Characters of Big-Time Sports

IT HAD BEEN THE MOTHER of all wake-up calls.

I had been *so sure* that simply taking some time off to spend with an old friend—golf—would make everything right. The rest of my walkabout would be a victory lap. Once again secure in the knowledge that my relationship with sports had been only slightly tarnished instead of completely rusted over, I would luxuriate in the total sports fan experience. Have a lot of laughs, take a few priceless photos, collect some souvenirs. Head back to work rejuvenated. The rest of the IGTS Tour would be like a montage in a feel-good movie: me mugging for the camera in a bunch of zany, goofy clips spliced together and set to an upbeat pop soundtrack. Think *Hard Day's Night* with sticks and balls, and me playing the roles of John, Paul, George, *and* Ringo.

If I knew how to produce a text-based version of the sound a needle makes when being ripped across a record album, I would do that here. For things had come to a screeching halt. The punch bowl had been unceremoniously removed from the party. Feel free to insert your own cheesy cliché or sound effect here. The point is this—I was starting over. Not only from scratch, but from…whatever is less than scratch. Pre-scratch?

In retrospect, it had all been right there in front of my nose, if I had ever paid attention. Golf—the *game*, not the business—was like an old friend who lived just down the street. Over time I had gotten busy, and more than a little lazy, and I hadn't stopped by to hang out with Golf in a while. Even though it was a two-minute walk to his door, we rarely saw each other for any longer than it took to exchange pleasantries. Then one day I noticed a For Sale sign on his lawn. A few weeks later I was standing in his driveway shaking his hand, just before he climbed into his car to follow a Mayflower moving van headed out of town.

Sometimes you get lulled to sleep in your own life, and it takes a two-by-four between the eyes to wake you up. Sometimes you need to lose something. Golf as I had known it was gone, and it wasn't coming back. The evidence was overwhelming.

I had succumbed years before to a common occupational hazard—people who work in golf tend to stop playing golf. That lethargy had spread. As a result of the Tour de Golf Tours, I realized that I really had no interest in going to another golf tournament, no desire to slouch onto the couch on a Sunday afternoon and watch the drama play out at that week's PGA Tour stop. I hadn't a clue what number to push on my remote to bring up Golf Channel. I was not positive Golf Channel was even part of my cable package, for that matter. And the topper? The previous year I hadn't been able to motivate myself to drive the 90 miles to see an LPGA tournament (a major, no less) in which women whom *I knew and had enjoyed working with for years* were competing.

Check, check, check, and…check. Golf had checked out of my life.

But that didn't mean that this had to be the case with the whole of the sports world. If Golf was indeed a good friend I had taken for granted and let drift out of my life, there was still time for contacting longtime buddies I'd similarly subjected to benign neglect—and to let them know how much I valued their friendship.

These were my oldest and dearest pals. The ones I'd grown up with. Those who had played a major role in shaping who I am today. I hadn't seen many of those friends in years and years, and communication had tapered off, to put it mildly. But that was about to change. It was time for a major reunion. All of the bosom buddies of my youth would be there: NBA basketball, NCAA hoops, the NFL, Major League Baseball, college football. I could hardly wait to see what they'd been up to during the ten years I had spent head down, focused laser-like on building my new career. Nothing would soothe the soul and rejuvenate the spirit better than to spend some in-person quality time with my old gang, the Big-Time Sports.

Here's the thing, though. The IGTS Tour had turned out to be a finicky creature. And a fiercely independent one as well. As such, there was little I could do to make the Tour's schedule bend to my will. In fact, more often than not, it controlled me. The logistical challenges of attending 100 sporting events in a year weren't necessarily that daunting—even when it involved assembling the necessary cross-section of events by gender and level of play (pro, college, high school, Team USA, etc.). But! Layering on top of that the requirement that 50 different sports were to be represented...well, that added a complexity to the mix that I hadn't fully appreciated until it came to sitting down and mapping it all out. This was part of what made this a true walkabout—if one were to base an opinion solely on a visit to my website's *Schedule* page, my journey truly would appear to have had no rhyme or reason to it.

For example...the Badminton U.S. Nationals in SoCal, followed by Major League Baseball in New York City, the National Synchronized Swimming Championships in Charlotte, North Carolina, and professional polo's U.S. Open in West Palm Beach, Florida. All within a span of nine days. See what I mean about the schedule actually running me?

The point is this: within this seemingly random framework of successive experiences, impressions tended to accumulate without laying themselves out into fully formed conclusions. My Tour de Golf Tours had been a unique opportunity to gather perspective as I moved through a connected string of events. More typically, though, all I could do was hang on for the ride, write down everything I saw or felt, and assimilate it all at a later date...hopefully.

As a result, I had to patiently settle for the fact that my major reunion with Big-Time Sports would be more of a collection of experiences interspersed with…well, with things like badminton, synchronized swimming, and polo. A single gala reunion would have to be replaced by a loosely connected series of happy hours, so to speak.

Except that most didn't turn out to be so happy.

* * *

I grew up a Red Sox fan. You may be relieved to know that I eventually recovered, but throughout my childhood and adolescence I fully took part in the shared neurosis. Long before there was Red Sox Nation, before "Sweet Caroline" and the trendy pink hats, being a Red Sox fan consisted only of deep-rooted angst, interrupted occasionally by interludes of spasmodic joy—which were quickly arrested by Faustian levels of agony. I am not exaggerating, as any Red Sox fan, circa 1919–2003, will attest, and page upon page has been written about this phenomenon by better writers than I.

During this period of time I used to really, really care whether the Red Sox players—*my* players—were happy with their lots in life. Did they feel loved and appreciated? Did they like Boston and New England? Enough to want to join the community and raise their families in my humble corner of the world? Did the applause showered on them make them go to sleep feeling comfy and cozy? The word that comes to mind when I recall that line of thought now is "innocent." Or maybe "delusional."

Many, many elite professional athletes long ago left the realm of reality as it exists for the average American. Sad to say, I now think of them as more cartoon character than human being. And I probably wouldn't cross the street to have a conversation with any of them. What would we possibly have to talk about—what strand of a common bond?

Me: "So, umm…how's the exotic car collecting going?"

Pro athlete: "Do I hear a noise? I thought I heard a noise…"

Jerry Seinfeld once did a bit on sports in which he mused that, given the trend just described and the rapid turnover of rosters at the professional sports level, in essence we're all just rooting for the laundry when we cheer on "our" teams. It's tough to refute that point.

That's why, over the years, I've migrated from rooting for teams to rooting for the *fans* of teams. Give me any random match-up in the major "stick and ball" sports, and I will always pull for the team that I perceive to have the most deserving fans. Admittedly, coming up with the definition of "most deserving" is somewhat less than scientific, but like the judge trying to define pornography said famously years ago—"I know it when I see it."

In the months following the Tour de Golf Tours, though, as my walkabout continued to pile up disconnected collections of impressions, two disconcerting threads began to emerge and intertwine: (1) The sports fan experience had gotten decidedly worse; and (2) Sports fans themselves might just be the ones to blame.

* * *

Every six weeks or so I make the pilgrimage to see Joanne Harris. My primary motivator is the need for a haircut, but equally important is the better-than-even chance that I'll learn something new. See, Joanne has seen it all—and then some. She has the whole Hollywood hair *artiste* aura down pat, having worked with some of the most recognizable stars of stage and screen. I always enjoy viewing her Wall of Fame, which is populated with miniature posters of the movies and television shows for which she has done the hair of the leading actors. My favorite, though, is the picture of a beaming Joanne holding the award that her peers in the Hollywood Makeup Artist and Hair Stylist Guild have bestowed upon her. But is she overly impressed by the lifestyle that surrounds her on a daily basis? Not in the least.

During the typical haircut, Joanne will engage in a more or less continuous monologue that runs the gamut from passionately ranting to waxing poetic. And every visit unveils a different set of topics. But I've never heard her tell a single "juicy" story about the stars. To her they are just people with heads of hair waiting to be made fabulous. I once asked her about her complete lack of interest in talking about celebrities—and why, on the other hand, America is positively obsessed with the subject. She paused in mid-snip for effect and then said matter-of-factly, "Celebrities are America's royal family." Then she was off on a different tangent.

That tidbit stayed with me and crystallized as I attended sports events that drew crowds ranging in size from the tens of thousands to…well, to just me and the players' moms. I came to realize that during the previous ten-year span of time during which I'd logged hardly any "grandstand time" to speak of, Americans had elevated professional athletes to the exalted status of Celebrity, which in this country is as high on the food chain as it gets. Yes, the truly elite athletes had crossed over into this realm long ago, with Michael Jordan the obvious example. But these days the net is cast a little wider, as I discovered at a swimming pool in Irvine, California.

The morning session of the ConocoPhillips National Swimming Championships had been a pure pleasure. As I sat in the sun-dappled outdoor stadium watching the preliminary qualifying heats, I couldn't have been more content. It was a well-produced event that moved along briskly, offering me the opportunity to see in a relatively short period of time almost the entire cadre of top-ranked American swimmers. It was pure athleticism unaccompanied by fanfare. But what I remember most vividly is what took place during the three-hour break between the preliminaries and the Finals.

For every top dog there's a perennial contender. For every Roger Federer, an Andy Roddick. For every Tiger, a Phil. And for Olympic hero Michael Phelps there is Ryan Lochte—a swimmer who would most likely be the king of the pool were it not for Phelps. Lochte has come agonizingly close on many occasions to unseating Phelps as the top American in multiple events and has a pretty good winner's résumé of his own. But if you say "swimming" to any random American in the post–Beijing Olympics era, they will reply, "Phelps."

If at this point you are beginning to feel the least bit sorry for Ryan Lochte, let me spare you the effort. First of all, the guy is by all accounts a truly classy competitor who is well respected by his peers. And nothing that I saw in my admittedly limited personal exposure to him appeared to contradict that reputation. He's also getting more than his fair share of endorsements—in fact, Speedo was using these championships as a vehicle to launch a new line of Ryan Lochte footwear.

And then, of course, there are the girls.

The word went out during the morning prelims that Lochte and fellow swimmer Peter Vanderkaay would be appearing at 4:30 in the Autograph Zone, a tent set up in the expo area that fronted the event venue. I happened to be returning to the site for the Finals session right around that time and was greeted by a line of about 300 people, roughly 297 of whom were female.

Vanderkaay arrived in the Autograph Zone first and took his place without much fanfare. Lochte arrived a few minutes later—*with* much fanfare. It wasn't quite the Beatles at Shea Stadium, but let's just say that if you happened to be in the vicinity of the Woollett Aquatics Center at that time…you noticed.

OK, a little unusual for that level of attention to be paid to a swimmer who was relatively anonymous to the general public, but I chalked it up to his good looks and charisma. Hey, I'm comfortable enough with my masculinity to admit that even *I* was on the verge of a swoon.

But how to explain what happened at Skate America?

I was on the back end of a day-night doubleheader involving two different events in two different cities. The latter of the two had brought me to the Rose Garden Arena, the centerpiece of Portland, Oregon's Rose Quarter entertainment district, where I would take in the Skate America stop on the ISU Grand Prix of Figure Skating tour. Right from the start, everything seemed a bit odd.

Maybe it was the dark and stormy film noir–esque night outside. Or maybe it was because I was inside a professional sports arena and there was no discernible buzz. It had been difficult to locate a Rose Garden entrance that wasn't locked, and once finally inside, I made my way around an eerily quiet concourse. It almost felt as if I'd wandered into the wrong building. The concourse wasn't fully lit, and only a handful of concession stands were open. And in a horrific sight that I hope to never again have to behold, *all* of the beer taps at *all* of the beer stands *had been removed!* The word that best characterized the entire scene was "subdued." And perhaps that was on the charitable side. "Somber" might be a more apt description.

I finally rounded a corner and came upon a small cluster of tables and pop-up display booths that had been set up by staffers of U.S. Figure Skating, the national governing body of the sport. And the centerpiece of this oasis of activity was an autograph-signing station at which three pairs of skaters attended to a continuous line of about 50 people. Curiously, most of the people in the line were adults, as opposed to the usual cast of teens and kids I'd found in similar setups. There were no signs or placards identifying the skaters, and the advance promotion of the event didn't mention the appearance of any Olympic champions. No Evan Lysacek, no Sasha Cohen, no Michelle Kwan. Not even a Tonya Harding with lead pipe accessory kit.

People were queued up for autographs from six fresh-faced athletes who were essentially unknown to them. It occurred to me that had I been a little smaller and a little younger, I could've sat down at the table and somebody would've asked *me* for an autograph. OK, a *lot* smaller and younger— but you get the point. The Paris Hilton–ization of sports, in which wealthy athletes become famous merely for being wealthy athletes, is looming ever closer. If it isn't already here.

In and of itself, this pedestal-placing of athletes in which America increasingly engages is all very benign. Self-indulgent, narcissistic celebrities have been with us forever. The next case of a celebrity *completely* torpedoing his or her career as a result of boorish behavior, though, will be the first. As I write this, Mel Gibson has a successful new movie out—enough said.

But when that behavioral carte blanche extends to America's newest group of celebrities, professional athletes, the ramifications are a little bit more widespread. The vast majority of kids aren't presented with many situations during the course of their daily lives that might lead them to mimic a Hollywood actor. For young athletes, though, almost everything they do is with the intent of emulating their favorite pro. And from what I've witnessed, that's not necessarily a good thing.

It was an early round singles match at the ATP Farmers Insurance Classic. Germany's Rainer Schuettler was pitted against American Robby Ginepri. I didn't recognize either of those names as dominant forces on the men's pro tennis circuit, but I was comfortable in a great seat that I had "upgraded" myself to during the prior match. Besides, a quick review of my event program revealed that on June 23, 2003, Ginepri had become "the first player to compete at Wimbledon with a sleeveless shirt." I ask—could *you* pass up seeing such a seminal sports figure?

Right from the outset, Ginepri struggled to overcome a string of unforced errors. Finally, in a fit of pique, he slammed his racquet to the ground with such force that it bounced off the surface and somersaulted into the stands, where it struck the shoulder of a spectator. A ball boy hustled over to retrieve the racquet from the stands, and Ginepri drifted over behind him. I naturally assumed that he had gone over to apologize to the woman hit by the racquet, so I was stunned when Ginepri turned his full attention to inspecting the racquet handed back to him—without so much as acknowledging the woman.

To my mind, the crowd reacted quite unusually to all this. At first there was a groundswell of heightened murmuring that, had it been almost any other sports setting, would have grown into a boo. It quickly died down, however. For to boo would be uncivilized, and such rude behavior in this setting would probably be cause for ejection. Unless, of course, you are a professional tennis player. And an American. This is John McEnroe's legacy to the game.

The scene now shifts to the California Interscholastic Federation (CIF) Southern Section Boys Tennis Championships, where during a change-over in a tense title match between Palm Desert and Brentwood it occurred to me that any doubts about pro athletes being role models can be quickly dispelled by successively attending and comparing high school contests involving completely different sports. Something which, it may not surprise you to learn, I was in the middle of doing.

Each sport has its own set of cultures and mores, based largely upon the personalities of the titans of that game at the professional level. For example, the El Dorado High School baseball team that I saw in a CIF playoff game the previous day clearly took its lead from the New York Yankees. Their uniforms bore a strong resemblance to the Bronx Bombers, and the numbers that the players had chosen to wear were largely those of the Yankees stars. And the high schoolers comported themselves according to the uniforms they wore. They were the embodiment of the icy cool of A-Rod, Jeter, and Rivera. They celebrated their own good play but not excessively—and they gave the opposition no mind whatsoever, other than to congratulate them at the end of the game.

In contrast, the Palm Desert tennis team that I was observing the next day had obviously embraced the classic tennis "bad boy" persona. They exuberantly exalted in almost every point earned and loudly shouted the call when their opponent's shots landed out of bounds. It was borderline "in your face" stuff, which, in another sport, would probably have drawn at least a "Dude...seriously?" About the only thing missing from one Palm Desert mini-tantrum after another was a "Double-turds!" outburst in the grand tradition of Spaulding Smails at Bushwood Country Club.

On one particularly close call that a Brentwood player had signaled "out," his Palm Desert opponent went through an entire passion play, ending with hands lifted to the heavens, beseeching his coach, "Can't we get a line judge here?" If I had been the Brentwood player, I'd be thinking, *This guy just called me a cheat.* But everyone in attendance pretty much shrugged and carried on.

To my mind, though, I couldn't help but think that such divergent framing of high school athletic events has to come from somewhere—and in my opinion it's taken from the pros that play those sports. Either that, or from rap stars. Then again, I find it pretty easy to blame rap music for everything, up to and including gingivitis. But that's just me.

It would have been easy to write off the behavior of the Palm Desert team as an isolated example of overexcited boys who were relatively new to both testosterone and playing under pressure. That is, if I hadn't observed much the same thing from the girls.

On a completely different occasion, I attended the CIF Southern Section Girls Tennis Championships, where the Division I title showdown matched two iconic high school programs, Campbell Hall and Dana Hills. The former was riding a 33-match winning streak that extended back into the previous season, while the latter was making their fourth consecutive appearance in the Finals. In a nonleague regular-season match earlier in the year, Campbell Hall had prevailed 10–8, tagging Dana Hills with their only loss of the year. That slim 10–8 margin was, coincidentally enough, the same score by which Campbell Hall had earned the CIF Championship they were now there to defend. Their opponent in that epic match? The Dana Hills Dolphins. These two teams were no strangers to each other, and nerves were definitely set on edge.

While there were many differences between the Boys and Girls Championships, there was one marked similarity—the same heart-on-sleeve emotion and the same bland acceptance of outbursts of temper and other petulant behavior. Not 15 minutes into the first doubles match that I witnessed came the first racquet heave of the day. I hadn't yet had enough time to evaluate the *tennis* skills of the players involved, but I can tell you one thing—at least one particular player from Dana Hills certainly had a great arm!

As her racquet slammed against the chain-link fence and rattled to the ground, it struck me as a teachable moment for all concerned. But the coach and the crowd double-faulted miserably on the opportunity. Their reaction? Shouts of affirmation like, "Come on, shake it off—you can do it!" and, "That's OK, you'll get the next point!" Alrighty, then.

I admit it. I'm old-fashioned (or, as The Bird delights in calling it, "crotchety") when it comes to this topic. But the tacit acceptance of this lack of sportsmanship and self-control bothered me. Don't get me wrong. At the vast majority of high school- and collegiate-level events that I attended, I was struck by how respectful the athletes were to each other and how well they handled both victory and defeat. But not in tennis, a sport in which

American professional athletes do things like *physically threaten* a line judge (see "Williams, Serena") or fail to apologize to a fan who could have been physically harmed by that athlete's tantrum. And where few onlookers act as if behavior like this is too far out of the ordinary. Does anybody but me see a connection here?

Sports fans have the ability to shape the behavior of professional athletes every bit as much as the inverse. And sadly, from what I was witnessing with increasing regularity, they have. Everything from silently condoning boorish behavior, to celebrating it, to out-and-out *emulating* it adds to the distancing of celebrity athletes from the fans of the actual games. And as I ping-ponged around the world of spectator sports, I began finding it harder and harder to root for either the coddled Big-Time Sports stars *or* the fans who contribute more and more to their cluelessness.

Sigh. That wasn't supposed to happen.

NINE

Just Add Alcohol and Stir

AS THE IGTS TOUR'S schedule of events flew by, I sadly came to comprehend how it is that sports fans have enabled today's professional athletes to become larger-than-life not-so-superheroes. What truly came to mystify me, though, was how so many fans at Big-Time Sports events have lost all sense of perspective. And in many cases, self-control. Trust me when I tell you that there's a lot of misplaced passion out there. Where does that come from? And why are so many sports fans so willing to put up with the behavior of these "passionate" fellow fans?

As I roamed the country on my walkabout, an occasional companion of mine was a book entitled *The Fix Is In*, written by an earnest author named Brian Tuohy. To my periodic distress, Mr. Tuohy had some very unflattering things to say about my old friends, the Big-Time Sports, which he annoyingly backed up with reams of good old-fashioned, roll-up-the-sleeves research. The nerve. The unmitigated gall. I wouldn't be surprised if his Sports Fan status were revoked as a result.

Tuohy summed up quite neatly the entire topic at hand when he wrote, "Have you ever stopped and asked yourself why do professional sports matter to you? Why do you care if a bunch of guys who happen to call them-selves the New York Yankees win or lose a simple baseball game? You didn't play in the game. You may not even have witnessed it in person or watched it on your television. You probably don't know any of the Yankees personally, nor they you. So why does what they do out on the field affect your life in any way, shape, or form?"

In contrast to a certain walkabout participant, Tuohy was actually able to follow up his questions with well-framed answers. In his book, he quotes scholarly publications that describe psychological factors that make perfect sense—the most compelling of which is people's innate need for belonging and affiliation with a group. But not just any group. No, we want to belong to *distinct* groups that more or less provide us with additional validation for claiming that we are not—and I'm paraphrasing here—pathetic losers.

But Tuohy was just getting warmed up. Drawing largely on a study done by Vassilis Dalakas, Robert Madrigal, and Keri Anderson that was published in 2004 in the journal *Sports Marketing and the Psychology of Marketing Communication*, Tuohy introduced me to the concept of BIRG: Basking In Reflected Glory. In a nutshell, people have a natural tendency to try to make themselves look better in both their own eyes and the eyes of society by latching onto the success of somebody or something else—and a well-known local sports team is a perfect instrument. You can tell when BIRGing is taking place when somebody says, "We really kicked butt yesterday!" when in fact their personal contribution to the home team's win consisted of turning on the television and consuming a bag of heavily salted snack food.

According to the BIRG study authors, this is all very normal and harmless. Who among us has not had a spring put into their step when their favorite team wins a big game? Things start to get out of hand, though, when people begin to lose their actual identities and immerse themselves too deeply in their team's identity. As Tuohy succinctly puts it, "This is the realm of the fanatic." And that of regular callers to sports talk radio. And more often than not, as I made my way through the world of Big-Time Sports…the bulk of the people who occupied my particular section in the bleachers.

Admittedly, sometimes this phenomenon enhanced my overall

enjoyment of a game. If the home team was winning, everybody was happily BIRGing away to their hearts' content. Euphoria reigned. High fives were exchanged with total strangers. And even when the home team was losing, it wasn't unusual for the fans to pull together for a reverse BIRG—affiliating and bonding with each other as they loudly berated their team for its poor performance. I believe that researchers call that latter phenomenon "Attending a game in Philadelphia."

Where things got dicey, though, is when the stands consisted of large numbers of people actively BIRGing in opposite directions.

* * *

When I began to map out the summer portion of the schedule for the Tour, I remember thinking to myself, *How cool would it be to have a regular-season football game under my belt before any of my NFL-crazy fellow American citizens have even started to focus on training camp—even before the media sets up its annual vigil outside Brett Favre's house?* Intoxicated by the thought, I turned my attention north of the border, where the Canadian Football League operates almost completely off of the radar screen of American football fans. And the next thing I knew, The Bird and I were crossing the border into British Columbia.

Perhaps it was because it was the first home game of the season. But I don't think so. I get the overwhelming feeling that a B.C. Lions football game is always a *big deal* in Vancouver. As far as the eye could see, everything and everybody was draped in orange. Except for the fans with the watermelons on their heads. They were either there to support the visiting Saskatchewan Roughriders or were fresh from a local farmer's market gone berserk. I sat in the stands puzzling over that one until I was distracted by a major case of anthem envy.

My nephew Devin is a gifted singer, and I defer to him on the musical structure and intricacies of "The Star-Spangled Banner." But this I know for a fact: it's wicked hard to sing—especially that lung-collapsing "rockets' red glare" part. Anybody remotely capable of carrying a tune can sing "O Canada," though. And I'm here to tell you that in Empire Field, the interim home of the Lions, they belted it out with gusto. As I looked around the stadium it was hard to spot anyone who *wasn't* singing. The easiest gig in Canadian show biz has got to be performing the national anthem at a CFL game. All you really have to do is show up and lip-synch, because even your amplified voice won't be heard over the crowd anyway.

In terms of game-day atmosphere, there is virtually no difference between the CFL and the NFL. Fans in both leagues closely and vocally identify with their teams. I could have closed my eyes and listened to what was going on around me and been unable to identify whether I was in Vancouver or any of my previous NFL haunts in New York, San Diego, or Charlotte (well, OK, the Southern drawl might've tipped me off to that last one).

There was one thing about the environment at Empire Field that did give me pause, though—in fact, I did a full double-take. For there, right in the middle of the surrounding concourse, literally just a few feet away from the tunnel through which I would enter to take my seat, was a tent bearing the name SportsAction. It was a legal gambling service, taking bets on, among other things, the very game that was just about to start! But wait, there's more…

Two minutes into the game, a SportsAction promo announcement came over the PA system, during which they announced the over/under for the game and encouraged people to stop by and place a wager. Later I noticed that all video-board replays were "brought to you by SportsAction." And then this—the padding wrapped around the base of the goal posts also bore the SportsAction name and logo. *A gambling company is a major sponsor of a pro football team!*

Somewhere Pete Rozelle was spinning in his grave. NFL commissioners past and present, Paul Tagliabue and Roger Goodell, were staggering around clutching their chests. And Pete Rose was *verklempt*—"How come *they* can do it and I couldn't?"

On-site gambling aside, the most immediately noticeable thing about

CFL football was the size of the players. It was as if somebody left an NFL team in the dryer too long. But as the game went on, it became obvious that size was pretty much the only difference between an NFL and CFL squad. The pure athleticism on display in Vancouver looked every bit as good as that found on autumn and winter Sundays in the Lower 48.

As for the rules of the game, other than a 110-yard field (I got a kick out of the scoreboard informing me that the ball was on the 54-yard line), the single biggest difference in the way the CFL game is played is that they use a three-down rule instead of the four downs used at all levels of American football. I initially took this as simply an exchange-rate thing, but the idea grew on me. Hell, if you can't make ten yards in two plays, give it up and let the other team have a crack at it. This almost forces the pass—and indeed I saw a lot less of the NFL smash-mouth football strategy that's built around three yards and a cloud of synthetic turf.

As this football cultural exchange unfolded, there turned out to be a lot of unique things about the game that I got a kick out of. For example, the CFL play clock is 20 seconds, versus 40 seconds in the NFL. Time between snaps is, well…snappy. As a fan of the passing game, I liked the fact that the receivers get a head start up the field, moving toward the line of scrimmage before the ball is snapped. Almost all of the pass routes run seemed to be of the "Go deep and I'll hit you" variety. The Fe-Lions dance squad also brought a smile to the face—but not necessarily for their lock-step rhythm and timing. I'm going to charitably assume that they each have demanding day jobs that don't allow them much time to practice, because in most of their routines, any synchronization that occurred was completely accidental.

But perhaps the most enjoyable contrast between the two brands of football experience? No matter how hard they tried, the handful of fans interested in starting a wave were completely unable to muster up enough interest from their fellow spectators.

Amongst all the differences, however, one scenario began to develop that had begun to grow wearily familiar to me. I speak, of course, of what happens when visiting fans infiltrate a stadium…and their team starts to thrash the home team. Seated all around me were Roughriders fans, clad in all kinds of bizarre attire, not the least of which were the aforementioned watermelons perched like football helmets on their heads, à la the old leatherneck days. At first there was much peaceful coexistence. Friendly jibes, in fact. A harmonious society of sports fans bonded by their love of Canadian football on a perfect summer night. Then Saskatchewan started to blow out the Lions, and it was only a matter of time before a watermelon-head or two started BIRGing just a bit too much. I could see it coming a mile away—just add alcohol and stir.

As pushing and shoving escalated into punches being thrown, stadium security invaded our section. With only a few minutes remaining in the game, The Bird and I took advantage of the fact that everyone was on their feet and craning their necks for a better view of the fracases popping up all over. We slipped down our row toward the exit, getting a jump on the postgame traffic—and finishing up an otherwise enjoyable evening with a sour taste in our mouths.

Little did I know at the time that this would simply be the first course in a sour-taste smorgasbord.

Sunday morning came early to the lavish World Headquarters of the IGTS Tour. As soon as the first rays of light filtered through the blinds, I was wide awake and headed for the executive locker room to shower. What prompted this burst of energy on the sleepiest morning of the week? I was going to an NFL game!

My mind wandered back to the dozens of enjoyable times I'd spent at NFL stadiums in the past—both inside and out, tailgating with friends. And as I thought more about it, I was genuinely surprised to realize that it had been more than a decade since I'd been to an NFL game. Technically speaking, in fact, I hadn't seen live NFL football since the previous century! My pulse quickened…

Many hours later, I rolled my car slowly back into my garage, shuffled up the stairs to my living room, and wearily sagged into an overstuffed chair. There was no question about it. In the intervening time between my last two visits, the NFL product had...ahem...evolved, shall we say?

It hadn't taken long to be introduced to NFL football in the new millennium. I was greeted at the gate of San Diego's Qualcomm Stadium by a veritable blanket of security, featuring not one but two checkpoints at which I received a full pat-down. Nothing says "fun" more than being frisked. Twice.

By modern standards, Qualcomm might as well be the Roman Coliseum in terms of appearance and amenities. Discussion of renovating or otherwise upgrading the stadium had been well under way when I had first attended a Chargers game there—in 1999. Those conversations clearly haven't proved fruitful quite yet.

But there was one big change in Qualcomm that jumped right out at me—the escalation in the number of outlets at which one could buy a beer. At nine dollars a pop. Then again, fans really *need* a couple of frosty ones to avoid thinking about what they just paid for a plastic bucket seat in an ancient stadium. In my case, it was $74 (plus the usual assortment of "convenience fees") to sit halfway up a section in the upper deck of the end zone. Otherwise known as the "cheap seats." I can't even imagine what it cost to sit in the "Sorry sir, you appear to be over your credit limit" seats.

I was fully aware that the game against the Oakland Raiders was a rivalry game, and I knew that Raiders fans have a reputation for "making their presence known" when they visit another stadium. So I was attuned to the potential for the...exchange of contradictory opinions. A little counterBIRGing, so to speak. But not to worry—everyone seemed to be getting along famously. Did I mention that I was there early?

In the lower concourse, all was calm and harmonious. The Official Chargers Band played, and sporadic bursts of "Let's go, Chargers!" were offset by shouts of "Raiiiii-Ders!" All in good fun down there. As I ascended the escalator and made my way around the upper ring, though, there was a marked difference in the atmosphere. You could see the tension on the faces of the security guards as they prepared for their afternoon's work. Up there the exchange of team-supporting chants were more like challenges—people marking their territory.

When I got to my seat I was amazed to find my section almost unpopulated, just 20 minutes prior to game time. Kickoff came and went, and still the upper deck was just over half full. And then the tailgaters arrived.

I know that Commissioner Goodell and the team owners who employ him are intelligent people. Which is why it greatly surprises me that all of them appear to have had the wool pulled over their eyes. See, despite what their good friends at Anheuser-Busch InBev and MillerCoors might have told them, not everybody who drinks beer remains the charming, quick-witted character that populates every beer commercial. Some of them actually become a bit contrary after their first six-pack. And belligerent after their second. Curious, I know.

The first brawl came in the break between the first and second quarters. It was not an isolated incident. Throughout the game the air was continuously full of profanity-laced tirades spewing from heavily tattooed bodies and angry mouths. And the *guys* were even *worse*. By the two-minute warning of the first half, police were permanently stationed at the foot of each section in my end zone. On a regular basis, they would wade up the stairs and come back down with some staggering character who was often already in handcuffs.

I wouldn't say that I ever actually felt threatened, but I did spend the game feeling uneasy and uncomfortable—certainly nothing approaching happy and entertained. Others seemed to revel in the combat. As soon as someone yelled "fight," everybody was up and rubbernecking for a better view of the stands—no matter what was taking place down on the field. People took cell-phone pictures and videos of every conflict and then busied themselves sending these gems along to their friends. That was probably the most disturbing thing of all.

I truly felt badly for the father who had brought his young son to the game. Arriving well in advance of kickoff, they sat right in front of me and reveled in their surroundings. It was likely the kid's first NFL game, and his dad was proud to be his host. They were gone by halftime. That got me to thinking. I took a lengthy look at the portions of the stadium within my view and became genuinely surprised at how few kids were in attendance. The next generation of NFL fans, at least on that day, had taken a pass on pro football.

And I myself couldn't wait to leave.

At one point in the festivities, I remembered that the NFL is hell-bent on establishing a franchise in Los Angeles. For those of you scoring at home, this would be attempt #3 to make a go of pro football in a city that has never shown anything other than a lukewarm appetite for it. God forbid that the team that does wind up relocating to Los Angeles is anyone *but* the Oakland franchise. Otherwise, every time the Raiders come to town, it will be like having two competing "home" teams playing. I envision *Colors*, with concession stands and valet parking. People will eventually resort to beating themselves up, just to get it out of their system.

On the way home, I felt like I'd lost yet another old friend. I'd always loved the NFL game-day experience. Heck, I even *proposed to The Bird* while tailgating prior to a Carolina Panthers game (romantic, I know). But things have unquestionably changed.

I drove for the first hour with uncharacteristic silence in the car—no postgame radio show, no music, no nothing. When I reached the stretch of I-5 that closely parallels the Pacific for several miles, the sun was setting majestically over the water. On any other day, everything would have been just right with my world. Finally breaking the miserable stillness, I addressed the last few rays of daylight: "What in the world happened to sports fans?" And then a little later in the darkness, "Do I even *want* to be a sports fan anymore?"

I went on a sports walkabout to find out one thing: do I still love sports, and was my decision to commit my career to this business a foolhardy one? OK, that's two things—or as a lawyer might argue, one thing with two clauses. Whatever the case, there's one thing I certainly did *not* set out to do, and that's to perform sociological field research or analyze societal trends. OK, that's two things also, but let's stop with the quibbling, already.

The important thing is that, in the wake of a string of Big-Time Sports events that had been at least somewhat tarnished by reprehensible fan behavior, I really couldn't escape posing the question: why do sports fans have such little regard for other sports fans and, to a certain extent, for spectator sports as a whole? What exactly happened during the gap in time that separates today from my heyday as an avid spectator? I've already touched on the deification of athletes and the apparently growing need for people to attach themselves to a winner, but that doesn't explain the alarming trend toward intimidation, confrontation, and even outright violence I'd witnessed too many times over the preceding several months.

I surveyed a few friends for their take on the matter, and each independently came back with the same answer—to paraphrase Bill Clinton, "It's the alcohol, stupid." At which point I scoffed. I have it on pretty good authority that alcohol has been sold at stadiums and arenas for about as long as there have been stadiums and arenas. And somehow people have managed to remain civil throughout the two or three hours it takes for a game to be played and watched.

"There's a difference now," one friend replied. "Before, it was made available for purchase. Now it is *sold*. Hard." An excellent point, and one that I could certainly verify.

Shortly after that conversation, I came across an online blurb that caught my attention. A team of intrepid researchers, working on a grant from the hyper-legitimate Robert Wood Johnson Foundation, had taken it upon themselves to see if they could aggregate some hard data about how much alcohol people actually consume at professional sporting events. Camping out at 13 different baseball games and three football games, they managed to get 362 fans on their way out of the stadium to submit, in the name of science, to a breathalyzer. Lo and behold, eight percent of those tested were found to have blood-alcohol contents that were in excess of .08 percent, the legal limit on the books in most states. And here's the thing—these were the ones who were *willing to be tested*. In an understatement that would win Olympic gold in such an event, lead researcher Darin Erickson of the University of Minnesota pointed out that, "The true percentage of uncooperative inebriates may be higher."

May be higher? How about rock-solid, lead-pipe lock, take it to the bank, absolutely higher. According to that conservative eight percent figure, 5,720 of the 71,500 fans who had recently shared Qualcomm Stadium with me were legally drunk. In a stunning coincidence, *all of these people* happened to be sitting in my section—along with a generous smattering of "uncooperative inebriates." Seriously now, what were the odds?

Because it's much easier to toss off "simple" solutions that are logistically unfeasible than it is to actually put some thought into it, allow me to suggest a quick fix to the whole matter. Install breathalyzers at beer stands. Initially unwieldy, yes. But I have enough faith in American ingenuity to believe that it could be done. The bigger problem, though, is that doing so would make it next to impossible for team owners and concessionaires to pocket all of the money currently being made selling beer to people who really, truly don't need another. And that would never do.

TEN

The Monster

I WAS RAPIDLY REACHING THE POINT at which it appeared that every Big-Time Sports event was destined to be yet another irretrievably disheartening mess. Instead of hotly anticipating the marquee professional games on the IGTS Tour schedule, I began to skeptically approach them as more representative of aggravation than entertainment. I distinctly remember warily eying the upcoming NHL game on the schedule and thinking, *Great. Another testosterone-charged sport with stands undoubtedly full of fans on a drunken BIRG binge. Are we having fun yet?*

The defending Stanley Cup-champion Chicago Blackhawks were coming to Anaheim to take on the Ducks. Once again, I would be attending a pro game after a long hiatus from that particular sport. Once again, I would be in an environment in which fans celebrated hostility within the game. Once again, there would undoubtedly be a significant presence of fans in vocal support of the visiting team. And once again, alcohol would be readily available. Sigh. I knew what was going to happen.

Which is why, when it didn't, I wound up becoming eternally grateful to the original framers of the game of hockey. Allow me to explain.

As expected, there were tons of Blackhawks fans in attendance at Anaheim's Honda Center, proudly displaying their Stanley Cup Championship shirts, hats, coats, and boxer shorts (OK, so they weren't actually displaying the latter—but I just *knew* they were wearing them). We were seated in a section that housed almost equal numbers of Ducks and Blackhawks fans, so I was resigned to sitting through yet another afternoon of abusive language and escalating confrontation.

But a funny thing happened on the way to the brawl. Fans of both teams coexisted peacefully throughout the game. In fact, they were downright *cordial* to each other. It was a pleasure to sit among this knowledgeable, mutually respectful group of fans, especially after having witnessed so much mean-spirited behavior of late.

I would have to look up the final score, but I recall it being an exciting game that was decided by one goal. The following, however, I do remember with crystal clarity…

Just as the game was finishing up, a freak storm rolled into the area. The rain was coming down in sheets as the Honda Center began to empty. It had been a promotional-item game, and Time Warner Cable Sports had sponsored a free giveaway of Anaheim Ducks hats. These were nice hats—a couple of quality notches above what I've come to expect from freebies. So it was with amazement that I watched two people decked out in Ducks regalia turn at the exit portal and generously offer the hats that they'd received to two Blackhawks fans whose heads were otherwise unshielded from the downpour. The hats were accepted graciously.

At that moment, I knew how the Grinch must have felt as he puzzled over exactly why the residents of Whoville were belting out Christmas songs below in the town square, even though he'd stolen everything the night before—*including the roast beast, for God's sake!* My own puzzler grew as sore as his as I tried to figure out what had made this crowd behave so differently than so many others. The comparison between this game and the Chargers game was particularly intriguing. Two professional sports venues in fairly close proximity to one another—so the difference wasn't regionally based. Two highly physical sports—so it wasn't a testosterone-mismatch thing. Two crowds made up of vocal, avid supporters of opposite teams. Two facilities fully equipped with ample opportunities to buy alcohol. Two games played on a Sunday afternoon. And two games at which I sat in the upper-deck cheap seats. So why did a pro football game devolve into a drunken mess, while a pro hockey game did not?

And then it hit me: Time. Pace. Flow.

An NHL hockey game starts and doesn't stop for more than a minute or two at a time until 20 minutes have been played. An intermission allows just enough time for a trip to the restroom and a concession stand before another 20 minutes of more-or-less continuous play starts again. Sixty minutes of playing time takes between 120 and 130 minutes of running time to complete. In contrast, an NFL football game consists of the same 60 minutes of playing time—but takes *well over three times that long* to finish.

Here's the critical difference: The periods of on-ice inactivity at a hockey game are consolidated into two large chunks. In football, they are parsed out in four- and five-minute segments, spread out over the course of the afternoon or evening.

That's a lot of dead time. And with an outlet for the purchase of alcohol never more than a few steps away in the average stadium, the opportunity to dash out for a quick beer run is always at hand, without having to miss much of the game while gone. In fact, one could easily make the case that there's not a whole lot else to do at times. In short, at an NHL game *one doesn't have time* to become drunk and obnoxious, while an NFL game is almost the ideal environment for doing so. Time. Pace. Flow.

Normally I'm only good for one revelation per day, but for some reason this whole line of thought kept turning over in my head, even long after I had arrived home. And finally the other half of this epiphany came to me. I had been pretty rough on my fellow sports fans for months, holding them primarily responsible for the demise of my enjoyment in attending live Big-Time Sports events. And don't get me wrong—I wasn't about to let them off the hook completely. But another perspective had emerged: ultimately, fans are simply guilty of something over which they have no control. They possess eyeballs.

Stay with me on this…

* * *

A lot of stuff can happen in ten years. In fact, the world can change completely. And it can happen right under your very nose, without you recognizing that it's even taking place. For example, while I had been toiling away to make the world a better place for golfers, a monster had emerged to wreak havoc on much of what is near and dear to me. This particular monster was amorphous, lacking all tangible physical characteristics but two. First, it was green. More specifically, it was multiple shades of green-on-green. Like a dollar bill. Second, it was huge—and growing larger by the day. Single-minded, not all that bright, and none too subtle, this monster exists solely to seek out and gobble up eyeballs.

I first took serious notice of the Monster at an NBA game. I was on my way to L.A.'s Staples Center to watch the Lakers play the San Antonio Spurs, when I realized that the opponent on my last visit to see the Lakers play in person had also been the Spurs. Except that game had been in Inglewood's Fabulous Forum, and the Lakers on that night had been led into battle by their twin superstars, Kareem Abdul-Jabbar and a youngster that went simply by the name of Magic. So it had been a while.

The experience of making my way to my seat and absorbing the atmosphere had been undeniably impressive, as The Bird and I had arrived in the middle of the full-on L.A. spectacle that is the Lakers pregame. Even when the arena was darkened—save for the spotlights trained on the court during player introductions—a bonanza of visual stimulation continued to wash over me. And the place was loud. Very loud. In fact, conversation was next to impossible almost throughout the afternoon, but for the scant intervals of actual play that temporarily interrupted the day's thumping soundtrack. It was as if we had gone to a rave at which a basketball game had broken out. A sloppily played basketball game.

Evidently, during my sabbatical between Lakers games, any shot that was neither a dunk nor a three-pointer had been outlawed. As had passing of the basketball. If somebody had tossed four more balls onto the court at any point in the contest, the players would have been only too pleased to engage in five simultaneous games of one-on-one. Yes, there is still no *I* in *team*... but *narcissism* certainly contains a couple of them. I became concerned that at some point a player might actually injure himself thumping his own chest.

Finally, at the point at which I began to crave something comforting and familiar about basketball, a timeout was called—and *they* took the floor.

The Laker Girls are a sports institution, much like their football alter egos the Dallas Cowboy Cheerleaders. Watching them perform during time-outs is like getting an extra show-within-a-show. That's always been part of the overall experience that makes a Lakers home game so unique. They are talented, they are gorgeous, and they are as classy as you can possibly be while wearing outfits the size of cocktail napkins. Even The Bird was hard-pressed to find anything negative to say about them. Not that she didn't try, of course.

That first Laker Girls timeout routine of the day was choreographed to a song with a distinctive Latin flair. I wasn't quite sure, but I thought the lyrics included the word "tequila." Sure enough, at the end of the routine a woman who appeared to be one of the Laker Girls was featured on the video board hawking 1800 Tequila—under the standard guise of a "Please drink responsibly" PSA. *How's that for coincidental program positioning?* I thought.

All thoughts of subtle coincidence were blown out of the water in the second quarter, however, when the Laker Girls romped onto the court for their next routine, clad in clingy white shirts that said FIOS and THIS IS BIG. Now I'm not saying that any innuendo was specifically intended, but let's just say that had the second line been plural in nature...well I think you get my drift.

The next routine brought the dance team out in mini-jumpsuits featuring a well-placed Carl's Jr. Burgers medallion, and it became starkly plain—the enterprising minds of the franchise have monetized the iconic Laker Girls, selling sponsorships to individual dance routines. Making them, in essence, real-time commercials. To my mind, it was akin to slapping a sandwich board on the *Venus de Milo* statue.

Don't get me wrong. I had been selling sports sponsorships for some time, and part of me was irrefutably jealous that I hadn't come up with the idea. I clinically admired the ingenuity of my marketing brethren. After all, what infinitesimally small percentage of the crowd—particularly the male portion of the crowd—could *stop* themselves from watching the Laker Girls perform? Somewhere in the recesses of my brain, however, I couldn't help feeling that I had just been sold a corporate lap dance. In retrospect, I shouldn't have been that surprised. The Monster has to be fed.

* * *

It used to be called "advertising." Then "marketing." Then "branding." The most accurate name now, though, would be "overkill." The denizens of Corporate America have determined that if you are conscious, there is no justifiable reason why you shouldn't be processing their messages. I'm sure we're not too far away from litigation that will deem your eyeballs to be wholly owned subsidiaries of Madison Avenue ad agencies.

There's just one tiny problem. As the tidal wave of advertising messages grows ever larger, people have gotten better and better at tuning them out. And not just passively, as has been the case for decades. In the last ten years or so, technology has emerged that has elevated the art of actively ignoring advertising messages to a science. In fact, it has delivered the Holy Grail of advertising avoidance—the FF button on the DVR remote. Just like that, people in great numbers are now able to short-circuit the carpet-bombing of television commercials. Zipping through commercials in this way is part of what's become known as television "time-shifting." But to the scions of capitalism it may as well be called Communism.

What to do? What to do?

At the risk of oversimplifying, it appears to me that the advertising counterstrike has two main prongs. The first consists of a carefully crafted strategy not unlike that of your average five-year-old at the beach: "Mommy, look at me… Mommy, look at me… Mommy, look at me… Mommy, look at me… *Mommy, look at me!*" In addition to television, advertisers have branched out to saturate almost anything that people see, hear, taste, touch, or smell. If you are capable of finding some small oasis of tranquility in your day-to-day conscious world, count on the fact that it will be bulldozed and "monetized" in the not-too-distant future. Your eardrums and eyeballs are far too valuable for you to be running off and hiding them.

The second prong brings to mind the scene in *Star Wars* where Luke Skywalker infiltrates the Death Star, navigates his way to the one tiny weak spot that the Rebel Alliance has identified, and squeezes off two well-placed proton torpedoes that eventually destroy the entire humongous space station.

There is a similar chink in the armor of the advertising-avoidance empire—the live sporting event. People do not tend to time-shift sports, because chances are pretty good that by the time they get around to watching that Big Game, they'll already know how it turned out. Which ruins the unscripted drama that sports so wonderfully provides. Have you ever been around someone who is desperately trying to *avoid* learning the score of a game currently being played because they've set their DVR at home to record it? It's sad, really. Lots of flailing of arms, covering of ears, and panicked flight from both television screens and any semblance of normal conversation. I learned long ago that this is a futile endeavor. A single glance at The Bird is enough to tip off the score, inning, and pitch count of any L.A. Angels game that she is privy to while I am not.

Once this Achilles heel was exposed, the all-out assault commenced. Corporate America proceeded to shred their collective rotator cuff throwing money at it. Through painstaking effort and ingenuity, they developed a formula whereby if one advertising message embedded within a sporting event doesn't do the trick, certainly 1,298 will. Most are clumsily blatant, but some, as the now-for-sale Laker Girls taught me, are delivered in a manner more like wrapping your dog's medicine in bacon.

Thus was born the Monster, bred to consume at all costs the eyeballs of every last sports fan—and fueled in that crusade by an endless supply of money. And nothing delivers eyeballs in bulk better than television. If the seminal band the Buggles are right, and video did indeed kill the radio star, it is well on the way to doing the same to the live sporting event—while beating, maiming, and torturing it along the way.

Of the many intriguing ideas introduced within the previously mentioned book *The Fix Is In*, one in particular stuck with me. Brian Tuohy at one point referenced a different book, *Out of Bounds*, which was published back in 1992. In that book, the authors, Congressman Tom McMillan and Paul Coggins, share an anecdote about Ted Turner, who at the time was relatively new to the professional sports ownership world. According to McMillan and Coggins, Turner "once remarked that he wouldn't need a live audience to make his sports ventures profitable, and in the not-so-distant future, could foresee *hiring* spectators to provide local color and to cheer on cue, as if acting like a laugh track for a television sitcom."

It turns out that Turner was only half right. The not-so-distant future is now here with regard to the inversion in importance of the live audience and the television audience. Amazingly, though, the other half of Turner's prophesy has gone the other way. There seems to be no cap in sight on what people are willing to pay to be part of the "local color." I'm sure that virtually no one who goes through the turnstiles of an arena or stadium actually perceives that this is the case, but in some instances it is blindingly obvious.

Take the PBA World Series of Bowling, for example.

* * *

It's a funny thing about Las Vegas—the city seems to be suffering through a chronic and debilitating shortage of chairs. If you don't believe me, try this simple experiment on your own: enter any Vegas casino and sit down—but not in any of the 12,594 seats at which doing so requires placing a bet or ordering food and drink. See what I mean? Spooky, huh?

So it was that I found myself luxuriating in the comfort of a cement bench at the taxi stand outside of South Point Resort Casino, waiting for the gates to open for the PBA World Series of Bowling. Actually the phrase "gates to open" is a bit of a misnomer here. The "gate" in this case was a fold-up banquet table, covered smartly with an attractive linen tablecloth and attended to by two kindly older women. Upon my earlier arrival they had informed me that the "set" wouldn't be open until shortly before the "show" was to begin.

The event was being conducted within the huge bowling complex on the mezzanine level at South Point, and on this particular day the action was confined to a half-dozen lanes surrounded by an ominous black curtain at the far end of the facility. That was where ESPN had set up to tape the championship finals for broadcast at a later date. And once the magical time arrived for us to slip inside the black curtain, it was instantly clear that those of us in attendance on this day were not so much sports fans as we were a live studio audience.

Any ambiguity about that notion was immediately dismissed by the continual presence of the sizable crew working the event/show. At the average sporting event, the game-day operations team does its best to make itself invisible, in order to keep the spotlight fixed firmly on the game. Here there were no qualms about it—if you were there watching, you were merely a prop. A prop who had paid $20 *per session* to be there.

"Attendance" was approximately 75 people perched on two sets of temporary bleachers that faced each other and flanked the two lanes used for the competition. While it was fun to be right there on top of the action, in practical terms we were farther away from it than would be anyone who tuned in to watch ESPN's taped broadcast. The culprit was the audio...or lack thereof. Every word uttered before, during, and after each match was fed into the recording of the show—but not shared with the studio audience. We saw mouths moving, and if it was particularly quiet we could make out some of what was being said into microphones, but otherwise it was a purely visual experience.

The one voice that we heard during the day was that of Mike J. Laneside (I'm going out on a limb here and guessing that's an alias), the member of the production team who doubled as studio host. He was the stereotypical on-site host, complete with the requisite glib deejay persona that was identifiable as soon as he uttered the words, "Who's ready to party with Jackie Bowling today?" Jackie Bowling (the alter ego of one Jaclyn Marinkovich) was on hand to play the role of fan liaison and sideline reporter. She shared the latter duties with Miss USA 1999, Kimberly Pressler. For the record, I never actually did get the opportunity to party with either Ms. Bowling or Miss USA. I did, however, receive detailed instructions on exactly how and when to cheer, capped by a short practice session on same.

We even had arts and crafts! In preparation for our arrival, blank white placards and markers had been placed on the bleachers, in the hopes that enterprising souls among us would make signs. And to prime the creative pump, there were even a few "homemade" signs done up in advance. Being the sheep that we were, many of us took the bait. So at the risk of being placed on the PBA's "Enemies List," I'm here to tell you that if you tuned in to watch the World Series of Bowling, don't be fooled. Those signs were not brought from home by rabid fans. Sorry.

Come to think of it, I'm already on the PBA's Enemies List. And it's all Scott Norton's fault. Norton was a PBA Tour rookie who hadn't exactly been setting the bowling world on fire coming into the World Series. But the lefty got on a roll in the WSOB Chameleon Championship and vaulted into the #1 seed going into the finals. This enabled him to kick back and watch the other competitors battle it out for the right to meet him in a one-game, winner-take-all match.

That match was packed with tension throughout. Not over whether Norton would win—which he did handily—but whether he would roll a perfect game in doing so. After tossing strikes in the first eight frames, a 300 game was well within sight. That drama ended with a spare in the ninth frame, but shortly thereafter Norton was celebrating his first professional win with his mom, Women's Hall of Fame bowler Virginia Norton.

I thought a nice little Flip video of that moment might be appreciated by the general public, so I did the honors and posted it on both the It's

Game Time Somewhere website and my YouTube channel. The PBA was… not amused. I received a terse email from those happy-go-lucky folks, who were apparently upset that I had taken it into my own hands to promote their sport. When I was a little tardy in ceasing and desisting, they somehow barged into my "private" YouTube site and vaporized the video. Come to think about it, that performance was almost as memorable as Norton's. Let's say I'll never think about bowling in quite the same way again. But I digress.

For an event that was taped and then edited, the production was wildly interruptive of the bowling. As if it were actually being shown live, the action stopped periodically, and everyone watched (but did not hear) Kimberly Pressler interviews of…well, other than one of the bowler's wives, we never knew who she was chatting with. So to recap: The show's producers wanted spontaneous exuberance but left us staring for long periods of time at people talking who could not be heard. We were even implored to stay and cheer during the televised presentation of the winner's trophy and check, even though we couldn't hear the ceremony. Just a thought, but shouldn't they have been paying *us* $20? Ted Turner would have.

Blessed with the fruits of the epiphany that had followed the Ducks-Blackhawks hockey game, my eyes were now wide open to the insidious effects of Televisionus Interruptus. A veil had been lifted, and from that point on I viewed every event I would attend—or had attended previously—through a different lens. So to speak.

Looking back on the rumble that had been the Chargers-Raiders game, as much as the rolling melee detracted from my own enjoyment of the game, in the spirit of fairness I took a look at it from the perspective of the fans participating in the extracurriculars. First of all, in the *A-Z Fan Guide* that the Chargers publish on their website, it states, "We strongly encourage fans to arrive at least two hours before game time." The stadium lots open at 9:00 AM for a 1:00 PM game, and they "can be expected to reach capacity and close an hour before kick-off." So once you're on-site, you've got some time on your hands. What to do? What to do…?

But in comparison to the time given over to television timeouts during the game, that four-hour pregame window was a relative eye-blink. I'm sure that people who have regularly frequented NFL games over the years haven't really noticed the gradual increase, but with more than a decade intervening between my last two visits I was *stunned* at how much more dead time now exists. Clearly the advertising folks at the NFL's network partners have been effective at selling commercial time, bless their enterprising little hearts.

Unlike a baseball or basketball game, a football game does not lend itself to fan promotions and interactivity during timeouts. So those in the stands spend an inordinate amount of time staring at a bunch of players standing around waiting to start playing again. What to do? What to do…?

I got it! Let's break up the monotony with a beer and a quick fistfight!

When *Monday Night Football* premiered in 1970, there were 18 commercials in a game, a number that even the folks at ABC Sports felt might be pushing the envelope a bit at the time. Since they had paid so much to the NFL for the television rights, though, they felt they had no choice. Eighteen commercials. How quaint.

Fast-forward to 2003, when researchers Dan Brown and Jennings Bryant conducted a study that was eventually published as part of a piece titled "Sports Content on U.S. Television" in the *Handbook of Sports and Media*. Brown and Bryant randomly selected the CBS broadcast of a regular-season game between the Indianapolis Colts and the Denver Broncos and tracked everything that appeared on screen. That "everything" included 29 commercial breaks, featuring 78 advertisements and 34 promos for other CBS broadcasts. One hundred twelve commercial messages. How quaint.

I'd be willing to bet my now-exclusive video of Scott Norton's World Series of Bowling victory celebration that the number of commercial messages broadcast during the Chargers-Raiders game that I suffered through was in excess of 150. Those watching at home had the luxury of doing something else while the Monster ate their television sets. We at the game…did not.

Lest one think that this is purely an NFL phenomenon, let me put that thought to rest for you. Televisionus Interruptus is alive and well at a wide cross-section of live sporting events, extending all the way down to ostensibly the purest and most innocent of events that I attended, the Little League World Series.

Anybody who has ever seen a baseball game knows the rhythm of the game. At the end of each half-inning, the teams swap places on the field and at bat, the pitcher throws half a dozen warm-up pitches, the first baseman tosses practice ground balls to the other infielders, and the outfielders play catch. It's a natural routine that has existed in baseball since Abner Doubleday and his buddies first scratched out a diamond to play on.

If you attend pro baseball games with any kind of regularity, you've no doubt been exposed to a wide range of promotional activities—from the brilliantly clever to the embarrassingly bad—that take place while the players engage in loosening up each half-inning. You may or may not be paying attention, but imprinted upon your brain is the general amount of time that this whole ritual takes. More to the point, if the proceedings start to exceed that subconscious norm, you notice.

At the televised final weekend of the Little League World Series, I noticed. Mostly what I noticed was that the people selling advertising for ESPN were doing a remarkable job. Judging by the amount of time that elapsed between innings, there were roughly double the number of commercials shown to television viewers than is the case with an average Major League Baseball telecast. After the first couple of changeovers, it got to the point where the coaches kept the kids in the dugout for what would normally be the standard between-inning time period before then sending them out to conduct their normal routine. During the fourth-inning stretch (remember, Little Leaguers play just six-inning games) we got the full "Take Me Out to the Ballgame" sing-along and *then* a long-play version of "The Chicken Dance." Several of the players completed puberty in the time it took to get the game back under way.

And while I'm normally not a big mascot fan, my heart went out to Dugout—a mascot dressed in a bear costume that danced and mugged his way through each game. One particular bit had him dressed up as a prize-fighter, shadow-boxing to the theme song from *Rocky* for the full interminable duration of a TV timeout. I'm sure that in the 90-degree heat of the afternoon, Dugout joined me in wondering if that *Rocky* bit would *ever* be over. If it was left solely up to ESPN, they surely would have run four more commercials, after which time they would've had to drag Dugout's spent carcass off on a stretcher, accompanied by at least two intravenous fluid feeds.

While that particular rendition of Televisionus Interruptus stretched the boundaries to the limit, it didn't technically impact the playing of the game. The producers of other events weren't as shy about letting television actually change the flow of their respective games, however. And thus, I often found myself torn between two competing lines of thought. The entrepreneur in me wanted to secure the exclusive rights to a No-Doz concession in the stands. The beleaguered sports fan in me wanted to stand up and pull a Peter Finch in *Network*: "I'm mad as hell, and I'm not going to take this anymore!"

For example, anybody who has ever attended a college basketball game that is being televised is familiar with what I experienced at the Pac-10 Men's Basketball Final. Even though the game was closely contested throughout, instead of feeling like we were hurtling toward a thrilling conclusion, the game felt more like a trudge to the finish, thanks to television timeouts. The combination of actual timeouts that the teams used down the stretch and those of the TV variety served to suck the life out of an otherwise great game. I found myself actually *yawning* while waiting for the conclusion of a game that featured buzzer-beaters at *both* the end of regulation and overtime! Nothing heightens drama like a period of 15 minutes during which seven seconds of actual live basketball takes place.

On the bright side, we did have so much downtime there were not one, not two, not three…but *four* occasions on which promotional items were tossed into the stands during a break in play. My favorite was the Pacific Life Whale Toss—the furry stuffed variety, not the full 100 tons of slimy blubber. Just in case any animal-rights activists were concerned.

While we're (sort of) on the topic of fish being out of water, it brings to mind my trip to see the USA Sevens Rugby Championship, the lone North American stop in the IRB Sevens World Series. As a total newcomer to the sport of rugby, I was enthralled by the game but totally confused by the process by which the tournament winnowed down the 16 competing teams into the championship game. Being the egalitarian sport that it is, a rugby sevens tournament has four different "Finals." And at the USA Sevens, for some odd reason the big one—the Cup Final—was anticlimactically the *first* of the four to be played. Hmmmm…

If there was just one thing I had learned by that point in my often head-scratching expedition, it's that when something doesn't quite square at a sporting event, start looking for television trucks. And sure enough, there was my answer. It turned out that the ultimate match was being played in the fourth-from-ultimate time slot because…well, because NBC said so. So there.

And the event's producers weren't shy in the least about this. In fact they came across as breathlessly devoted to a strategy that revolved around getting on television at all costs. The tournament preview in the official event program laid it right out: "Another factor affecting the teams is the schedule. To accommodate NBC coverage, teams that make the Cup quarterfinals will play their quarterfinals on Saturday evening. This means that the top teams will play four matches in one day. Such a schedule is not unheard of, but certainly has the potential to change how teams approach the games and their recovery throughout Saturday's action."

Allow me to translate. What they are saying is "Woo Hoo! We're on *television! Live television!!* So what if the integrity of the competition is compromised?" in a manner that underscores that one hour of live television squeezed into the middle of a Sunday afternoon is far more important than legitimizing the outcome of the tournament or maximizing the experience for poor slobs like me.

It was just another baffling instance of a mind-set whereby so many people in the sports industry accept it as a *fait accompli*, that if their games are not on television, their sport is irrelevant—and in no way capable of growing and being enjoyed. There's already a lot of clutter on sports television as it is.

Do they really, honestly think that an hour or so of live coverage a couple of times each year provides value that is worth jeopardizing their live product for?

Even still, television apologists could correctly claim that, while completely taking over the margins of so many of the events that I attended, their broadcasting policies didn't necessarily *directly impact* the games. And I was with them on that. That is, until I attended the NCAA College Cup—collegiate soccer's answer to basketball's Final Four championship weekend.

I had been unexpectedly warming to the game of soccer—in person, anyway. Watching on television…well…it *was* gaining on watching paint drying. But as I headed to the national title game between the Louisville Cardinals and the Akron Zips, an added bonus was that I would be viewing it with a real, live knowledgeable fan. My buddy Chris was along for the trip to Santa Barbara, and I knew that he, having played soccer at the collegiate level, would undoubtedly be able to answer the burning questions that had entered my mind while watching previous games.

For example, how do soccer players come about their *astonishing* recuperative powers? I have witnessed players somehow progress from writhing on the turf in absolute agony to miraculously dragging themselves to their feet to limping around in unsteady circles to running down the field at full tilt—all in the space of less than two minutes. That is *remarkable!!*

I have to admit to somewhat uncharitably wondering if this phenomenon had anything at all to do with the fact that a foul just might be called on the opposing team as a result of the egregious assault visited upon the innocent player. Chris cleared that up for me, though. "No connection whatsoever," he said with a broad grin. "How could you *think* such a thing?"

As we were savoring the first half of the well-played contest, I began to extol the virtues of a game in which there were no stoppages of play when, for no apparent reason, everything came to a halt. I looked to Chris for guidance, and he suddenly recalled with much irritation that the NCAA is unique in sanctioning what it refers to as "media timeouts." He went on to say that this doesn't happen anywhere else in the world; not in Major League Soccer, not in the English Premier League, not in either of the UEFA leagues—all of which are heavily sponsored professional entities. This clearly did not sit well with Chris, who summed it up succinctly: "Soccer doesn't *stop*," he spat out with disgust.

That particular media timeout happened to have come when neither team was on the offensive, so it was no big deal in the grand scheme of things. Later on, however...

The game was scoreless deep into the second half. Louisville had held the game's early advantage, narrowly missing on two scoring opportunities in the first half. Akron had survived, however, and was in the process of taking over control of the game. A two-on-one breakaway for the Zips resulted in a shot that rolled just barely wide of the Louisville goal, but it was just the beginning of an offensive onslaught for Akron. In short order, Cardinals goalie Andre Boudreaux was called upon to make an acrobatic save off of an Akron corner kick—which in turn led to another corner kick opportunity for the Zips. You got the feeling that a goal was imminent. It was just a matter of which one of the Akron stars would convert and how they would do it. The excitement in the air was palpable; it was...

And now, a word from our sponsors.

The ESPN advertising sales department served as the defensive stopper that Louisville needed, and the Cardinals cheering section couldn't have been more pleased. They stopped just short of a standing ovation—for a television...oops...I mean, a "media timeout." Among Akron supporters and fans of soccer in general, there was palpable revulsion in the stands. And sure enough, when the game resumed after the television timeout, the field that had been so strongly tilted the Zips' way subsequently evened out.

In the end, Akron proved to be the much better team on that day. In the 79th minute, the Zips' Scott Caldwell found his own shot deflected right back to him, giving him the opportunity to settle the ball and take another shot. He deposited that second chance into the net, just over the leaping Boudreaux. On the strength of that goal, Akron won the College Cup title 1–0. It wasn't lost on either Chris or me, however, that the outcome of the game could easily have been directly impacted by television—and that it's almost inevitable that at some point in the future it will indeed happen. At which point the Monster will have succeeded in eating an entire sport's national championship.

None of this had ever occurred to me while watching sports in my living room. Television timeouts came in handy, in fact, for using the bathroom…doing chores…reading *War and Peace*. But here's the thing—the very same commercials that are benignly ignored by anyone watching at home are *absolutely killing* the experience for those of us sitting in the stands at the game. The lack of respect for our time has grown to be nothing less than infuriating.

So don't go, is what I'm confident you are thinking at this point. But I ask you—isn't all of this hassle ultimately worth it to see the Big-Time Sports played in person? To be able to say "I was there"?

Isn't it?

ELEVEN

X-Treme Product Pitching

THE SCENE COULD BE ANY of the 6,000-plus days that made up the nearly two decades leading up to the It's Game Time Somewhere Tour. An alarm clock sounds, a coffee pot is propelled into action by its timer, and I sleepily reach for the TV remote to turn on *SportsCenter*. It's tip-off time for another day, and whether I'm home or away, ESPN is tossing up the ball to get things started. And if I'm slow on the draw on the clicker, I know The Bird has my back.

Back in the early '90s, I first got hooked on starting my day with *SportsCenter* because I wanted...no, make that *needed*...to get information about the previous night's games. No, Virginia, there wasn't always an Internet. *SportsCenter* was the epicenter of scores and highlights, and the Rosetta Stone of the genre was the Dan Patrick/Keith Olbermann sports carnival affectionately known by devotees as "The Big Show." In fact, for one blessed stretch of time, Patrick and Olbermann helped to blunt the impact of each Monday morning with *90 freakin' minutes* of highlights, interspersed with truly clever, often downright hilarious commentary.

Right around the time that I began my walkabout, I got to thinking about "The Big Show" with more than a little bit of nostalgia. It was a normal day, and having turned on *SportsCenter* per usual, I was greeted with a segment on the "Top 10 Developing NFL Stories for Next Season." Earlier in the week there had been the obligatory saturation coverage of the Super Bowl and its aftermath, culminating with highlights of the Saints' victory celebration in New Orleans. The football season was over. There was nothing more worth saying. Honestly. And certainly no such thing as a "developing story" about a sport that wouldn't see its first day of *practice* for months. But that's what they gave me.

I clicked over to ESPN2. Nothing but talking heads—Jay, Dana, Skip, Guest Debater Whose Name I Did Not Recognize. At one point the talking heads were engaged in serious discussion about…other talking heads. *Click.*

ESPN Classic. Cue Beethoven's "Ode to Joy"—I was greeted with images of *actual athletes engaged in an actual game!* Unfortunately, however, that game had originally been played some time ago, and I already knew the particulars.

How about ESPNU? I thought. *That channel was theoretically created specifically to cover college sports! Click.* And there, much to my dismay, was a simulcast of an ESPN Radio show hosted by the Entitled One.

I had been vaguely aware of the existence of the Entitled One for some time. Occasionally during the middle-of-the-weekday dead spot in programming I had caught bits of his show on my car radio. He was nothing special to listen to, and his material never struck me as very original. What he had in spades, however, was smugness—hey, he had his own ESPN Radio show, while we…did not. Did that not put him on par with the elite athletes that he discussed?

What put me over the edge into full boycott mode, though, was a show of his that I had heard (again while in the car) the previous October. When I tuned in, the Entitled One was in the midst of a whiny rant about how, given the dispersal of broadcast rights, it had become tricky finding the Major League Baseball playoffs on television. He freely admitted that he had seen only a few innings of the recently concluded Angels–Red Sox ALDS series and "not a second" of the Colorado Rockies NLDS series against the defending World Series-champion Phillies. He capped off his diatribe by declaring that he didn't have time to track down which game was on what network, with his final words on the topic being, "Hey, I have a social life!"

I almost drove off the road.

Over the years I'd had the pleasure of meeting and working with a great number of people just starting out in their careers as sports journalists and sports management professionals. Their stories were all different, but they shared the same common bond: they would die for a job like the one held by the Entitled One. There are quite literally hundreds, if not thousands, of people capable of doing his job who would not consider it an imposition on their time to look up a listing for a game—and then watch it from beginning to end, "social life" be damned.

That was the first day that I began to suspect that the lunatics had taken over the asylum in the sports-media biz, much to the detriment of the sports fan. And now, having spent months venturing out into the world of live sports, it occurs to me on an almost daily basis that the biggest culprit is ESPN. This is not an easy realization to deal with. It's kind of like finding out that your best childhood friend is now swindling little old ladies for a living. Or even worse, has become a hedge fund manager. Redundant, I know, but hang with me here.

In the storied history of the Walt Disney companies, there have been many days in which they've presented the public with truly transformative original entertainment ideas. Then again, there are the 1,893,902 other days on which they've simply worked to repackage, rehash, or otherwise bludgeon us over the head with those once-brilliant concepts. With their acquisition of ESPN in 1996, they brought that particular approach to the sports world. Things have unfortunately never been the same for sports fans.

In case you think that Disney's ESPN is the least bit shy about the "streamlining" of its daily coverage of sports, well…you would be mistaken. Once again on an ESPN Radio show that I listened to with slack jaw and bulging temples, the host (whose identity I can't recall) patiently explained to a caller that the company does intensive research to identify the handful of topics that appeal to its target demographic, and then floods its networks with programming that highlights this narrow range of topics.

The host went on to describe a strategy that focused on being able to say or type "Dallas Cowboys" or "Lebron James" a set number of times each hour and day. It was the concept of the old 80/20 rule taken to an extreme—to the point where I'd bet that 95 percent of daily programming on ESPN's "Family of Networks" addresses five percent of the news in the sports world that day. And to borrow a phrase from *Casablanca*'s Captain Renault, you may be shocked, *shocked* to learn that comfortably tucked into that 95 percent of daily programming is saturation coverage of the sports properties to which ESPN owns at least a portion of the television rights.

Were I a betting man, I would wager that the Monster's first formative words were, *"DaDaDa, DaDaDa."*

In the spirit of full disclosure, I will admit that part of my irritation with ESPN is the fact that, according to the crack team of actuaries that they have on staff, on February 12, 2009, I ceased to exist. For that is the day that I graduated from the 18-to-49-year-old demographic. Evidently, when sports fans turn 50, storm troopers invade their homes and confiscate all of their discretionary income, because they clearly have no intention of using it anymore. At least that's what the automatons of the advertising business appear to believe with all their hearts.

Shortly after the day I turned 35, I came to terms with the fact that I was no longer coveted as passionately by advertisers. But at least I was tolerated. Now…they…*sniff*…they don't even want my eyeballs anymore. I feel used—and a little dirty.

As emotionally debilitating as dealing with the revocation of advertiser love may be, I've adopted a brave face and soldiered on. Much more difficult has been having to live in the blast radius when the ESPN television trucks roll into town to cover a sporting event that I am attending. For, having completed a hostile takeover of the entire sports world, the self-anointed Worldwide Leader in Sports simply bends normal on-site game-day event production to their will. But don't cry for me—cry for plucky little mascots like the Little League World Series' Dugout, who risk collapsing into dehydrated exhaustion every time they try to fill an entire ESPN television timeout with a spirited dance routine.

Sadly, after almost 20 years, my morning routine no longer includes *SportsCenter*. Ironically enough, these days I turn on *The Dan Patrick Show* immediately upon awakening. The same Dan Patrick who helped usher *SportsCenter* into my breakfast nook in the first place. Apparently free to pursue what often become hilarious tangents, Patrick and his on-air staff (the Danettes) provide little in the way of game results or highlights, but it is refreshing to listen to them talk about sports the way that real sports fans do. But the biggest bonus I've received from watching the show is learning the moniker that Patrick has bestowed upon his former employer.

He refers to ESPN as simply "the Mothership."

Brilliant. Never has a nickname so aptly captured runaway hubris in a single word. I use it frequently. I've even converted it to a verb, as in, "Well, the game itself was entertaining, but of course ESPN was there Mothershipping another perfectly good event."

And nowhere—*nowhere*—does the Mothershipping reach greater heights than at the X Games, where athletic competition serves as merely a flimsy front for one X-traordinarily long advertisement for X-cessively caffeinated energy drinks.

Originally called the Extreme Games, the inaugural event was undeniably goofy. But also undeniably fun. In the mid-'90s some forward-thinking sports-production types at ESPN decided to take a chance (we're talking pre-Disney here) on a new concept for filling hours of airtime in midsummer, the slowest time of the year for sports. "Why not," they reasoned, "hold an Olympic-style competition featuring the types of activities engaged in by those kids who…well, who aren't quite right. And to go really off the wall, let's stage it in Providence, Rhode Island." A partial lineup of the sports that made up the first Extreme Games reveals how eclectic the event was when it debuted: Bungee jumping. Sky surfing. Sport climbing. Street luge.

Seriously—street luge.

I actually happened to be living in downtown Providence when the first Extreme Games site was being built out, and I remember being alternately fascinated by and horrified at the route chosen for the street luge course. I couldn't imagine anyone surviving a crash. And I wondered, *Where exactly does one* practice *street luge?*

But what started back then as delightfully offbeat and viral is now so contrived you would assume that even the most naïve of kids would sniff out in a heartbeat that the X Games is one big infomercial. Indeed, if you look up the X Games on Wikipedia, the first subheading that greets you is "Economics." But evidently the kids are OK with it, as I learned when I made the trip to Staples Center to see the Moto X competition. Moto X...Moto-Cross...get it? These guys slay me.

"Stealth marketing" was the phrase that came to mind when I first arrived on-site, but as the evening wore on I came to realize that there was nothing even remotely "stealthy" about this event, right down to the shameless plugs provided none-too-subtly by the cyclists themselves. One particularly inelegant scenario occurred during a close-up shot of one of the riders upon completion of his heat. Once he was cued that he was on camera, he extended front and center into the picture a water bottle bearing the Monster energy drink logo and then gave an animated wave—exposing a Target logo on the palm of his glove. And if you still didn't get it, he pointed to the logo with his other hand. I'm guessing even the inveterate hawkers among NASCAR drivers would have blushed had they witnessed this entire product pitch disguised as a competition.

I couldn't help thinking about the fact that the entire X Games franchise was originally built around attracting the kids who were continuously being shooed out of public parking lots with their skateboards because they were too scruffy and antiestablishment. And now the next generation of that kid is a walking, talking billboard. Can I please have some sullen, uncommunicative attitude here?! For God's sake, some of the competitors *didn't even appear to have any tattoos!*

Despite their disquieting level of respect for the Establishment, I have to admit that these kids are enormously good at what they do—the moto-cross riding part, not the corporate shill part. If you are a motocross racer—and especially a motocross stunt racer—you absolutely, positively *cannot* mail it in on practicing your trade. If you decide to slack off in preparation for a competition, you might as well spend the time you saved by adding every ambulance service in town to your speed-dial list. These athletes are dedicated to both their craft and to putting on a good show.

And it was indeed a good show. At least the bite-sized pieces of action that interrupted looooooong stretches of staring into space. Make no mistake about it—this was not a sporting event that ESPN happened to be covering. This was a made-for-ESPN television event. How else do you explain this scheduling:

At 5:30 the qualifying round for the Moto X Speed & Style competition began, with the objective of narrowing the field of 11 racers down to 8 finalists. Each cyclist did just one run.

At 6:20 the qualifying round was concluded.

At 7:40 the first quarterfinal heat began.

For the mathematically challenged, that is a break in the action of exactly *80 minutes*. During which time we were held captive. Literally every Staples Center exit door was clearly labeled NO RE-ENTRY. If you had a notion to sample the Street X-Po outside or simply go for a walk in the brilliant evening sunshine during the break, you either forfeited the right to see the finals or coughed up the money for another ticket.

Did I mention that each and every one of the vast number of bars inside Staples Center was fully staffed and conveniently open for business throughout this "halftime"? I invite you to close your eyes, lean back, and envision what a healthy portion of an "extreme sports" crowd is like after literally having nothing to do but drink for well over an hour.

Why the preposterous time gap? Because ESPN had shifted its coverage to a skateboarding venue. And because this X Games was billed as "all live all the time," we motocross fans had to wait until the skateboard competition had concluded before we could get back to business. It wasn't like we had *nothing* to keep us occupied, though. For about 45 minutes we were enraptured by the sight of maintenance workers packing and smoothing the dirt track. Then we got the ESPN feed of the skateboarding, which, through Staples Center's clarity-challenged PA system sounded like: "And thienonfne klsvintgish fnnnuugled klipstonsssssnnng! *WOW!*"

The one thing that *was* decipherable during this mind-numbing interlude was a series of clips shown on the video board. In another sport it would have been a "bloopers reel," but this being motocross, pretty much the only thing that qualifies as a "blooper" is a wipeout. Thus we were treated to video of one horrific spill after another—much to the delight of the crowd. For me, though, it brought back a memory that I would have preferred not to revisit.

Many years ago, I was attending a Syracuse University basketball game inside a frenzied Carrier Dome. The Orangemen had just scored on a breakaway dunk, causing their archrival Georgetown to call a timeout and, in turn, the Syracuse cheerleaders to take the court. They were performing a complex pyramid stunt, and because nobody in the building could hear themselves think, the entire routine was based on a timing count. Michelle Munn, the cheerleader at the top of the 15-foot human pyramid, counted wrong. Per the routine, she let herself fall blindly backward into the waiting arms of two male cheerleaders. Except those male cheerleaders weren't there yet. A crowd of more than 20,000 people went from wild exuberance to shocked silence as she hit the floor, head and neck first.

I will never, ever forget the eerie sound of her agonized wails echoing through a pin-drop-quiet arena as she lay there. Worse, though, was when she abruptly stopped. As an EMT team carefully moved her onto a backboard and gently loaded her into an ambulance right there at center court, I was convinced that I had just watched someone die. An amazingly wide range of emotions washed over me—each one worse than the last.

Amazingly, Michelle Munn not only survived, she came away with nothing "worse" than a slight skull fracture and separated shoulder. But as I sat in Staples Center listening to people squeal with delight over the video of one crash after another, many of those raw emotions returned. At that moment it appeared crystal clear to me that *inevitably* someone doing a motocross stunt—perhaps even in the X Games—will be either permanently paralyzed or killed in front of a live audience.

Indeed, unbeknownst to me at the time, in the previous day's Best Trick competition, motocross rider Paris Rosen had missed the landing on a jump and wound up lying motionless on the Staples Center floor for ten full minutes before being taken off on a stretcher. He suffered a Grade Two concussion, a bruised right lung, and a liver laceration, as well as other injuries to his hips and ribs. This had the effect of "quieting the stunned crowd," as the *L.A. Times* phrased it. No kidding?

So I had all kinds of feel-good mojo going when it appeared that the next round of competition would finally commence. Setting aside the cavalier discounting of danger and the shameless huckstering, the qualifying round had provided a good taste of the excitement this sport could potentially deliver. The first couple of runs had been really impressive, as I started to get a feel for just how hard motocross racing is. Shortly thereafter, though, every run started to look the same, with two or three variations on a theme about what the rider would do in midair coming off of a ramp. No matter what was done, though, it elicited a Pavlovian "Ooooohhhhhh" from the crowd—almost as if they had forgotten that just a few minutes earlier they had seen basically the same thing. It was like 18,000 four-year-olds screaming "Do it again!" over and over and over. And I thought *I* was easily amused.

I anticipated that the eight-man, bracket-style finals portion of the Speed & Style competition would offer a little more in the way of drama, given that it would feature actual one-on-one races, as opposed to solo rides scored by judges. You can usually count on the unexpected when athletes go head to head—even *without* motor vehicles involved. I had a feeling there would be some sparks, both actual and figurative.

What actually transpired, though, was that, in all but one race, one rider jumped out to an immediate lead and increased it throughout—resulting essentially in separate stunt rides, each of which was pretty predictable. If I had an ounce of cynicism in me, I might think that things were actually arranged that way…like, say, when one rider wiped out and his opponent's bike suddenly stalled mysteriously, refusing to start again until the other rider had caught up with him. Nahhh—it had to have been pure coincidence.

While not as interminable as the break between qualifying and the finals, the timing between the seven races that comprised the quarterfinals, semifinals, and finals couldn't remotely be described as brisk. And as I had seen so often of late, the combination of boredom and excess lubrication started to take its toll on the environment. In the section below my mezzanine seat, a young man began dancing—evidently to the beat of his own drummer. A drummer on amphetamines, that is. His nonstop, spastic flailing effectively cleared the area around him, as people expected him to either: (a) stumble and fall into them, (b) throw up on them, or (c) both.

Because he somehow succeeded in avoiding actual physical contact with anyone, the security personnel on duty seemed frozen by indecision; after all, he was merely dancing, wired as he was. When, after some time, it didn't appear that he would be stopping on his own, though, two uniformed ushers made a tentative move to lead him away. Naturally this resulted in a shower of boos from those looking on.

With half the arena now a rapt audience, two women took full advantage of the attention and alternately lifted their shirts for the benefit of the crowd. A less charitable correspondent might suggest that this was about the closest thing to a compelling competition all evening. Whatever the case, they drew thunderous applause. Until they were escorted out. Triggering, of course, thunderous booing.

If you're getting the impression that this was more sideshow than sporting event, then I have accurately portrayed the X Games for you.

When the evening was mercifully over, I was struck by the ultimate irony—of all of the sporting events that I had attended up to that point in my walkabout, it was an Action Sports event that offered the least in the way of…well, action. On the field of play, anyway. When I had originally penciled the Moto X competition into the IGTS Tour, I expected loud. I expected annoying. I *didn't* expect boring—but that's what I got from my stint in the studio audience at the most tightly packaged and mass-marketed "counter-culture" sports gathering on the planet.

Dolly Parton once famously said, "It costs a lot of money to look this cheap," and the X Games is living testament to that. It takes a gargantuan effort to pull off a full slate of events that ESPN would have you believe sprang up virally amongst the dudes down in the local 7-Eleven parking lot. At the end of the day, I wondered why ESPN didn't just put together a tasteful video piece featuring the entire advertising sales staff on their knees, pleading with kids to buy more of their client's stuff. They would have saved a bundle on event production costs.

TWELVE
Working the Count

IT HAD BEEN A TOUGH SUMMER and early fall of 2010. My quest had begun many months before with optimism and buoyancy. When I got together with friends to describe what I had intended to do—and why—there was universal support and confidence. "This is exactly what you need!" was the standard refrain. "You'll get your groove back…and you'll have a blast doing it." The word "fun" was bandied about more often than not.

Now, as the leaves prepared to turn in the places where leaves turn, those same friends conveyed concern when I ran into them. "Wow," they'd say. "You don't look so good." And once again the word "fun" would make its way into the conversation. Only this time in a different context, as in: "This hasn't been any fun for you, has it?" It was almost inconceivable to them—and to me—that the reaffirming walkabout that I had embarked upon with such high hopes would yield such disillusionment, cynicism, and disappointment to date.

Of course there had been episodes of enjoyment and even delight, typically at events at which they were least expected. But the overriding mission, which was to rediscover the joys of a childhood and infuse them back into my career in sports, had been…well, there's no other way to say it…a complete bust. The worst part of it was that my unpleasant discoveries were not combining to show me a new way. There was thus far none of the "When one door closes, another one opens" thing going on. No making lemonade from lemons. It was all bad.

OK, I lied. That wasn't the worst part. "Worst" was reserved for something that I desperately tried to avoid admitting, even to myself: I had helped to nourish the Monster.

Granted, operating as I have from a very small corner of the sports universe, I wouldn't even qualify as an unindicted co-conspirator in the ruination of spectator sports. But there was no denying that the path I had taken through the sports business had led to a place where what I do for a living is less about delighting sports fans than it is about exposing them to a tidal wave of advertising. In my own small way, I've contributed more to the problem than the solution.

And whatever way you choose to look at it, I was certainly a hypocrite.

I had begun to recall with increasing frequency a conversation that I'd had with a senior executive of one of my former employers. In a moment of clarity I had said to him, "The eyeballs we're delivering will never justify the ask." In essence, we were selling sponsors on the concept that their message would be effectively delivered to their desired market in great numbers. And we couldn't honestly lay claim to our ability to do that. I waited for some words of wisdom to counter my statement—a description of some measure of return on investment that I hadn't considered. But all I got was a silent nod of assent.

So I had that going for me as well. Sigh.

I've heard it said that the opposite of love is not hate but indifference. I had never really grasped what that meant until this point in my life. But now I got it. One after another, I had revisited the sports properties that I had been crazy about during what was looking more and more each day like a former life. And, one after another, these cornerstones of sports in America had let me down.

The sting from each encounter with the Monster had been fresh right after each experience, but a certain numbness had been setting in more and more rapidly after each game. It became easier and easier for me to reconcile the losses. I became indifferent. More a sports zombie than a sports fan.

But if I was afraid that I had lost all passion whatsoever, I could always count on college football to get my pulse racing again. For this is where love and hate occupy the same turf, so to speak. I love college football. To me it is unparalleled as a uniquely American spectacle. Which is why I hate the Corleone family of college football, the BCS. Passionately.

Sports fans have always had a working agreement with their sports. As long as they are fun to watch, provide us with the opportunity to choose and root for our favorites, and culminate in a compelling chase for a championship, we're pretty happy campers. Otherwise…there's a disturbance in the Force. In college football that disturbance is the poll-and-bowl system, which takes a perfectly good sport and turns it into a three-month popularity contest followed by a bunch of exhibition games.

I'm all ears if someone can tell me of any other game played at an elite level anywhere else in the world that determines its champion based almost entirely on the votes of semiqualified "experts." Even professional boxing eventually gets it right more often than a blind squirrel. Which means that the people who run college football lag behind *Don King* on the Sports Integrity Meter. I could rest my case right there. But I won't.

Last year, a total of 35 bowl games were played, involving 70 teams that qualified for postseason play simply by: (a) winning more games than they lost, and (b) avoiding the combination dartboard/lazy Susan process that the NCAA uses to decide who is and who isn't on probation at any given time. These teams got invited to travel to exotic locations like Detroit, El Paso, and Mobile to play in tension-filled games in which the winner gets… well, nothing other than the right to give their coach the requisite Gatorade shower. This smacks vaguely to me of the "everybody gets a blue ribbon for participation" approach to competition currently in vogue in kindergarten classes throughout the nation.

Per the basic sports-fan pact described above, this doesn't work. It is our considered opinion that we are all but constitutionally guaranteed a system that will determine the champion of college football on a field instead of inside a conference room. Evidently our sentiments were shared by a group of very large colleges and universities, who several years back got together over cocktails and decided to "fix" college football. Granted, they did have a good concept to start with. Instead of the ludicrous system of polling that had determined college football's mythical "national champion" for decades, these forward-thinking leaders felt that it might be a good idea to actually have a National Championship *Game*. On a real gridiron, with real players and everything! They even thought of taking four existing bowl games and making them Extra-Special Also-Ran Games!

"Bravo! Great idea!" we sports enthusiasts responded. "But how will you determine which teams will play in the Extra-Special Also-Ran Games and what two teams will play in the National Championship Game?"

"Don't worry about a thing," came the reply. "We'll just use the existing poll system to pick them. Only we'll use computers to make it *better!*"

"Outstanding!" we cried.

"Oh, and by the way, only teams from the six conferences that we represent will actually ever be selected to play in the National Championship Game."

"Come again?"

And so it came to be that premier college football was hijacked by the Bowl Championship Series. While every other sport that the NCAA presides over (including football in three smaller-school divisions) uses a playoff to determine its national champion, "big-time" college football uses a process cleverly co-opted from your local high school, which originally established it for selecting their prom king and queen. That is, those who are already popular are the only ones in the running. If you're thinking, *This system appears to be rigged,* I must admit that the thought has crossed my mind on occasion as well.

What in the world could possibly justify such a ludicrously subjective way to identify our nation's best college football teams, including its champion? Money. Lots and lots of money. Big heaping piles of money large enough to hide an entire *neighborhood* of small children. But not democratically allocated money.

The BCS is run by an iron-clad coalition of the "haves" and the "have mores," and these schools are not of a mind to share, if it means losing out on that next ivory back scratcher. In fact, six privileged conferences walk away each year with roughly 85 percent of the total BCS revenue, despite the outcomes of any of the BCS games. Their annual take of almost half a billion dollars (that's *billion*, with a *B*) has actually resulted in serious talk of antitrust scrutiny, something almost unheard of in pro sports. Oops…wait—this isn't "professional" sports, is it now? Wink, wink.

But as I was combing through the schedule of marquee college football games to find just the right one for inclusion in the IGTS Tour, the following truly unfathomable notion occurred to me: they could get their grubby paws on *even more money* if they instituted a playoff system. A playoff system that would make March Madness look more like March Mild Neurosis. To wit, each spring, a group of my oldest and dearest friends gather for three days to eat, drink, reminisce, and laugh at each other's bad jokes. This gathering *always* occurs during the NCAA college basketball playoffs. It is tradition, and despite having to cross the country to be there, I wouldn't conceive of missing it. I also annually play in at least two March Madness pools—yet another way to stay connected with friends. And since the age of 12, I have missed watching just one Final Four Championship Game, and that was only because I was stuck circling LaGuardia Airport in an endless holding pattern. (1997. Arizona over Kentucky. In overtime.) Get the picture? I am heart, soul, and (here's the important part) wallet invested in the college basketball playoffs.

In contrast, unless a college football bowl game is on television in a bar I happen to be in, I typically don't watch any of them. Why? Because I don't care who wins. The games are meaningless. I only tune in to the BCS

Championship Game if my favorite team happens to have been voted into it. Otherwise, a spirited game of lawn darts is more compelling to me. I've attended a couple of bowl games but only because the ticket was free and I didn't have to travel more than ten miles.

But here's the kicker—all things being equal, I am a *much* bigger fan of college football than I am of college basketball.

The point is this: if college bowl games were incorporated into a playoff, I wouldn't think of missing a single one. In fact, with gun to head and the choice of watching either the Super Bowl or a legitimate college football title game, it would be no contest—I'd take the latter every time. I am just *dying* to lavish my money and affection on college football, to incorporate college football playoff traditions into my life much the same way I've done with college basketball. And I know I am not alone. This is why the BCS system befuddles me so. I get the "it's to make money" part. I just don't get the "we're not interested in making even *more* money" part.

I humbly submit that the Real College Football Playoffs would surpass even March Madness in terms of popularity, ratings, and—here's the key—advertising revenue. The sheer volume of eyeballs available for gobbling over the course of a gripping monthlong drama involving America's favorite sport would give even the Monster indigestion.

But year after year goes by with no hint of any meaningful change. The BCS is hunkered down with all of the hubris and arrogance of the Nixon administration during the Watergate days. Whenever I hear BCS executive director Bill Hancock go through his propaganda-laden shtick on how college football has the "best, most compelling regular season of any sport," I feel the sudden need to shower.

But perhaps I should be grateful to Hancock and his henchmen, for it turns out that they have bestowed upon me a perverse benefit. My urge to closely follow college football grows each year as I invest time and energy each autumn weekend, mulling over matchups and figuring out which games have to end in what way in order to create long-term, crippling embarrassment for the BCS over their deeply flawed system. Then I root actively for those games to play out in such a way as to shed the maximum amount of bad light possible on these greedy good old boys who currently hold college football hostage.

I revel in watching the BCS committee squirm each time they are forced to feverishly spin their justification for anointing two teams as "unquestionably the best in the country" when often they just plain aren't. Which is why, with everything else on my walkabout going so badly, I began to take heart in the notion that a perfect storm was developing, in the form of the Boise State Broncos.

Not in the history of the current system had there been a team with more potential to spotlight the inequity in which the BCS traffics. See, Boise State plays in a conference other than one of the Privileged Six. But they'll go anywhere to play anybody in their nonconference games. And they rarely lose, no matter the opponent. In fact, the previous year's team had been undefeated, winning each one of their games in convincing fashion, including a shutout of Oregon—the team that would go on to win the Pac-10 championship and receive gobs of money for playing in the Rose Bowl.

In the measured opinion of the BCS, however, Boise State had not been one of the two best teams in the country. Thus the Broncos were sent to play in the least esteemed of the Extra-Special Also-Ran Games. They won that, making the season essentially a repeat of 2006, when they had beaten heavily favored Oklahoma in the very same bowl game. Evidently, I wasn't the only one to notice this trend.

This particular season had been projected to be an off-year for dominant teams in college football, and experts were in agreement on the following: an undefeated season would most likely land a team in the BCS Championship Game; and few, if any, of the traditional powers appeared good enough to pull off that feat.

As for Boise State…well, the Broncos had all but one starter back from the previous season's unblemished squad, and they had been able to schedule not one but two games against teams included in the nation's preseason Top 25. Virginia Tech was considered the stronger of those two ranked teams, so it stood to reason that if Boise State could travel across the country and post a nationally televised dominating win against a Top 10 team from a Privileged Six conference…and then take care of business per usual the rest of the season…well, there could be *no conceivable defense* for excluding them from the mega-money National Championship Game.

Other than, of course, that Boise State would then have to be paid like a national championship team, an unpleasantness that the BCS system had thus far studiously avoided. See, that money would have to come directly out of the pockets of the six glamour conferences that have reserved the windfall from that game for themselves. That would mean a dramatic drop-off in ivory back scratchers, not to mention the unbridled indignity suffered.

But if the scenario laid out above came to fruition and Boise State was once again left with their noses pressed against the championship-game window…well, as Ricky Ricardo might say to the BCS, "You've got some 'splainin' to do."

Which is why I was almost giddy with excitement as I arrived at my hotel on the day before what I considered to be the college football game of the year: Boise State vs. Virginia Tech, at the neutral site of Washington, D.C.'s FedEx Field. According to my admittedly blue-sky way of thinking, I would be present for the beginning of the end of the BCS. My dream scenario involved a Boise State blowout victory, an undefeated season, and the inevitable indefensible snub followed by a media firestorm, antitrust litigation, financial scandal, forced resignations…and ultimately the replacement of the BCS system with a college football playoff!

A guy can dream, can't he? Besides, I was running out of success stories to be gleaned from the Big-Time Sports. If I was going to grasp at straws, I might as well concentrate my energies on saving one of my very favorite sports on behalf of sports fans everywhere. And lest we forget, let's get back to what's truly important here: me.

I still hadn't found the definitive answer to the question that had set me on this quest. But that reckoning was looming on the horizon. And it wasn't pretty. This game could stave that off. It *had* to. It was the last of my cherished Big-Time Sports events to appear on the IGTS Tour schedule. After this…well, I was out of options for turning my whole wretched undertaking around.

Truth be told, there was another reason for giddiness as I checked into the Courtyard Marriott in Aberdeen, Maryland. Lack of sleep will do that to you. This was the tail end of a 12-day, five-city IGTS Tour swing, and the attendant planes, trains, and automobiles weren't adding a lot to my already flagging enthusiasm level. My once-buoyant walkabout was giving way to a weary stagger.

It was, in fact, to mitigate the pain of what shaped up to be an *extremely* long day of travel on the day after the football game that I chose to stay halfway between Washington and Philadelphia—where I was to board a morning flight for the long trip back home to Los Angeles. Aberdeen just happened to occupy that halfway point. So the irony was delicious when I pulled into the entranceway for my hotel and discovered that the full name of the property was the Courtyard Aberdeen at Ripken Stadium. Yes, my hotel, chosen by a virtual pin in the map, was the center of a baseball complex, flanked on one side by the Cal Ripken Academy and on the other by Ripken Stadium, the home of the Aberdeen IronBirds, a Class A minor league affiliate of the Baltimore Orioles.

How appropriate. The night before my pivotal trip to see Boise State save college football would be spent here, wrapped in the confines of a complex dedicated to sports.

Local legend had it that when Cal Ripken broke Lou Gehrig's record of 2,130 consecutive games, he received a $75,000 honorarium from the MLB Players Association, which he used as seed money to build the Ripken Stadium and Ripken Academy complex in his hometown of Aberdeen. Undoubtedly someone of Ripken's fame and fortune could have funded the construction of the complex with seat-cushion change, but the honorarium thing does make for a nice story.

The impeccably groomed baseball diamonds and grandstands on the north side of the complex are used largely to support instructional camps and competitive destination play, including the Cal Ripken World Series, which is the highest level of play in youth baseball's Babe Ruth League. And, in 2002, Ripken acquired the rights to the Utica Blue Sox franchise, negotiated the current affiliate arrangement with the Orioles, and moved the team to Aberdeen. It is, by all accounts, a marriage made in heaven.

I knew none of this when I made my lodging plans. And even if I had, it would have been irrelevant, given that I had already checked off a minor league baseball game earlier in the Tour. But embedded in my DNA is the compulsion to watch any baseball game conducted remotely within eyesight. And as luck would have it, the IronBirds were playing on the afternoon of my arrival—*well* within eyesight. In fact, directly across the driveway from my hotel. So what would I do on my "day off" from attending sporting events? Attend a sporting event, naturally.

There was one tiny problem, however. "How much do they charge for admission over there?" I asked when checking in. "Well, they sell out pretty much every game, and they started playing about a half hour ago," the desk agent said. "But let me check something." She disappeared around the corner into her office, and when she returned she bore a broad smile and a ticket to the game. "Here you go. Our last ticket—to the last game of the season. Have fun!"

A hint of sunshine had appeared among the storm clouds that had been gathering ominously on the horizon of my walkabout. And as for the actual weather that day in Aberdeen, it was perfect. This would be a nice diversion.

Ripken Stadium is not your typical minor league ballpark. The best way to describe it is that a modern major league stadium was architected and then scaled down to a capacity of 6,300. There are several different tiers of seating, including skyboxes that appeared to include all the amenities of say…Camden Yards, for example. Also, in the fashion of the newer MLB stadiums, the areas adjoining each of the foul poles are set up as party decks that offer loosely assigned seating as well as an assortment of different-sized tables shaded by umbrellas. My ticket got me a seat in the pavilion in the left-field corner, and I joined a bunch of people who were picnicking and basking in the warm late-summer sun.

One other feature of Ripken Stadium that is pure major league is the scoreboard, which features sophisticated graphics and tons of information about the game and about each of the players who come to bat. Using that and an equally information-drenched game program, it didn't take long to acquaint myself with the home team.

I had arrived in the top of the fourth inning of the game between the IronBirds and the Connecticut Tigers. Having steeled myself for the onslaught of cheesy antics considered *de rigueur* in minor league baseball for attracting fans who theoretically can't get through an entire inning without being "entertained," I was quietly thrilled to find that the emphasis at Ripken Stadium was almost exclusively on the action on the field. As the game progressed, there were a couple of musical snippets and one "Everybody clap your hands!" exhortation, but otherwise the focus was purely on the baseball being played.

Intermittent promotional activity took place in between innings, but it wasn't assaulting, and it was spaced out well throughout the game. The host for all this activity was quite the opposite of the super-glib "personality" that I had been suffering through at events all summer. Slightly reminiscent of the late Chris Farley, he was a chunky, happy-go-lucky sort who dispatched his duties with the bemused, sweetly sarcastic manner that Bill Murray employed with his Camp North Star CITs in *Meatballs*.

The Wawa Food Markets Hoagie Throw was charming, as was one between-innings "base scrub," performed with giant toothbrushes and sponsored, of course, by a local dentist. All in all, it was the same blueprint used at minor league stadiums across the country but blessed with more creativity and performed with understated humor and better props. I began to melt into my surroundings.

I got to talking with another fan about what I considered to be a lively and sizable crowd, especially for the final game of the season. "When do the playoffs start?" I asked. He almost snorted his beer through his nose.

"Well, whenever they do, we won't be there!" Much to my amazement, I learned that the IronBirds were dead last in their New York–Penn League division, a position they'd occupied for most of the year. In spite of this, though, a full house was the norm. In fact, every ticket for every game had been sold that season. Sure enough, in a trip around the concourse later in the day, I came across a card table that had been set up to facilitate sign-ups for a spot on the next year's season-ticket *waiting list!* Clearly the team had unlocked the secret formula for keeping their fans happy.

Down on the field, nobody had been able to unlock the secret formula for scoring in quite a while. There had been plenty of that early on, and when I arrived, the game was tied at four runs apiece. Shortly thereafter, however, a pitcher's duel broke out, and neither team had been able to push across the tie-breaker. It remained 4–4 into the ninth inning, despite Connecticut having 14 hits to the IronBirds' six. Compounding their frustration, in the top of the ninth the Tigers got a runner to third with nobody out and couldn't get him home. When the IronBirds went down quietly in the bottom of the ninth, we were headed into extra innings, even though the game was less than two and a half hours old. Now *that's* baseball.

In the 11th, Connecticut finally broke through with a run and took a 5–4 lead into the bottom of the inning. Then, with a runner on first and down to their last out, Aberdeen got a gift when the Tigers' pitcher threw wildly on a pickoff attempt, allowing the runner to advance to third base. Pinch hitter Joe Oliveria promptly singled him in to tie the game and send it into a 12th inning.

During the short break, I looked around in amazement. Here in extra innings, on the last day of a disappointing season, not only had the bulk of the crowd stuck around, they were heavily into the game. Nobody needed to be prompted to make noise when, in the bottom of the 12th, Manny Machado, the Orioles' top pick in the recent amateur draft, led off with a single. The decibel level increased when *cleanup hitter* Kip Schutz unselfishly dropped down a perfect sacrifice bunt. But a two-out shoetop grab of a sinking line drive to right field ended the threat and cut the crowd off in mid-celebration.

At long last, in the top of the 13th inning, Connecticut strung together several of their eventual 20 hits in the game and scored two runs. Fans finally started heading for the exits, and I thought I could vaguely hear the sound of either a bus starting up or a fat lady singing. I chose to hang around because it was a gorgeous evening, because by then I had managed to migrate down to a field-level seat near third base, and because…well, because I had no other place to be until the following evening.

The IronBirds' Jeremy Nowak struck out swinging to start the bottom of the inning, and Joe Oliveria followed him back to the dugout after looking at a called third strike. Mychal Givens staved off the inevitable when he was hit by a pitch. Then the fun started.

Blair Dunlap, who had struck out with the bases loaded to end the 11th inning, came to the plate representing the potential final out. He dug in and worked the count. And worked it. And worked it some more. As he fouled off pitch after pitch after pitch, somewhere in the deep recesses of my fried-to-a-crisp brain a light went on. There was something to what I was seeing, but I couldn't put my finger on it. Finally, with the team's season just one strike away from being over, Dunlap fought off yet another tough pitch and dumped a single into right field. A great at-bat had kept the IronBirds alive.

It didn't take long for Manny Machado, batting next, to show why he is regarded as the Orioles star of the future. His triple into the outfield gap drove in both Givens and Dunlap, and yes—we were implausibly tied once again. But not for long. Kip Schutz singled to left field, delivering Machado home with the game winner. After 13 innings and nearly four hours of season-prolonging baseball, the last-place IronBirds celebrated their walk-off victory as if they'd just won the World Series.

"That was just what the doctor ordered," I said to myself while negotiating the three-minute commute from my grandstand seat to my hotel. The window in my room looked out over the infield of Ripken Stadium, and I watched as the shadows spread over the grounds crew performing their postgame duties. It had been a pleasant surprise. Although it was just a Single-A minor league baseball game, it had been truly enjoyable. And I was hopeful that the football game the following night would follow suit with an experience that would get me back on track toward reconciling my differences with the Big-Time Sports.

As I mulled over that possibility, the sense of déjà vu that had appeared during the game kept nagging at me. It was nothing that a quick dinner and a good night's sleep wouldn't take care of, though.

"How about those IronBirds?" I chuckled to myself as I drifted off that night.

THIRTEEN
Déjà Vu

THE ANNOUNCED ATTENDANCE at FedEx Field the next night was 86,587, which I figured had to be close to a complete sellout. From my vantage point, every last seat seemed to be occupied—and I definitely had a bird's-eye view from which to make that assessment. I had secured my ticket for the game between the Boise State Broncos and the Virginia Tech Hokies only recently, so I didn't expect premier seating. And I was right. I did a quick count of the number of rows between me and the absolute apex of the stadium.

"Let me see…there's the one right behind me, and…well, that's it. One."

I had chosen to park in the suburbs and take the Metro to the stadium. Bad decision. To my chagrin, the trip wound up entailing two long train rides sandwiched around a transfer and then a walk of more than a mile just to get to the stadium parking lot. As I waded up the walkway toward the main gate, side-stepping empty beer cans and broken bottles the entire way, it was hard to believe that FedEx Field was less than five years old. If there had once been any attractive plaza or landscaped area, it had long ago been ruined. What was left was a big impersonal cement bowl, a lot of chain-link fencing, and scores of barricade horses. Once inside the gates, it didn't get much better.

Many would describe the evening's environment as "spirited," and it certainly was that. The word "plastered" also came to mind. This was more or less a home game for Virginia Tech, even though FedEx Field's Landover, Maryland, location is almost 300 miles away from the Blacksburg campus—a campus that I'm guessing was a virtual ghost town on this night. Each and every last Hokies student appeared to be there with me. And while most of them were drunk, at least it was a good-natured drunk. In the time leading up to kickoff, they welcomed me with open, albeit erratically gesticulating arms. We were all in this together up here, weren't we?

Shortly before the game had even begun, I jotted down a cogent observation: *Hokies are loud.* At kickoff, the stadium was airplane-taking-off loud. When Boise State kicked a field goal to go up 3–0, it had diminished to eardrum-piercing loud. But when the Broncos completely stuffed Virginia Tech's first possession, blocked their punt, and scored shortly thereafter, things ratcheted down considerably—to merely extremely loud. When Boise State took the ball right back and scored again to make it 17–0? Well...not quite so loud.

Hokies fans as far as the eye could see were collectively melting into their seats. And by then the yelling was mostly *at their own team*. I could even start to make out the voices of the vastly outnumbered Broncos contingent across the way. As for those of us in the nosebleed section, I was certainly the only one who had a wide grin adhered to my face as the final seconds of the first quarter ticked away. As the saying goes, Boise State's 17–0 lead over Virginia Tech wasn't even *that* close. The Broncos had held the Hokies to *negative* cumulative yards thus far, while in turn scoring each time they touched the ball.

My fiendishly clever plan for the overthrow of the BCS was coming to fruition. The entire football-watching country was tuned in for the thrashing that Boise State was administering to one of the nation's top-ranked teams. Make no mistake—I had nothing against Virginia Tech, and in fact I had grown kind of fond of my enthusiastic neighbors. But what must be done needed to be done. The BCS must be toppled if I were to reclaim at least some measure of Big-Time Sports fandom.

To their credit, the Hokies fans in the house managed to take the full punch in the nose that had been the first quarter and regroup. They were a resilient bunch, and many of them appeared to actually believe that they would come back to win this game. They were passionate. And being well lubricated, they were also a little delusional. But their faith was rewarded.

For whatever reason, the ferocity with which Boise State ruled the first quarter dissipated rapidly. They started giving up yardage in big chunks, especially through the air. And once the Hokies passing game had been established, it opened up the line of scrimmage for their running attack. A Virginia Tech touchdown was answered only by a Boise State field goal. Not long after that, it took the Hokies just five plays to convert a Broncos fumble into another touchdown. The insurmountable lead looked downright...well, surmountable. It had been cut to 20–14 by halftime.

Sloppy in the first half, the game got even messier after the break. And Boise State's messes in particular became more frequent and more impactful. Fumbles. Dropped passes. A missed field goal from gimme range. An extra-point try that was blocked. Dumb penalties at the worst possible times. All of these, combined with Tech's sudden discovery of an offense, enabled the Hokies to take a 30–26 lead late into the game.

At which point I got Mothershipped.

When I had exited the train that had brought me to within "easy walking distance" of FedEx Field, we had been told rather stridently that the last train departing from that location would leave promptly at midnight. No problem. The game started at 8:00. *Plenty* of time for me to watch the game and then negotiate my way out of the stadium and back down the road. Except for one tiny thing I didn't take into account...ESPN was televising the game.

All night long, the timeouts had been far lengthier than anything that I'd witnessed at any other televised sporting event—*including* an NFL game. And as the game wound down to its tense conclusion, it began to dawn on me that if I stayed to the end I would risk missing the last train, a train that was leaving *four hours* after kickoff. Incredibly, I found myself weighing my options. How serious were they really about that midnight deadline? How much could a cab cost? The train ride over had been circuitous, so I had no idea how far I actually was from the parking lot where my rental car sat. And never mind cost…would I even be able to *find* a taxi? FedEx Field had proven to be pretty short on amenities, so the chances that a taxi stand existed were 50/50 at best.

I finally came to the conclusion that I had no choice but to leave early. My newfound and now-rejuvenated friends were stunned. They razzed me with all the requisite jokes about fans in Los Angeles as I crawled over and around them to get to the aisle.

As I speed-walked through the parking lot outside, I heard a full-throated groan of anguish, followed by a long stretch of eerie silence. That was all the external stimuli I needed to know that Boise State had scored a last-minute touchdown to snatch victory away from Virginia Tech. I didn't know which was worse: the fact that I'd missed seeing the Broncos' dramatic game-winning drive at the final hour or the fact that it basically didn't matter. For even though Boise State had managed to pull off a 33–30 win, the damage had already been done. They'd had their foot planted firmly on Virginia Tech's—and by extension all of college football's—chest. But they never got around to pressing down.

Put it this way: Boise State had owned the first quarter and the last one and a half minutes of the game, outscoring Virginia Tech 24–0 during that time. But in the nearly three quarters of the game that intervened, they were themselves outscored 30–9. By what I had to admit was a good but not great Hokies team. I knew that in the grand scheme of things, this Broncos win would be tarnished enough that it would dissolve in significance before the season was over. Yes, Boise State would most likely finish undefeated. Again. And yes, once again they would be sent to play in the most invisible bowl game that the BCS committee could conjure for them. And, come January, each member school of the BCS's Privileged Six conferences would receive their regular shipment of ivory back scratchers.

College football would continue its downhill slide toward irrelevance in my life. I had run out of Big-Time Sports to love.

I thought about this during the train ride to L'Enfant Plaza. I thought about this during the 30-minute wait for my connecting train. I thought about this on my wee-hours drive from the Greenbelt commuter rail parking lot in College Park all the way to my Aberdeen hotel. It was the first thing I thought about when my alarm went off to begin a long day of spawning westward to the Pacific. And it was still in the forefront of my mind as I gazed out my plane window during the first of three flights that would eventually take me home.

I was defeated. Demoralized. Depressed. All the rest of the bad *de* words. And whatever word captures the perfect balance between anger and sadness. Not in my worst nightmare had I considered that this walkabout would turn out so badly. This was supposed to be a triumphant quest that would jump-start the next stage of my career in sports—hell, my *life* in sports. All the demons of self-doubt would be exorcised. Never again would I have to think about how big my bank account would have grown to if I hadn't decided to "pursue my passion." A passion that was now more or less nonexistent. The crash and burn was complete. While golf and I had simply drifted apart, I was headed toward a nasty divorce from the Big-Time Sports. Irreconcilable differences.

Having traced my way back through all of my fandom roots, I was now forced to face the fact that sports are not what they once were to me. Not even close. All that my trip through the world of "stick and ball" professional sports events had revealed to me was that I no longer shared the same planet as the caricatures that inhabit stadiums, arenas, and sports talk radio. Those fans are, for whatever reason, willing to overlook the damage that mountains of money have done to spectator sports as long as they have "their team" with which to validate themselves. Me? No thanks. No more. The cost and aggravation of attending Big-Time Sports events isn't remotely worth the psychic payoff.

And then a new emotion—embarrassment. Had I bothered to think about it, or pay the slightest bit of attention while on my ten-year leave of absence from watching the games that I grew up with, all of this would have been so self-evident. Instead, it took months of wading through the remains of what I had remembered Big-Time Sports to be before I saw the writing on the wall. I ruefully remembered the punch line to an old joke: "Denial ain't just a river in Egypt."

Whatever the case, things had now become abundantly clear.

The Monster long ago swallowed the professional athletes who ply their trade within the major sports properties and who now live like Jonah inside the belly of the beast. Only this particular belly houses multiple gated homes, each well stocked with expensive toys and legions of sycophants. Celebrity-worshipping fans took it from there. And the public drunkenness and deteriorating lack of civility that I kept discovering in marquee sports venues were merely the vestiges of societal trends at large. And I wanted to stay in this business because…?

As things had slowly unwound over the past few months, I hadn't mentioned any of this to The Bird, of course. When this whole miserable journey was through, though, there would be plenty of time for a "come to Jesus" career discussion. And this time I would choose a line of work that was as far away as possible from any leisure pursuit that I held remotely dear. Assuming, that is, that I had any of those left.

Last in the cavalcade of uninvited emotions, dread began to set in as I began to fully contemplate a future in which sports would nourish neither my wallet nor my soul. Was I doomed to start all over again on *both* fronts?

It was finally sheer exhaustion that put me at least temporarily out of my misery. The endless journey from FedEx Field back to my hotel had left me with just four hours of sleep, and none of them had been remotely restful. I leaned my head against the window, and despite the fact that I'm rarely able to sleep on planes, I nodded off fitfully. The way things were going, I'm sure I embarrassed myself by snoring loudly.

I was awakened by the rumble of turbulence. I'm not a nervous flier, so I didn't jolt immediately into a panic-stricken state of full consciousness. Instead, I found myself groggy and dazed, struggling to figure out exactly where I was. And with my conscious mind temporarily on the disabled list, the subconscious reigned. I floated from one random thought to another for several moments before something discernible took form. To my surprise, it was that nagging feeling of déjà vu that I'd felt at the IronBirds game. But this time all of the dots were connected.

Now it was clear: just as I'd felt in my bones that evening, I *had* been there before—just not "there," as in Ripken Stadium. Physical location aside, though, all of the circumstances that had presented themselves to me in Aberdeen bore a striking resemblance to a game I had seen played months prior, in the early days of the IGTS Tour. As I emerged from my sleepy haze, the details began to come back to me.

Given how much had happened since that Saturday afternoon at Jackie Robinson Stadium in Los Angeles, it seemed almost as though Game Two of the NCAA College Baseball Super Regional between UCLA and Cal State Fullerton had existed outside the realm of the Tour. To start with, I had been downright lucky to gain access to the game in the first place, rescued from having my nose pressed against the proverbial window by a chance encounter with a gentleman named Jim Winn, who just happened to have extra tickets to the sold-out game. Third row tickets, right behind home plate, to be precise.

The NCAA Super Regionals are the rough equivalent to the Sweet Sixteen round of the annual March Madness basketball tournament. At each of eight Super Regional sites across the country, two of the 16 teams still alive after the national tournament's Regional stage are matched up in a weekend best-of-three series, with the winner moving on to play in the College World Series in Omaha.

While UCLA was the higher-ranked team as a result of the Bruins' school-record 46 wins, among those in the know, Cal State Fullerton was the favorite to win this Super Regional. In the 30-plus years in which the

Titans had played Division I collegiate baseball, they had *never* had a losing season. In fact, quite the opposite—with 16 trips to the College World Series, Cal-Fullerton had averaged a visit to that ultra-elite tournament pretty much every other year, walking away with the national championship on four different occasions.

In contrast, despite UCLA's rich tradition of athletic excellence, not a single one of the school's 100-plus NCAA championships had come in baseball. In fact, the Bruins had only *been to* the College World Series twice, with the last trip occurring back in 1997. Why such a hard time getting to Omaha? Well, if you play baseball on the West Coast, you eventually have to go through Cal-Fullerton to reach Nebraska. And going into that night's second game of the Super Regional, UCLA had beaten the Titans just three times in their last 22 meetings.

Having lost Game One of the series the night before, every Bruins fan in attendance knew full well that they were one loss away from having their season ended by Cal-Fullerton. *Again.* As I surveyed a somewhat somber collection of UCLA fans, it was hard to miss the guy sitting right smack in the middle of the Bruins section wearing a Titans-orange T-shirt that read simply, CAL STATE OMAHA. He couldn't even get a rise out of the Bruins faithful. After all, his point was irrefutable.

It was a pitching duel for the first half of the game, but things heated up considerably in the later innings. A flurry of scoring eventually wound up with Cal-Fullerton taking a 6–4 lead into the eighth inning—a lead that, based upon history, looked much larger than two runs. The energy slowly drained from the UCLA bleachers as Bruins fans began resigning themselves to yet another loss to their arch-nemesis. Even when Cory Regis hit his second solo home run of the game to cut the eighth-inning deficit to 6–5, the response was muted. UCLA had Cal-Fullerton on the ropes a couple of innings earlier but had failed to put them away. And of course there was that whole "lost 19 of the last 22 to the Titans" thing. Defeat was clearly considered inevitable.

And so it was that the Bruins fans orchestrated an "everybody up" cheer for their team after its second out of the ninth inning. They were justifiably proud of this winningest-ever UCLA baseball team and were determined to show their appreciation for a great season. They were on their feet and clapping for quite a while, though, because the last Bruin standing was not about to go down without a fight.

And *that* was the image that kept trying to sandwich its way into my consciousness as I was delighting in Aberdeen IronBirds baseball over the weekend. That final UCLA batter had worked the count every bit as valiantly as had the IronBirds' Blair Dunlap—Aberdeen's own last man standing.

The count went to full and stayed there for one foul ball after another. Finally, the by-then visibly irritated Cal-Fullerton pitcher missed his mark. Ball four. A walk prolonged the fans' final serenade. A great at-bat had kept the Bruins alive.

They were still applauding that display of resiliency when...hey, wait...is that...? Could that *possibly go out?* Yes, it could—"it" being a majestic fly ball by UCLA's Tyler Rahmatulla that cleared the left-field wall with just a few feet to spare. And just like that, the season was *not* over. In fact, this was just the beginning.

"This" being UCLA vs. Cal-Fullerton, the Titans naturally came back to tie the game in the bottom of the ninth and send it to extra innings. Now emboldened, however, the Bruins exploded for four runs in the 10th, winning the game and evening the series. A series that they won the next day, earning them their first trip to Omaha in much more than a decade. And once there, having never won a single College World Series *game* before, UCLA clawed themselves all the way into the finals against South Carolina before midnight struck and the Cinderella run ended. National runners-up. Not bad for a team one pitch away from being eliminated in the Super Regional.

As I sat there on the long plane ride home from a generally disastrous trip, I still couldn't help but smile at the combined memory of the UCLA and Aberdeen games. It was eerily remarkable how similar the two scenarios had been. In both, a team was literally down to their last out of the season when a scrappy, determined at-bat staved off defeat and set the stage for a dramatic comeback win in extra innings. "And neither of the games was interrupted for a television timeout," I chuckled sardonically to myself.

Since it was the first remotely enjoyable moment of the day, I decided to revel in it a bit longer. I dug my event notebook out of my backpack and, flipping through notes taken at dozens of sporting venues, I eventually reached the pages that I had scrawled upon while in my third-row seat at Jackie Robinson Stadium. My enjoyment of that game was evident in my style of writing. Exclamation marks and underscored phrases had increased in number as the game went on, and by the time I had gotten to that ninth inning it was obvious that...

"What the...no *way*...I'll be *damned!*"

I didn't even realize that I'd said this out loud until my startled neighbor looked up suddenly. Amidst the other scribbled markings on the opened notebook page in my lap was the name of the UCLA batter who had worked the count so heroically for the walk that kept his team alive:

It was Blair Dunlap.

Stunned by what I'd read, I rummaged through my backpack once again, fishing out the program from the IronBirds game. I flipped to the Player Information pages and scanned the roster. Sure enough, listed next to Blair Dunlap's name, under the column heading of "Last Team," was the simple acronym, "UCLA." Evidently the Baltimore Orioles organization had shared my enthusiasm for Dunlap's grittiness, for they'd claimed the Bruins' graduating senior in the MLB amateur draft that spring and assigned him to start his pro career—for the Aberdeen IronBirds.

A chill passed through me. This was not mere happenstance. There were far too many intertwining coincidences for it to be just that. I hadn't planned on attending an Aberdeen IronBirds game. I hadn't even planned on being in Aberdeen, for that matter. I *had* planned on being at the UCLA game but had been turned away when the game sold out—only to find someone with an unplanned pair of extra tickets directly behind me in line. And all of that merely *set the stage* for the parallel series of events that led each game to the point where Blair Dunlap would cosmically intercede in exactly the same way twice. The realization hit me full force at 30,000 feet. I had been sent a message.

Those who know me best will verify that I am the last person on Earth to believe in things that can't rationally be explained. Not one for omens or signs, I pay little heed to mysticism, karma, astrology, etc. But there was simply too much here to write off to chance. On the very day that I had reached the nadir of my walkabout and was considering turning my back on a lifelong passion, a message was delivered: Go in the other direction. Embrace the small and the humble in sports. Seek out the experiences that draw spectators interested in pure athletic competition, instead of those that simply want to claim "I was there."

Somewhere in the air between Philadelphia and Chicago, everything had turned around. I found myself saying goodbye to the Big-Time Sports—but without rancor, frustration, or sadness. It was just time. My thoughts turned toward many of the events that I had attended with the single-minded purpose of merely crossing them off my checklist of 50 different sports. Five minutes ago, they had been novelties—amusements to pass the time between the "real" sporting events. Now *they* were the real thing. My entire perspective had changed dramatically, and for the better.

I booted up my laptop and opened the spreadsheet that listed the upcoming IGTS Tour schedule. Kayaking…surfing…a triathlon…cycling. I couldn't wait to get home and get started. In fact, I started getting downright antsy. *Can't this plane fly any faster?* I wondered.

FOURTEEN

Apparently, Size Does Matter

JUST FOR THE RECORD, I believe in karma now. Destiny, kismet, predetermination—yup, I'm all in. I promise to never again roll my eyes when The Bird pronounces, "Things happen for a reason, you know." Because this particular "thing" that had just happened had retrieved from the cosmic dumpster my recently discarded passion for sports. Which was a pretty big deal.

As the airplane engines droned along in the moments after my epiphany, a long, slow wave of relief enveloped me. *Enormous* relief. I felt like a neighbor had stopped by a yard sale I was holding and whispered to me, "You may want to rethink selling that dusty old painting over there for ten bucks. I'm pretty sure it's an original Van Gogh."

What had been hiding in plain sight for months was now magically unwrapped and presented for me to behold. The source of my disillusionment was not the Big-Time Sports themselves—it was (and most likely always will be) the *trappings* of the Big-Time Sports. Baseball is undeniably one of the biggest of the Big-Time Sports, drenched in money and hubris at the major league level. But taken down a notch in visibility, to the collegiate and Class A minor league levels, baseball had delivered to me a pure sports treasure of charm and innocence—twice, no less. The setting of a Big-Time

Sport had been relocated to someplace outside the purview of the Monster…
and *voila!*…baseball had reverted back to what made it so desirable to me way
back when.

I recalled that a hundred years or so earlier when I was a fresh-faced
Ithaca College psychology major, there had been a depiction of a famous illu-
sion in my Cognitive Psych textbook—a drawing that looked at first like a
pretty young woman with her head coquettishly turned away in a gaze over
her opposite shoulder. When you stared at it for a while, though, it morphed
into a completely different image, that of a much older woman who…
umm…well, let's just say she wasn't a "looker." The point is this: the sudden
discovery of my bicoastal Blair Dunlap encounter had similarly transformed
my perspective completely. Up until that midair moment somewhere over
the Heartland, I had been viewing my walkabout as the unattractive elderly
woman. And then, seemingly in an instant, I could see the entire experience
for all of the beauty and charm of the young girl.

Make no mistake about it—there is undeniable ugliness in the world
of spectator sports. I hadn't merely imagined it. Spectating in many situations is certainly not what it once was, even as recently as ten years ago. The
hassle involved in attending highly visible sports events at the professional
(and nominally amateur) level makes them far less appealing than I can ever
remember. I had made mental note of this several times during the IGTS
Tour to date but had always written it off as an unavoidable trade-off. You
want the Big-Time Sports thrills, you put up with the Big Hassle.

In the months since I had set out on my quest, I had taken notice of
increased media discussion on the topic of fan safety and comfort. I chalked
this up to my personal immersion in the subject, kind of like being able to
clearly hear your own name spoken by someone across the room at a noisy
cocktail party. But still…it seemed to me that a nerve had been struck—and
that perhaps we are closer to the day of reckoning for professional sports than
I had imagined.

Although the initial conversation that caught my attention was
about protecting fans from random acts of violence, many writers, sports-

casters, and fans began to chime in with comments about how uncomfortable it is to go to a game these days because of fan coarseness and vulgarity. Now, nobody wants to be "that guy" who takes offense easily—the weenie who complains because somebody else is continuously yelling obscenities. But all it takes is a groundswell, something that will make all of those silent sufferers (or conscientious objectors who never raised a hand to say why but who just stopped going to games because they didn't want to deal with it anymore) feel more comfortable about voicing their opinions out loud. And based on my experiences, we may mercifully be closer to the tipping point than I had previously considered.

Think about it: Continuously rising ticket prices in a deeply sluggish economy. Millionaires squabbling with billionaires about how to split up obscene amounts of money. The complete absence of "heroes" among professional athletes. Technology that makes the viewing experience at home more comfortable and compelling than the viewing experience at the game. Total disregard for the on-site fan experience, as evidenced in the form of Televisionus Interruptus. When you top that off with plain old discomfort about one's surroundings, why would *anyone* choose to attend a game? The answer, no doubt, lies deeper within the human psyche than I am qualified to comment on. Perhaps the drive to be able to say "I was part of something big" is far more pervasive than I had imagined.

As my midair musing about all of this continued, I recognized that just 15 minutes prior, I would not have wanted to face this topic. But with the benefit of my newfound perspective, it became remarkably easy to size up the whole matter pragmatically and pronounce the following: Smaller Is Better. In many, many cases the benefits of attending "lower-level" sports events are on par with those of being on hand at "top-tier" events—without the associated increase in cost, discomfort, and aggravation. Now possessed with a level of equanimity that had been absent while my disenchantment with sports had been progressing toward outright panic, I knew with absolute certainty that there was a vast untapped world of enjoyment in the 98 percent of sporting events that fly under the radar screen of the major sports media and public awareness.

And as I gazed out the plane window considering this, it occurred to me that at that particular moment in time, there was probably nobody more qualified to comment on the topic than me. For I had seen sports played at all levels, with the only constant factor being the effort expended by athletes striving to win. At the lower levels I had been presented with one treat after another, and all the while I had been dismissing each of them as something less than a true sporting event because they didn't have the requisite big-league trappings. The very trappings that I now plainly saw as the biggest impediment to the pure enjoyment of authentic athletic competition.

The notion that I had been an idiotic sports snob did not escape me.

I remembered with a mix of amusement and embarrassment one of the first "second-tier" sporting events that I had attended, back in the early days of my walkabout. With my laptop computer still sitting at silent attention on the tray table in front of me, I decided to search my document archives and revisit the material I'd compiled during my trip to the U.S. National Synchronized Swimming Championships. Sure enough, based on my write-up of the experience, it was plain that my perspective at the time was that every sporting event should be conducted with the primary goal of maximizing fan attendance and reach, with every other objective of much lesser importance:

> *I never expected the Goodyear blimp to be hovering overhead. But a small directional sign might have been nice. I was attempting to attend the U.S. National Synchronized Swimming Championships, and so far the sledding was tough. I knew enough to travel to Charlotte, North Carolina, for the event, but more specific information was hard to come by. A Google search on the event's name yielded little other than a link to an Internet clearinghouse for matching volunteers to various activities. Only when I went to that site did I discover that I needed to find the Huntersville Family Fitness and Aquatic*

Center. Yes, it was actually easier to find out how to volunteer for the event than it was to attend it.

Google Maps got me to the property, but from there I still had to triangulate my way all the way into the actual pool being used for the competition. No directional signage of any kind did I encounter, and in fact the venue was still fully open for daily business, despite the presence of a national-level championship in the house! I got behind a guy in line at the front desk who was checking in for his workout, purchased a ticket and a program, and was directed to a door that led to the Promised Land. I feel justified in saying that I've witnessed a new standard set for hiding your light under a bushel, as they say here in the Bible Belt.

Clearly I had zoomed right past the outlook of the sports fan and allowed the sports marketer in me to take over. And the latter noticed with increasing distress that the environment surrounding the championship was more "private party" than "compelling sporting event featuring elite athletes." And while it had been done with a tongue-in-cheek approach, I had taken it upon myself to suggest a few tweaks to synchronized swimming's (or "synchro's") marketing image and event-production techniques:

Let's start with the name. Or, to be more specific, let's start by changing the name. In comparison to the amount of gymnastic and acrobatic activity on display, there is notably less actual swimming involved in the sport. In fact, the Solo competition is basically a chlorinated gymnastic floor routine. If I were the Grand Poobah of All Sport, I would decree that synchronized swimming be renamed Aquatic Gymnastics (or its stylish abbreviation, AquaGymnastics). I was considering the name AquaSynchro Gymnastics, but with all those K sounds I figured it might scare small children out of the pool (which, of

*course, would now be called an AquaGym). Having now rein-
vented the brand, I will pass the baton to the PR experts while
I focus on event management.*

I yammered on and on about lighting, video monitors, underwater cameras, emcees, PA systems, athlete introductions, scoreboards, yadaya-dayada. Don't get me wrong—most of what I had written was relevant, and some of the suggestions actually had some merit. More important, I wouldn't have been so passionate about wanting to improve the visibility of the sport if I hadn't been so captivated by what I was seeing. It tragically looked to me as if the general disregard for marketing and promotion was comparable to a scenario in which the inventors of the Post-It Note made just a few pads to keep around the house for grocery lists and then called it a day.

But...yeesh. I had redefined the word *overzealous*. And I had also, as they say in the newspaper biz, buried the lead. Which is this: synchro is awesome to behold.

Admit it. When you read the words "synchronized swimming," one of two things came to mind: (a) a grainy black-and-white newsreel featuring the watery equivalent of the Hokey Pokey, or (b) the Caddies Day water ballet scene from *Caddyshack*. Something along the lines of *Little Miss Sunshine* with water wings. To be totally honest, I had initially thought the same thing. But I was really, really wrong.

The effortlessness of motion and coordination of movement required by synchro is an impressive athletic feat in and of itself, but when you take into account that these athletes are treading water the whole time, it is truly remarkable. Throughout the Nationals I found myself repeatedly checking the depth markings on the side of the pool to verify that the swimmers were never indeed coming in contact with the pool floor ("Yup, *still* 16 feet"). As the competition went on, I grew more and more amazed at both the athletic accomplishment and the casual way that competitors regarded what they had just done.

Like most washed-up jocks, I can easily delude myself into musing that if I were a little younger and so inclined, I could take up pretty much any sport and eventually play it at a decent level. When witnessing synchronized swimming, however, not for a nanosecond did I entertain the notion that I could ever, *under any circumstances,* make it through the first day of practice—even in my athletic prime.

Synchro is a seamless blend of explosiveness and grace. The former is best characterized by the height of the leaps that the competitors make from the water—it is not uncommon to see surges of power that bring the athlete out of the water from the waist up. Remember, this is done without pushing off of any solid base—the propulsion comes only from the force generated by the athlete's limbs themselves!

The grace of the sport is displayed throughout but is particularly embodied in a "common" move in which the athlete does the equivalent of an underwater handstand, slowly lowering herself further into the water, often in a slow twirling pattern until her toes deftly glide into the water, leaving not a ripple to mark where she once was. Again, this is done solely through body control achieved by treading water with her arms. And don't forget—this is done while she's holding her breath. I actually took that for granted initially—until I decided to count how long some competitors were under water. Fourteen, fifteen, sixteen seconds, all while exerting strenuous physical effort! Do not try this at home.

And by the way, most of this stuff is done either in perfect tandem with, or in perfect counterbalance to, one or more teammates. During full team competition, this coordination and split-second timing remarkably involves *eight* athletes.

But yours truly had chosen to focus primarily on why there weren't more people in the stands and what could be done to address that. There was, though, a glimmer of hope for me. Confirming that I hadn't completely thrown the baby out with the pool water, so to speak, was this one notation at the conclusion of the write-up of my day at the U.S. Nationals:

Perhaps the highlight of the day was an exhibition

put on by four young ladies who were learning synchronized swimming through a program in place at the club hosting the championship. They had only been at their chosen sport for less than a year, and their timing was less than…well…synchronized. But as they progressed through their routine, the crowd in the bleachers rose to show their encouragement and appreciation. And the musical number accompanying the performance? "Walking on Sunshine," of course.

As I read through all of my notes from that day, two things came to mind. First, it felt as if they had been written eons earlier by somebody to whom I was only distantly related. In looking back on it, I now realize that some sports won't ever be "Big Time," and that's OK—with both them and me. Don't get me wrong. I still believe that synchro is a vastly underpromoted sport with a tremendous spectating upside. It's just that I no longer feel that all sports that have a modest following are, by definition, underachieving. Small crowds *do not* necessarily equate to failure on the part of event organizers.

And the second thing that came to mind? An overwhelming urge to return to the pool for another synchro competition, with my priorities much more in line this time. Because rather than excoriate myself for sins of walk-about events past, it was time to relish in anticipation the dozens of suddenly compelling events that still lay ahead on the IGTS Tour schedule. I hit the flight attendant call button and ordered up another round of honey-roasted peanuts—for my entire row. And throwing caution to the wind, "While you're at it, bring me another CranApple—and leave the *full can* this time. We're celebrating here."

I'll be honest with you. I was concerned that the impact of my attitude-adjustment experience aboard Southwest Airlines flight #217 might dissipate in the days that followed. After the salty snack and sugar high, it stood to reason that the resulting hangover might blunt my resolve to approach the rest of my walkabout with a healthier mind-set. But any worries I might have had were soon carried away in the currents of the Potomac River.

Under normal circumstances, I wouldn't have been anxious to travel a great distance to spend a day on the grounds of an electric power-generation plant. But this *particular* electric power-generation plant housed the unlikeliest of sports venues, which was playing host to an altogether unique sporting event. The venue, the Bethesda (Maryland) Center of Excellence (BCE) is a manmade whitewater river course, and the event that I had come to see was the USA Canoe/Kayak Slalom National Championships.

The course itself is somewhat of an engineering marvel, measuring 40 feet across and a quarter mile long and featuring two dozen or more huge concrete boulders that had been selectively airlifted into place along its banks. An extensive series of guide wires and pulleys that extend from one bank to the other enable retrofitting of the course to create an almost limitless number of variations, from basic to "controlled chaos" as many of the athletes who train there describe it.

In fact, many elite paddlers—including past, present, and aspiring Olympians—have relocated to this rural outpost area specifically to take advantage of the BCE. Because what makes the facility *truly* noteworthy is that the water that tumbles through it is always at least ten degrees warmer than that of the neighboring Potomac River, whose western shore runs parallel to the course and serves as its runoff point. Which is where the relationship between Team USA Canoe/Kayak and its landlord, the Mirant Dickerson Power Generating Station, comes into play.

When looking for warm water, it helps to have friends who have an endless supply. And there's nothing that warms water better than running it through some electricity generators. Back in 1991 PEPCO, the electric utility that preceded Mirant as owner of the power plant, agreed to help create this Olympic-level training course within the concrete channel that returns discharged water back into the upper reaches of the Potomac—at a speedy

250,000 gallons per minute, no less. As you can imagine, when that kind of gush hits some strategically located concrete boulders, the result is some serious churn. Thus was consummated a marriage made in whitewater heaven.

Since I'm a sucker for love stories like this, it was inconceivable that I would miss the Slalom Nationals. On a Sunday morning that in previous years might have been spent agonizing over last-minute changes to my fantasy football lineup, I was headed to the upper reaches of the Potomac to watch the best whitewater paddlers in the country compete for a national title. I kept invoking my new mantra, "Smaller Is Better," as I drove deeper into the Maryland countryside on a cool, misty morning. But I couldn't help but wonder how the organizers of the event were going to deal with the fact that the whitewater course was buried deep within the multi-acre campus of an energy-producing company. The *secured* multi-acre campus of an energy-producing company.

The event website had basically said, "No worries—just follow the signs." So I did. And the faithful were rewarded. At the very first place that confusion may have occurred about where to turn, there was a manned checkpoint where I was welcomed, asked to register, and given further instructions. The half-mile from that entrance to the event parking lot consisted of several twists—and even more opportunities for wrong turns. Each of the latter was blocked off by orange cones, though, and I never went more than a couple hundred yards before I saw another simple handmade sign luring me along the correct route. Once in Spectator Parking, event personnel guided me to the proper place to park, checked me in, and informed me of the current status of the shuttle bus.

Those of you who are thinking, *So what? Simple stuff,* would be amazed at how few single-event venues effectively manage this process, even in the absence of the additional security concerns in play at the BCE. Put it this way: this was one of the few events I'd attended that provoked absolutely zero confusion or indecision about when and where I needed to go, how to get there, and what to look for when I arrived. I simply followed well-posted instructions and was led point-to-point—from directions to parking to shuttles to registration to obtaining event documentation. As the day progressed, I couldn't help notice that pretty much everything about these Slalom National Championships was decidedly grass roots, homemade, and low budget—but rock-solidly effective.

Take, for example, the event program. Duplex-printed on a single sheet of standard copier paper and folded to create a four-page, 5.5"x 8.5" handbill, it provided: (a) background on the origins of the sport and the venue, (b) a listing of the day's events, (c) a description of how the scoring system worked, (d) thumbnail bios on the "Paddlers to Watch," (e) a short description of the organizing body, and (f) brief logoed shout-outs to the event's major sponsors. Inserted into that handbill was a half-sheet—also printed on both sides—that listed the names, bib numbers, and hometowns of each athlete, sorted by vessel type and listed in the order in which the athletes would be paddling.

Given that each program probably cost a couple of pennies to produce, a quick calculation of the info-to-cost ratio was pretty near…well, infinity. Was it glossy? No. It wasn't even necessarily that eye-catching. But it was *exactly* what a newcomer to the sport needed to make the event more enjoyable.

The information that wasn't provided in the program was nicely supplemented by an emcee, who worked the event more or less nonstop to describe the backgrounds of the paddlers and how they were approaching their runs. He even worked in interviews of former Slalom Olympians and other luminaries of the sport who were on hand. A professional deejay had been hired to entertain during breaks and to keep a nice background vibe going behind the emcee's commentary. It was like being at a coffeehouse—with boats hurtling by on a regular basis.

Even the fund-raising had a unique, homespun charm to it. It appeared that the organizing committee had been able to lay their hands on a generous supply of potted chrysanthemums, and many had been used to decorate the venue for the event. And as the day progressed, the emcee periodically announced that these staples of autumn landscaping were up for grabs in exchange for a reasonable donation. By the time I left, nary a mum remained unclaimed.

Even more beauty in simplicity—there were no bleachers at the venue. Instead there were picnic tables scattered along the banks of the course. Folding chairs were also propped up along the fence by the venue's entrance, providing self-serve seating—literally. Pick a chair and pick a spot; you could change locations pretty much endlessly throughout the day. Or if you preferred a close-up view of the paddlers, as I did, you could climb down the hill to a prime fence-leaning location just a few feet from the water. My biggest spectating concern the entire day was whether the spray from the course would fog my camera.

The most impressive thing about all of this, though, was that it was facilitated by an almost entirely volunteer-based event-management team. Which is why there's a place reserved in Sports Heaven for those who toil in anonymity to produce events involving America's less visible sports. Without the dedication and commitment of these people there would not be such a thing as the U.S. Canoe/Kayak Slalom National Championships, for example. As I relaxed in my custom-designed VIP seating section, it occurred to me that a cheerful retiree effectively working their Volunteer Assignment checklist is probably of far more value to the future of sports in this country than is someone who happens to be gifted with preternatural speed, strength, or hand-eye coordination. Although, in either case, you can never eliminate the risk of having them make The Decision to "take their talents to South Beach." Or anywhere else in Florida, for that matter.

One person I knew wouldn't be heading to South Beach any time soon was Henry Hyde, a talented kayaker from Colorado. The reason for my certainty on that front was that Henry was just nine years old. The son of two elite paddlers, he had been in a kayak since the age of three and a half (well, other than for meals and bedtime stories) and had competed in junior events since he was six. But Henry was not at the Nationals to watch his parents take part. It was actually the other way around.

Aside from what this says about Henry Hyde, it also speaks volumes about the ascendant state of this sport in America, for while he was the youngest competitor to tackle the difficult whitewater course, he was by no means the only person under the age of 20. And all of them had earned the right to compete on the same course and under the same conditions as decorated Olympians.

From the very first run of the day, the competition was much different than I had envisioned—largely due to the dual direction of each paddler's run. Although one's performance is ultimately measured in the amount of time it takes to negotiate 20 or more slalom gates over a quarter-mile of rapids (with penalty seconds tacked on for touching or missing a gate), the biggest challenge of this sport is not simply generating pure speed. This is because many of the gates that the paddlers must negotiate require them to reverse course and paddle *upstream* against the current (have I mentioned a flow speed of 250,000 gallons per minute?). Therefore, should a paddler get going too quickly through the green-colored downstream gates, it's more than likely they'll give back all the time they've gained as they struggle back upstream to go through the red gates.

Even going downstream requires a battle with the current, as the key is to continually position oneself on the correct side of the river from which to attack the next gate. Steering oneself is *at least* as important as propelling oneself—and both require a great deal of upper-body strength and dexterity. Much like synchronized swimming, this is one of those sports that to see in person is to be awed by the athleticism that it requires to merely compete— let alone to excel.

Henry Hyde had an early draw in the kayak lineup, so I wasn't sufficiently up to speed on what constituted a good run when he first cruised by me. By the time his second run came around, though, I was a full-fledged kayaking connoisseur. And in that capacity, I deemed his second time down the course to be nearly flawless for the first 18 or 19 gates. The heavy churn of the water for the final three gates was too much for him, though—his upper-body strength just wasn't sufficient to successfully negotiate two of the final three gates. The resulting 100 penalty seconds wiped out an otherwise respectable time. While Henry never had a realistic chance of medaling, he acquitted himself well, and there is no doubt in my mind after watching him that he will compete for a spot on the U.S. Olympic Team as early as 2016. Unless, of course, he's grounded at the time for not doing his chores.

As for me, the entire day was a delight. The morning mist and drizzle had given way to late-afternoon sunshine, highlighting the dazzling color of the rapidly disappearing chrysanthemums. I had discovered yet another sport that I could never dream of competing in—and I was OK with that. World-class athletes had plied their trade mere feet from where I sat watching in admiration, and an enthusiastic crowd had shared their appreciation throughout.

On the drive back to Baltimore I turned on the car radio and hit SCAN. Sure enough, the first strong signal that came through was the Baltimore Ravens football game. The second was the Washington Redskins' flagship station. I left it there and drove along county roads framed by fields and forests that were starting to lose their annual battle to remain green. After a while I realized that I hadn't processed a single word of the NFL broadcast, despite the strident tones of the broadcasters covering the game. I really couldn't have cared less. There was nothing that they could have said that would have altered in any way my internal hum of contentment with the world of sports on that autumn day.

FIFTEEN
Teachable Moments

YOU DON'T HAVE TO HIT ME between the eyes with a two-by-four more than a half-dozen times to get my attention. It had taken me more than 50 sports events, months of traveling all over the country, and two memorable at-bats by a UCLA Bruin–turned–Aberdeen IronBird to come to the realization that maybe...just maybe...the so-called "second-tier" (or even more dismissive, the "fringe") sports could provide every bit as much sports-fan satisfaction as those currently administered by the Monster.

As long as you can figure out the rules of those sports, that is.

It was probably preordained that the first event after my Smaller Is Better epiphany would be produced so well and conducted in such a fan-friendly manner. The sports gods had worked way too hard to get me into the right mental space to then have it all unravel. So in the cosmic places that these details are hammered out, it was decreed that the USA Canoe/Kayak Slalom National Championships would provide me with a flawless spectating experience. Because in the Smaller Is Better sports world, that's not exactly a given.

Witnessing 50 different sports being played in less than a year is challenging. Comprehending what's going on at 50 different sporting events is altogether more formidable. Trust me on this—there's generally nothing out there that resembles a *Small Sports User's Manual*.

In retrospect, I should have bronzed my Slalom Nationals program, for it was one of the precious few times that I was given a document that explained clearly and concisely what I would be seeing and what specifically I should be watching for. And it also now strikes me that there's a fortune to be made in sports by enterprising sound-system experts out there. The difference in audio from venue to venue spans the full spectrum of quality, with most much closer to the ridiculous than the sublime. Generally when it came to assimilation at sporting events, I was left to my own devices. Sometimes that was frustrating, but more often than not it added another layer of enjoyable intrigue. Kind of like an information Easter-egg hunt.

Take, for instance, my afternoon at the USA Diving National Preliminaries…

It was a day whose name ended in *Y*, so traffic was heavy in SoCal—thus causing me to run a few minutes late. I couldn't say with absolute certainty, but based on the sub-low-key (no-key?) nature of the environment that I encountered, I probably didn't miss much in the way of opening-ceremony pomp and circumstance. In fact, within a few minutes of taking a bleacher seat in the Mission Viejo Aquatic Complex, I started to wonder if I had come to the right place.

Sure there was a pristine pool bordered by diving boards of various types and people springing off of them with a great deal of proficiency…but no signs, no banners, no printed material to pick up at the front entrance. Come to think of it, I never did figure out if there *was* a front entrance. A custodian had seen me standing on the sidewalk peering into the facility and came over to unlock the gate. I half expected to be hustled out by the Diving Police at any moment. "Nothing to see here, folks. Just an elite competition with national championship ramifications. Come on now, keep it moving."

Once I got comfortable with the idea that I wasn't going to be asked to leave, I started to focus more closely on my surroundings. As I sat there on a small set of aluminum bleachers with a smattering of other folks, this is what I heard from a disembodied male voice:

"David…107C…2.7." *Splash.* "Awards: 4½, 4, 5, 4½, 5."

And then, in full compliance with Title IX, I also heard from a disembodied female voice:

"Amy…403A…2.4." *Splash.* "Awards: 5½ Bingo."

For reasons never quite clear to me, both men's and women's competitions were being conducted at the same time. From where I sat, the women were to the left side of my view, diving from three-meter springboards, while to my right the men were competing from one-meter boards. Under separate tents set up on the pool deck were several judges who held aloft white scoring cards after each dive so that the hidden voices could read them off. I never did get a look behind the curtain at the great and powerful Wizards of Diving.

There was no denying it. I was a fish out of water. In over my head. Tossed into the deep end. Feel free to insert your own favorite water-based cliché here. Everyone else in attendance quite obviously knew their diving, because they saved any reaction whatsoever for the truly impressive dives— and didn't have to wait for the scores to be announced in order to identify and reward the special ones. This was usually done with a nod and a knowing glance at those around them. Your humble correspondent was never the recipient of either a nod or a knowing glance.

From some advance research I knew that, from this tidal wave of people, they had to narrow the field to 12 divers of each gender for the Finals—which would in turn determine who moved on to the AT&T National Diving Championships in Texas. I quickly surmised that in order to figure out the all-important "who's winning" thing, I had to pick up the scoring system on the fly.

I hypothesized that the announced numbers that preceded the individual dive consisted of a code that described the dive that they would be performing (and there were lots of alternatives). Then the numbers that came after the dive and the announcer's subsequent call for "awards" were the individual scores given by the five judges. I was particularly proud of deducing that "Bingo" described a dive in which the same score was awarded across the board—i.e. that "5½ Bingo" meant that each judge individually determined that the dive merited a score of 5½. These USA Diving folks are real cut-ups.

Things went along in this manner for about 90 minutes and, lulled into a daze by the repetitive, rhythmic nature of the competition and the sunny brilliance of the day, I slowly morphed into a dive-judging savant. Even though I was so relaxed I feared I might start to drool at any moment, I began mentally scoring dives frighteningly close to the numbers that wafted out of the PA system after each splash (or lack thereof). I was becoming the Rain Man of diving.

Suddenly the assembly line of women divers came to an abrupt end, and the female wizard voice informed the divers that the three-meter boards were open for practice, the top 12 divers would begin the final competition in 45 minutes, and their names would be "posted." Aha! Just as I suspected—somewhere, somehow, they were actually keeping score! Over on the one-meter boards, the men continued to cycle through their dives to the drone of the male wizard.

I took this opportunity to start asking questions. A couple of young ladies who were clearly in the know about competitive diving were sitting not far from me, so I ran by them my theories on how this whole thing was being scored. They were very sweet and patiently answered my questions, but since I am not fluent in either dive-speak or college-girl-speak, my full comprehension was lacking. It was kind of like asking someone for directions—after you mentally process the first few turns they describe, everything else becomes a random collection of word parts. "Well, you take a left onto Main Street, and then when you get to the Chevron station you go right onto Carter Road. You'll come to a fork in the road and you want to keep to the left, and follow kashmulsh ilt flivbrop orgjilish regnad kcin…"

I thanked them for their help and scribbled down what I thought they had described about how a winner was going to be teased out from the endless tangle of numbers that were still floating around in the air. Then, armed with that sketchy "knowledge," I approached the inner sanctum of the scoring tent to run it by an event official. Based on the look on her face, I'm not sure that the woman I talked to had ever encountered a real, live, uninformed sports fan in its natural habitat before. But she warmed to the task and eventually filled in the blanks for me. What I learned was this…

Everyone in this type of competition has to perform the same number of dives—five for women and six for men. The total body of work for each diver must include certain dive elements composed of variants on how they take off (facing frontward vs. facing backward), what they do while in the air, and how they enter the water (facing toward the board vs. facing away from it). The divers plan out in advance what specific dives to do and in what order to do them and submit their program to the officials prior to the festivities.

Now here's where it gets tricky—each dive performed carries with it a "degree of difficulty." To calculate an official score for each dive, the total of the scores awarded by each of the five judges is multiplied by the DD number specific to that dive. This calculation is done for each subsequent dive and added on to a running total—eventually yielding one single score per diver for the competition. The top 12 total scores go on to the Finals, where they do it all over again from scratch.

I'm pretty sure.

This explained the most puzzling part of the day to me—why the same dive was rarely performed by two competitors in a row. Granted, the process in use brought some competitive strategy and flexibility to the event, but if you ask me, I would much rather have seen everyone do the same dive in succession. That would provide some sort of comparative framework within which to assess the whole thing. When I asked the official why it wasn't done this way, I could tell she was starting to calculate the exact point at which it was appropriate to call security. If she had been a bank teller, the silent-alarm button would no doubt have been pushed.

Fearful that somebody at USA Diving HQ would soon be starting a dossier on me, I decided not to push my luck. I slunk back to my bleacher seat. And while the Finals that were contested later in the day were nothing short of dazzling to watch, I never did find out how many of the 12 finalists I saw of each gender actually did qualify to move on to the Nationals. I did, however, develop a nice healthy glow—both physically and mentally.

* * *

As much as I wanted to definitively declare that smaller is absolutely better, at this point the hypothesis still needed more testing—mostly because I was finding that smaller can also be a whole lot more work. And I soon found out that, on occasion, it can also be downright painful.

When I was growing up, my dad introduced me to two of his passions: sports and engines. Guess which one stuck. To what is I'm sure his eternal disappointment, my knowledge of the inner workings of a car never progressed much beyond the stray do-it-yourself oil change. So naturally the world of automotive sports never really beckoned. Until the IGTS Tour, that is. And to my surprise, I thoroughly enjoyed my first NASCAR race; so much so that I'm sure I'll return for another.

So I was pumped when it came time to head to the Auto Club Raceway in Pomona for the 51st annual NHRA Winternationals—the first Full Throttle Series event of the year. Although there had been cars on the drag strip for the previous couple of days, this was the actual "opening day" of the season, with heats taking place for both Funny Cars and Top Fuel Dragsters.

So as I entered the tunnel underneath the grandstands and heard the PA system boom, "…and the 2011 NHRA season is just about ready to start!" I was like an overeager Labrador. I could not believe what great timing I had. And look at that—an empty spot on the rail! I had *loved* being on the rail for my NASCAR race. I picked up my pace.

"This is so cool!" I virtually giggled as I approached the rail. "This is gonna be…*what the hell was that?!*"

You've probably seen the iconic Maxell print ad, where a guy is sitting in an armchair, pinned against the back cushion, with hair and scarf flying horizontally behind him. He's being blown away by the Maxell recording that emanates from the speaker in front of him, which is obviously a good thing. I'm here to tell you, though, that there is a yang to the pleasurable yin conjured up by that image.

Any veteran drag-racing fans who happened to glimpse my indoctrination to their sport were no doubt amused by it. In the split second that it took two Funny Cars at top speed to pass by me, I was literally blown back from the rail, staggering as I fully experienced the concept of "shock and awe." I distinctly remember seriously wondering if my eardrums were about to explode.

I can't even describe the noise, because none of the usual standards for loud, screeching, or otherwise horrifically annoying sounds quite compare. Not airplanes taking off. Not a group of jackhammers at work. Not a rock band at full volume with bad speakers. Not even an episode of *Keeping Up with the Kardashians*.

The noise of a full NASCAR field of cars racing by is impressive, to be sure, but it has a higher-pitched sound that I'm more familiar with. I had spent an entire race at trackside and never felt the overwhelming urge to seek earplugs or to otherwise cover my ears. That was more "fun loud." This new noise…was not.

A uniquely deep-throated rumble that shakes you to your core, it redefines the word "ominous"—like the gates of hell were in the process of erupting up through the ground. I had a fleeting thought that this was my retribution for sneaking a BlackBerry into a professional golf tournament.

I quickly abandoned all pride and covered my ears tightly for each and every heat that took place for the rest of the afternoon. And fortunately my doctor assures me that my resting heart rate will eventually return to normal. But it was a teachable moment: for those of you contemplating your own sports walkabout…be careful out there.

Time went by, and I got more skilled at taking the measure of any sport that I was covering, no matter how little knowledge I possessed going in. And truth be told, after a while I abandoned all efforts to educate myself prior to attending an event that shaped up to be a mystery to me. Half the fun was seeing if I could figure out the rules of any given contest before that particular contest ended. Teasing out sports rules turned out to be very nearly a sport in and of itself.

With none of the vestiges of the Big Hassle to deal with, virtually every game proved to be more enjoyable, with many approaching downright captivating status. The formula for an entertaining event experience narrowed down to a good vantage point, a more-or-less clear idea of the rules, and a compelling story line upon which to build a rooting interest. An event held outdoors on a sunny day got extra credit.

To master the art of watching second-tier sports, the following collection of tools is valuable: rudimentary event documentation, an intelligible public-address system (ideally manned by an intelligible public addressor), an informative scoreboard and, if all else fails, knowledgeable fellow spectators. More often than not, all else did indeed fail, so I simply transformed event appreciation into a group project involving those who didn't quite manage to avoid eye contact with me in time.

If I found myself confused by what I was watching, I would simply eavesdrop on surrounding conversations in order to identify the right mix of knowledge and approachability and then ask some kind soul for a quick rules clinic. If that didn't prove fruitful, more drastic measures were called for—like dropping into the official's tent at a national diving competition, for example. And then there are the times that you strike pure gold…

Having arrived early for the Collegiate Nationals of synchronized skating (the chillier sibling of synchronized swimming), The Bird and I took our seats during the latter stages of the Adult Nationals. And in so doing, we were welcomed to the confusing lexicon of competition that lives under the umbrella of the U.S. Synchronized Team Skating Championships. In consulting a basic schedule of events that we'd been able to scare up, we learned that in addition to the divisions listed above, a national title would be awarded in both a Masters and a Senior division. But here's the thing—as the day progressed, the skaters in all the divisions looked to be roughly the same age. I'm not exaggerating when I say that if one team each from the Collegiate, Adult, Senior, and Masters divisions were lined up, you would be hard-pressed to match team to division. Clearly, competitive skating keeps you young.

As previously mentioned, the process of acquiring on-site expertise is normally a bit of a crapshoot. On this day, however, information gathering was like shooting fish in a barrel. For, wandering all over the concourses—both inside and out—of Ontario's Citizens Business Bank Arena were women bearing medals won earlier in the championships. And who would know the rules better than one of the competitors?

What I learned from a conversation with an eagerly accommodating group of athletes was that in order to be in the Collegiate Nationals each skater must be an enrolled student. For a team to compete in the Adult Nationals, it must be made up entirely of skaters who are at least 21 years old—with the majority of the team over the age of 25. For teams in the Masters Nationals, the minimum age is 25, with a majority of skaters over 35 years of age.

OK, so far so good. But then this—skaters in the *Senior* Nationals can be as young as 14 (as long as they have passed "novice" status in a field test). And here's the kicker: the top two teams in the Senior Nationals represent the U.S. in the ISU World Championships—the pinnacle of competition in the sport. Huh? This struck me as AARP lobbying taken to an extreme. But I took this information to heart, given that nothing says "credibility" more than the gold medals hanging around the necks of my semicaptive panel of experts. And nothing compares to the sense of passion that athletes at this end of the sports-world continuum convey about their sport when they are explaining it to a novice. These particular ladies radiated enthusiasm and charm.

It's one thing to head off to an event knowing that virtually everything about the experience will be new to you. It's another when you think you've got it covered...only to find out that you don't.

The five-day USA Cycling Elite Track National Championships

offered a virtual crash course on the number of different ways you can set up a bicycle race. Scratch races, sprint races, Madisons. Something called Omniums. You get the point—they're doing a lot of stuff on a bike on a track. Hmmm…what to watch…what to watch? How about the Team Pursuit? Done and done. And I was off to the L.A. Velodrome.

Like many of the venues that were built originally for the 1984 Olympics, the Velodrome is still heavily used for Team USA training. It also plays host to cycling competition at the regional, national, and international levels. The largest indoor velodrome in the country, it's an impressively constructed and maintained building—and an arena used exclusively for cycling. There's no retrofitting of this place for the Globetrotters or Ice Capades tours.

I walked in the door literally seconds after the first heat in the Men's Team Pursuit had begun, and in no time at all I was drawn into the competition. There were four cyclists circling the track, spinning like crazy. As the name would imply, the three trailing cyclists were in hot pursuit of the leader, who led by the narrowest of margins and…what the?…he just veered off and rode up the steep bank of the track, allowing everyone else to pass him! When he finally righted the ship and came back down, he was in last place!! "This guy is an *elite* cyclist?" I scoffed.

I was sure the new leader was thrilled to be the beneficiary of that gaffe, because he began to…hey, what's going on here?—he did the *exact same thing* as the other guy! Didn't *anybody* want to win this thing?

I looked around. Nobody seemed to be fazed by this unusual behavior. I began thinking it might be me. So I started listening to the call of the PA announcer for clues that would help me sort out the motivation of these alleged world-class cyclists. He kept blathering on and on about the team's this and the team's that, and before too long I started to realize that the guys on the track weren't racing each other—they were a single unit, together in their pursuit. But what were they pursuing? I didn't see anything like Rusty the Rabbit, the little sock puppet that greyhounds love to chase. Curious.

After 16 furious trips around the track, they stopped pursuing. And it was revealed that they were in actuality simply pursuing a good time. No, not that kind of good time—I mean the *best* time. As in fewest minutes and seconds. And since they were the only ones on the track, they got it. Until, of course, the next group of four cyclists gathered at the starting line and began their pursuit of a good time. I wondered…why not just send the fastest guy on the team out and have him secure the best time while everyone else knocks back a Gatorade and cheers him on?

As I watched this scene repeat itself every five minutes or so, it slowly dawned on me. I remembered drafting. More specifically I remembered The Bird drafting off of me on long bike rides. It works like this—the displacement of air that a lead cyclist generates will create a vacuum that sucks along another rider who happens to be in close proximity. The operative word here is *sucks,* as in it sucks to be the person in front dragging along the person who's gliding blissfully behind you.

So that's what was going on here. These cyclists were forming their own little peloton, taking turns drafting each other along. After one had led the pack for a lap or two, he would peel off by turning his bike up the steep bank and then glide back down to the back of the pack, where he would be pulled along—resting before his next turn at the front. In this way, the team benefitted from stringing together successive sprints that, all told, would greatly reduce the time it would take one man to ride four kilometers (roughly two and a half miles).

But what about the name of the event? This "pursuit" thing…if all they were doing was competing against the clock, then wouldn't any competition based on securing the fastest time also be called a pursuit? The 100-yard dash…pursuit. The Boston Marathon…Pursuit. The Ironman Triathlon… Pursuit. Or is track cycling merely giving a nod to the age-old pursuit of happiness?

While I mulled this over, I started to zero in on the little idiosyncrasies that helped define the uniqueness of the event. This was not the type of cycling that the average Josephine on the street is familiar with. For starters, the bicycles themselves are really just first cousins to the road bikes that are used in the Tour de France—or the Tour de Coffee Shops that we recreational riders take part in, for that matter. For one thing, there are no brakes. While this could be problematic when out for a ride in the neighborhood, in the Velodrome it's pretty rare that some clown in a '96 Toyota Celica opens his car door into the middle of your bike lane.

There are also significantly fewer gears than the 21 (or so) that we're used to. There's actually just…well, none—unless you count the pure leg strength of a rider as a gear. In a somewhat smaller surprise, there are no kick-stands, wicker handlebar baskets, or little bells that you can ring with your thumb on these bikes either. Just so you know.

Cycling pursuit teams start their heats side-by-side from a standstill position, with their bikes on a progressively steeper angle. Consequently, it's easy to envision a scenario in which the outside rider on the most steeply banked angle might veer to the left on an initial move and wipe out the rest of the team in a domino effect. And I'm guessing that it's happened more times than anyone would care to count. That probably explains why each cyclist has his own valet starter at the beginning of each race—someone who holds them upright and then sends them on their way. Kind of like your dad did when you took that first ride with the training wheels off.

In the break between the qualifying heats and the medal races, I took a walk over to the far end of the Velodrome and leaned over the rail for a bird's-eye view of the track at its most steeply banked point. The angle here is listed as 45 degrees, but to me it seemed a lot closer to 90 degrees—i.e. straight up and down. Although I was seeing it with my own eyes, I still couldn't fathom how much the forces of gravity were being denied by the cyclists who came this far up the bank. Not to mention the slimmest of margins by which the rubber on the sides of their tires was keeping them from wiping out. During the competition that I witnessed, there were no crashes, but I could imagine that they can be pretty horrific. Someone traveling at a speed of more than 45 mph at an almost vertical angle and wearing no protection other than a helmet…I suppressed a shudder.

Even on the much flatter areas—the lower, inner part of the track that the team hugs during the race—the proximity in which they ride to each other can be unsettling to watch. Strung out in single file, the riders maintain a space of as little as a few inches in between bikes. Again, one hiccup, one false move, one random '96 Toyota Celica with an open door, and…well… just envisioning it made me wince.

Returning to my seat for the women's Bronze Medal race, I noticed that there was a good deal of milling around the track at both the starting line and also across the way on the back stretch. Completely confused by this, it was time to shift into research mode. I cast an eye over what was an especially sparse crowd, even by second-tier-sports standards. This would have to be an info-gathering cold call. I got up and sauntered over to my nearest neighbor to ask if he…umm…knew what specifically was going on down on the track. And wouldn't you know—he did. Justin was his name, and he just happened to be a local cycling coach.

"This is the pursuit part of the competition," he replied, clearly delighted to share his sport. "In the medal races, a team can win either with the fastest time or through the Catch."

Aha! The Holy Grail! The missing piece of the "pursuit" puzzle! In the Gold and Bronze Medal races, two teams actually *pursue* each other around the track. If one team can make up the half-lap needed to reach the tail end of the other, the race is ended. If neither team is able to win via the Catch, then the team that posts the best time for the 16 laps (12 for the women) wins the medal.

This was infinitely more fun to watch than the qualifying trials.

In the men's qualifiers, something called Team Ouch had blown away the field with a time of 4:22:217. Which, it was pointed out by my trusty PA announcer, was more than three seconds faster than the previous year's gold medal time. It came to mind that they might have peaked a bit early, and I wondered if they would have the energy to repeat that performance in the Gold Medal race. Not to worry. Team Ouch won by virtue of the Catch, not even three-quarters of the way through the race.

As dominant as was Team Ouch, they were matched on the women's side by a team dressed in uniforms so bright white they glowed. They were named Peanut Butter & Company Twenty12, and I can only imagine that their sponsorship comes from an amalgam of food groups and numbers, à la an episode of *Sesame Street*. On this particular evening they should have been sponsored by the number *1*, because that's how easily these three women—Hanan Alves-Hyde, Cari Higgins, and Ruth Winder—breezed through the qualifying trials. And in the championship race, they, too, won gold via the Catch.

As I headed to my car, fighting the urge to lean constantly to my left as I walked, a certain incongruity occurred to me. Months earlier I had stood shoulder to shoulder with thousands of fans at the final stage of the Tour of California bike race. That event, too, had included a loop that was repeated. But that circuit was miles long and therefore largely out of sight of the finish line. It had been exciting to witness the speed at which the riders came racing by to complete each of the four loops, but at the end of the day, we only saw a cumulative five or ten minutes of action. Yet the place was packed.

Now, having witnessed both world-class road-bike racing and track racing, it was no contest—the latter was much more compelling. But there were only a handful of people on hand. Granted, I had chosen to attend the Track Cycling Nationals on a weekday evening on the second day of the five-day championships, but I couldn't help notice that even a total sellout of the Velodrome would have yielded just a fraction of the attendance of the Tour of California.

This second-tier sports world is a curious place.

Why, if you are a cyclist, would you deliberately choose to ply your trade—work your butt off (in a manner of speaking)—in relative obscurity? As I thought about this on the way home, several questions about athlete motivation that I'd been trying hard to reconcile began resurfacing. And they all revolved around that key word: *Why?*

Full disclosure—when I first began to encounter them, I had initially thought that these second-tier sports folks were…let's see, how can I put this charitably…oh, the hell with it—I thought they were nuts. Throughout the early days of my walkabout, every time I came across a scenario in the sports world that could not be framed within the context of capitalistic or narcissistic motivations, I had chalked it up to a one-off—an aberration. *These people don't care about becoming wealthy? Or famous? That's odd.*

If it's conceivable that someone could be both jaded and naïve at the same time, that was me. It wasn't that my soul had necessarily hardened or that my worldview had become any more cynical than it had been prior to working in the sports business. I had merely become accustomed to the ubiquitous monetization of sports, as espoused by those who may at one time have immersed themselves in a sport for the sheer love of it—but had long since forgotten what that felt like. After ten years of sharing office space with the Monster, I just couldn't fathom why someone would invest great amounts of time and energy simply for the sheer love of a game and the camaraderie of those who shared that passion.

On this night, though, while navigating the unusually empty boulevards that led me home, I let it go. I no longer felt compelled to ponder this, to try to explain or quantify the motives or ambitions of these supremely dedicated athletes.

I finally acquiesced and let the track cyclists—like the divers, kayakers, canoeists, and synchro swimmers before them—teach me something. And I began to embrace the words of J.R.R. Tolkien: "Not all those who wander are lost." Certainly I myself had wandered far, far, *far* afield from where I thought I might be at this point in my own journey. Never would I have imagined that the vibrant sports world that I had been seeking in vain was not only existing—but thriving—well under the mainstream sports radar screen.

For the most part, the athletes I was encountering had never appeared on ESPN; it's quite likely they didn't even *watch* ESPN. They were too busy training and honing their skills in their chosen athletic pursuit. They were too busy achieving remarkable things simply for the love of competition and the hope that maybe—just maybe—they'd get to compete for their country in the Olympics one day. Despite tremendous levels of dedication and discipline, and advanced levels of skill, they mostly toiled in the sports world equivalent of Off-Off-Broadway. But they didn't seem to care. These athletes were actually *living* Nike's "Just Do It" marketing campaign.

And one more thing popped into my brain.

I recalled my day at the U.S. Table Tennis National Championships where, in addition to the scores of scheduled matches played on a vast vista of courts spread out within the Las Vegas Convention Center, great numbers of pickup practice games sprouted up organically on temporarily unoccupied tables. I remembered that when these games involved the highly ranked players, they were as much fun to watch as the real thing, because after a couple of games in which these players worked on technique, they would inevitably start goofing around, trying wild shots and yukking it up. And that triggered fond memories of doing just that type of thing when I played basketball competitively. (Well at least *I* thought it was "competitively.")

During open shooting times before and after practice, my teammates and I would often become sidetracked into a game of HORSE—which naturally led to half-court heaves, shots from behind the backboard, etc. As I think back on it, not only did doing stuff outside the routine improve my touch and feel for shot-making from all angles...it was *fun*. An interesting concept, this...Sports = Fun. Who would've thought?

SIXTEEN

The Mingle and the Mad Dash

As summer eventually capitulated to fall, an interesting thing began to happen—I noticed people edging away from me at cocktail parties.

Many months earlier when I had first announced my walkabout intentions, my friends, family, and colleagues were wildly intrigued. In addition to showing support at every turn, they were always anxious to hear the details of my travels to iconic venues and well-publicized events. A pivotal late-season Lakers game against San Antonio. Opening Day at Yankee Stadium. The U.S. Opens of both golf and tennis. March Madness. NASCAR. And being the attention-seeking miscreant that I am, I was more than happy to indulge their curiosity.

As time went by, though, I found myself consistently swinging the conversation around to all of the hidden jewels of the sports world that I had been discovering. My answers to their questions about the Big-Time Sports became perfunctory, as I was in a hurry to turn the discussion to things like pro surfing, water polo, and lacrosse. Some people humored me with much more skill than others, but the telltale glazing of the eyes eventually gave them away. They couldn't care less. And by the time I got around to sharing the delight I'd found at the Smaller Is Better events, it was *astonishing* how many people suddenly discovered something else that needed attending to. Right that second, in fact.

Oh, I'd hear the whispers. "No, seriously—he actually likes high school football more than pro." Or, "I hear he got up at 3:30 in the morning to go watch a *triathlon*, for God's sake." But it was cross-country that finally triggered mass exodus at social gatherings. For it was evident to most that I had finally lost my mind.

In 1959, British writer Alan Sillitoe published a novella titled *The Loneliness of the Long Distance Runner*. It was made into a movie in 1962 and ultimately received enough acclaim to land it on the British Film Institute's list of the greatest British films of the 20th century. I never read the story or saw the movie. In fact the only thing I've ever known about the plot line is that it revolves around cross-country running. And that one small nugget of knowledge has always framed my perception of the sport: cross-country = lonely.

That thought was lurking in the back of my mind as I arose very early on a Saturday morning in mid-November and began the two-hour drive from Portland to Springfield, Oregon. In the pitch dark. In a steady rain. With a temperature hovering somewhere in the low 40s. So was it any wonder that I expected to be one of, oh, maybe a *dozen* fans on hand to witness the NCAA's West Regional Cross Country Championships?

I was prepared to experience the Loneliness of the Long Distance Watcher.

So imagine my surprise when I arrived at Springfield Country Club and was redirected to a separate spectator parking lot at a local elementary school. And then my shock when I pulled into that lot and saw a line of people queuing up to board a luxurious shuttle bus. And then my absolute disbelief when I was dropped off back at the golf course and found hundreds of people already present for an event not scheduled to begin for almost an hour. Lonely? I was beginning to feel downright crowded. And confused. Why in the world would so many people show up on a cold and misty morning at a venue that, if it wasn't actually in the *middle* of nowhere, it certainly knew the ZIP code?

Actually, part of the answer did indeed lie within the ZIP code. For in Oregon, if anybody is running anywhere, there will most certainly be people on hand to watch. If you happen to find yourself somewhere in the Web-Foot State and sprinting to catch a bus at some point, it's more than likely that a small crowd will gather to cheer you on. But even though I knew in advance that I was venturing deep into the land of Nike and Prefontaine, it still didn't prepare me for the gorgeous build-out and pristine environment that played host to what has to be one of the lowest-profile sports in the NCAA lineup.

As I navigated my way down the 18th fairway toward the event's hub in the center of the golf course's back nine, a steady stream of runners going through their warm-up runs began to pass me. And, as if I needed another reason to be transfixed by the spectacle, I was captivated by the colors. A bright kaleidoscope of hues and tints was splashed against the emerald-green backdrop of the golf course. With 31 women's and 25 men's teams competing, all of the colors of the rainbow were well represented in the different teams' warm-up suits and uniforms. "Vivid" and "vibrant" kept elbowing each other out of the way for the lead in the adjective race.

Once I arrived at the Start/Finish complex, it occurred to me that, from the runners' perspective, it would've been impossible to carve out a small moment of *privacy*, let alone loneliness. I learned that the male competitors would be sharing the course with 178 close associates, while the ladies would start their race side by side with 221 others. Add to that more than 1,000 highly engaged spectators, and you had an atmosphere that was about as supportive and inclusive as could be imagined for a solitary pursuit.

The rules were straightforward. Each school could send up to seven runners onto the course, with the top five performances counting toward the team's score. Each runner crossing the finish line captured the number of points equivalent to their finishing order. In other words, the winner of the race scored one point for their team, the runner-up two points, and so on throughout the field. In the final tally, the team with the *fewest* number of points would win the meet. The first- and second-place teams gained automatic entry into the NCAA National Championships, and the next two or three would put themselves in the mix for an at-large bid.

The women went first, touring a 6,000-meter course (3.73 miles) consisting of two and a half loops around a carefully laid-out route traversing mostly golf course fairways. For their part, the guys would run much the same course, but with two loops added to make it a 10,000-meter (6.2 miles) race.

Considering the weather conditions when I left predawn Portland, the light drizzle in the air when I arrived represented major meteorological progress. And although it never warmed up, there was no precipitation at all when it came time for the women's race. As I watched them surge off of the starting line, two disparate notions entered my mind. First, it struck me that there are fewer things more basic to athleticism than running. And running when done well is beautiful in its grace and form, particularly when exhibited by women, who—this may come as a shock to you—have a huge head start on men in the grace department anyway.

The second thought that entered my mind was a knee-jerk reaction from the days in which my job made me ultimately responsible for keeping a golf facility as untarnished as possible. The sight of hundreds of people running with wild abandon around the course triggered a deep-seated sense of trepidation. I went into a mental duck-and-cover at nightmarish images of the good members of Springfield Country Club lined up outside my door to give me the *what for* in the coming days. Later on, as I stood at a bend in the 16th fairway facing toward what would soon be a thundering herd of male contestants beginning their race, I overheard a conversation during which— as luck would have it—the golf course superintendant, who was out with his young son to take in the event, was asked how he felt about the impact to the course. He responded in good humor and said, "No worse than usual, I guess." It was probably a good thing that I no longer worked in facility management.

Shortly after the men's race began, a light rain began to fall. In retrospect, it gained slightly in intensity throughout, but by that time I was completely enraptured by the competition. Had the rain not made it hard for me to take notes, I wouldn't even have noticed it, despite being underdressed for the occasion. For if the men and women competitors ran 10,000 and 6,000 meters respectively, we spectators probably logged a couple thousand meters ourselves, rushing back and forth across the interior of the course in order to see the field go by multiple times in each lap. As this went on, I couldn't help but note on the faces of my fellow fans the exuberance and glee that you normally see in little kids on the playground. Everyone was having a ball running as fast as they could to see others…well…running as fast as they could.

Sophomore Jordan Hasay of the University of Oregon added to her growing legend by winning the women's race, followed eight seconds later by teammate Alex Kosinski. Deborah Maier of California managed to sandwich herself in between the two Ducks. Despite taking the individual gold and bronze, though, Oregon fell short of the University of Washington, who sent five Huskies across the line in 21st place or better. The men Ducks one-upped their sisters in spikes, slipping past Stanford to take the meet by a score of 63–65 (remember—*lowest* score wins). The University of Portland's Trevor Dunbar took individual honors, outsprinting Stephen Sambu of Arizona by a mere third of a second.

Poignancy usually lives at the tail end of endurance contests, and to be sure, this race had its moments. I watched Luke Tonnemaker of the University of Idaho complete his run in obvious pain. After crossing the finish line he stood hunched over, grasping his shorts and attempting to collect himself. After several long moments he rose to scan the crowd of runners for a friendly face. None appeared, so he went back to hunching over. This repeated itself several times, to the point where *I* wanted to go out, pat him on the back, and tell him, "You did good." I think I understand that loneliness thing now.

The whole event went by way too quickly. It seemed I had just arrived, but soon all that was left was the Mingle. There is nothing in all of sports better than the post-event Mingle, where athletes, friends, family, and a random collection of other miscellaneous fans gather on the field of play and just hang out for a while, reveling in what has just taken place and making plans for later on. It's the essence of sports, a scene of pure Americana. I tried to capture the atmosphere on my handy Flip video camera but soon realized that it just wouldn't translate. You had to be there.

I'm blaming at least some of my cocktail party pariah status on the RV Goddess. She is, after all, the Internet's foremost ambassador of all things running and Oregonian, in addition to food and RV travel. If I hadn't met the RV Goddess, I may not have developed such a fascination with people running in circles, propelling themselves over stuff, and throwing various oddly shaped objects around—all in the name of sport. Truth be told, though, it would have been extremely hard *not* to meet the RV Goddess, given that much earlier in the IGTS Tour we were both part of the same unruly mob that had stormed the field at the Pac-10 Combineds. But I'm getting ahead of myself here.

First, a pop quiz. How many separate events make up a heptathlon competition? If you answered seven, chances are you are either a Greek scholar or you were one of the 75 or so fans on hand on Mother's Day in Cal-Berkeley's Edwards Stadium to witness the staging of the Pac-10's Heptathlon and Decathlon Championships (aka "the Combineds"). The event was actually part of the overall Pac-10 Track & Field Championships, but with 17 different activities going on between the women's heptathlon and the men's decathlon it can get pretty crowded on the track and field. Therefore, the talented multi-event athletes at each participating school get their own weekend in advance of the rest of the meet to showcase their stuff.

Except that…umm…there was nobody there to be showcased to.

To be fair, the morning's intermittent rain and chilly wind no doubt kept some people away, but even in those early days of my walkabout, I could recognize that we were occupying serious under-the-radar territory. This competition was so far outside the mainstream of attention, its title was misspelled on the conference's own website. Yes, we're talking about the one and only "Pac-10 Multi-*Evnets* Championship."

I didn't realize it at the time, but the Combineds proved to be pretty nearly a spectator's nirvana. Through a crystal-clear PA system, a golden-voiced announcer provided continuous updates on not only what had just happened but how it related to the competition. For example, instead of just saying, "That throw was 32.17 meters," he said, "That throw was 32.17 meters, but she has a better toss of 34.24 meters and another chance to improve upon that." Scoreboards, both electronic and manual, were also consistently updated. And then there was that surfeit of elbow room. All for a very reasonable admission price of…nothing. There's that price again.

The weather still looked a little iffy when I arrived, so I chose a vantage point high above the field, underneath an overhang that kept me warm and dry. From that spot I had a great overview of the action spread out before me and also a chance to take in my wider surroundings.

The first word that came to mind about Edwards Stadium was *imposing*. First of all, it's a hulking concrete structure built in the postwar era. No, not that war…no, before that one…keep going back…yup, the post-World War *One* era. Opened in 1932, it was at the time the only stadium in the world built specifically and solely for track-and-field use. A $3.5 million renovation in 2000 created Goldman Field inside the environs and restored the facility to its proper place in the track-and-field lexicon. Which brings to mind another word: *iconic*.

Twelve world records have been set there. Twenty-six American records. Twenty-four collegiate records. In 1940, the 15' barrier was cracked for the first time in the pole vault. The legendary Jim Ryun ran a 3:51.3 mile there in 1977. On a cinder track. This is pretty heady stuff, and you can feel an almost spectral sense of history as you sit in the stands. And just as I was thinking that things couldn't possibly get any better, the sun started to peek out.

So then, of course, I got greedy.

I wanted to get closer to the action. And I started to notice that there were people down on the field who didn't look all that much like competitors, coaches, or officials. They were just milling about at a respectful distance on one end of the field. I wanted to mill as well, so I relocated down to a spot near the rail for some reconnaissance work. As I stood there I had the opportunity to take in the finish of the women's 800-meter run, a closely contested race won by Ryann Krais, a sophomore from UCLA. With all eyes on the exhausted athletes gathering themselves at the finish, I weighed the odds of being hauled off in shackles for what I was about to do. Eventually figuring that I could fall back on the time-tested "But everybody else was doing it" defense if needed, I made my move.

As aggressive "storm the field" moves go, this one was pretty mild. If you were thinking, *Vault the railing and dash,* well, hold onto that thought. In actuality it was, *Climb the little set of stairs set up specifically for this purpose and amble.* I moved nonchalantly along the rail, up the three-step ladder, then down the six steps onto the field. A casual saunter over to where other interlopers had gathered to watch the men's pole-vault competition, and...*I was IN!* Then again, a quick glance back up into the stands revealed that pretty much every one of the fans who had ventured out to take in the competition that day was also "in." No matter. I was up close and personal with the action, feeling faster and stronger by simple proximity.

Once the adrenaline surge from my well-calculated but still courageous infiltration of the track and field world had subsided, I set about basking. The sun had wrested control of the day, combining with the relaxed, languid pace of the meet to create an aura so comfortable and tranquil I was barely aware of time passing. I found myself slipping in and out of a hypnotic state, emerging occasionally to watch with admiration as superbly conditioned men and women did a host of things better than I could ever do any single athletic thing with regularity. I began to consider weightier questions like, *What exactly is the thought process behind taking up the decathlon or heptathlon?*

There is little transfer of skills from one event to another, especially from track events to field events. And make no mistake about it, each event is extremely challenging—there's no gliding through any of them. That would probably explain why the Combineds are a sport practiced by a select few people. The entire UCLA team on hand that day consisted of Ryann Krais in the heptathlon and Trent Perez in the decathlon. I wondered if Trent, for example, just woke up one morning and said, "I think I'll try my hand at ten different sports today and see if I can excel in each of them."

For my money, the toughest and most humbling of the events had to be the pole vault. There are no degrees of success on any given attempt—you either clear the bar or you have failed. And if things don't go so well, you have a split second as you lie sprawled on the mat to reflect on your failure before the bar and/or your own pole most likely come crashing down on top of you. It brings to mind the scene in the movie *Airplane!* where everybody on the flight lines up for a turn at slapping the woman who has become hysterical.

And within the context of the Combineds, the pole vault (along with the high jump) carries even more pressure. While in all of the other events an athlete can stumble through, put up a score, and keep going, if one doesn't clear some height—any height—in the pole vault or high jump, that person would get no score of any kind. Which pretty much renders the rest of the entire two-day decathlon or heptathlon moot. Thanks for playing our game.

I became captivated by the efforts of Jeremy Marcinko, a freshman from Arizona State. As the height of the bar was inexorably raised, one athlete after another eventually failed on each of their three attempts to clear it, thus retiring from the competition. Marcinko crashed and burned on his first two attempts—sometimes badly—before somehow or another pulling it together and crossing the bar on his third and final attempt at one height after another after another. It was a seminar on persistence, and when it was over he had outvaulted all but one competitor. Ashton Eaton. Yes, *that* Ashton Eaton.

I had never heard of Ashton Eaton prior to that day. And as of May 9, 2010, chances are pretty good you hadn't either. That could be quite different by the time you read this. Truth be told, I'd be surprised if it isn't, because once I'd seen him, I couldn't for the life of me figure out why he had such a low profile. Ever since the days of Jim Thorpe, the title of World's Greatest Athlete has been bestowed upon the man who is the reigning Olympic decathlon champion. Does the name Bruce Jenner ring a bell? His gold medal in the decathlon at the 1976 Olympics catapulted him onto Wheaties boxes and into household-name status.

Bryan Clay is the current World's Greatest Athlete, having won the decathlon in Beijing in 2008, but when the London Olympics rolls around in 2012 he will be 32 years old. And everything that I saw that day at Edwards Stadium points to Ashton Eaton—the pride of Bend, Oregon, and the University of Oregon—taking Clay's place. Everything seems to come easily to him. Of the ten events that make up the decathlon, he won seven—and several by wide margins. He's charismatic, he's telegenic. And the name? Are you kidding me? It's right out of celebrity central casting. The man has presence.

None of this was news to the RV Goddess. I first got to chatting with the alter ego of one Terry Taylor after noticing her being hassled by an official for having a camera lens that could technically be used only by someone with a press pass. Risking confiscation, she wrote the whole encounter off to a case of "lens envy" and kept snapping—albeit a little bit more inconspicuously. This caused me to become an immediate fan of the RV Goddess. Quite naturally, for we shared the common bond of being sports-world fugitives that day.

Terry and her husband Dave go way back with Oregon Ducks track and field, what with Dave being a former All-American and all. From her completely objective, unbiased viewpoint, Terry shared with me that Eaton is pretty much unbeatable in the decathlon, citing as evidence a little thing like his *world record* in the indoor heptathlon. And, on top of it all, Terry said, "He's a really nice guy." The whole situation barely seems fair to the rest of the male population.

Thus was the RV Goddess drafted as a member of the IGTS Tour's support staff. As I lurched through the demoralizing Big-Time Sports fiascos of the summer and early fall, she kept in touch, feeding me snippets of information on the world of track and field. Which eventually delivered me to the NCAA Cross Country Regional and later on to the USATF Indoor National Championships—events that I probably wouldn't have added to my walkabout without her input. She must have known something.

SEVENTEEN

Dueling Acronyms

IT WAS RIGHT AROUND THANKSGIVING that I started thinking more and more about Vassilis Dalakas, Robert Madrigal, and Keri L. Anderson. You remember—the BIRG folks. The ones who published the study that had been so helpful to me when I was struggling to understand how ordinarily reasonable people can get so irrationally wrapped up in a sports event that does not otherwise touch them personally in any way, shape, or form. I wondered if the gang had done any work in the Smaller Is Better world.

I had been at this attending-sporting-events thing for quite some time. During that time I had shared viewing experiences with a full range of crowd sizes—from throngs of 90,000 to gatherings at which my arrival moved the needle considerably on the head count. Somewhere in between there is a dividing line that changes the entire complexion of the viewing experience. Somewhere there is a point at which BIRGing is brought down to a more intimate level, where the fan experience becomes less about rooting for oneself—which is essentially what BIRGing boils down to—and more about rooting for someone else. Not that anyone has asked, but just so you know, I have developed the metric.

It goes like this: if more than 50 percent of the athletes in any particular competition could theoretically, at a moment's notice, tap out a personal text message to more than 50 percent of the spectators, the event has crossed the line from BIRG-likely into the realm of SIOFFOLO (Sweating It Out for Friends or Loved Ones). Granted, it's not quite as elegant an acronym as that which Vassilis, Bob, and Keri L. might have been able to come up with—and if you prefer, we could go with a more social-media-savvy "Facebook Friends" event designation—but I like to think SIOFFOLO gets the job done nicely.

Either way, the point is this: if you happen to be someone on a one-year, 100-event, 50-sport quest to rediscover your inner sports fan, you are far more likely to encounter people in the stands at a SIOFFOLO event who are really and truly living and dying inside with the flow of the competition. A condition that is quite contagious, to say the least. For example, I made the acquaintance of the RV Goddess, who has a personal connection with Ashton Eaton. From that point on, there was no way I could *not* root for the guy (as if he needed my help). And I've kept tabs on him ever since. I will care deeply about the Olympic Decathlon competition in London, for reasons that include the simple desire to see Terry Taylor made happy. It's human nature.

This is what sports at the SIOFFOLO level are: More human. More personal. More captivating. Attending Smaller Is Better events creates the opportunity to connect more empathetically with the athletes. You bump into their friends and family members in the bleachers. You start to root for both the athletes and their dedicated followers as people, and their victories warm your heart. You vicariously experience unadulterated joy in victory and witness indomitable grace exhibited in defeat.

The 1980 Olympic Hockey Team's Miracle on Ice was tremendous theatre, but the story line of *Hoosiers* is more timeless. The former made every American proud—the ultimate BIRG. The latter connects with everyone who has ever wanted incredibly badly for the local team to win for the sake of the athletes. They want it for *them*—for the athletes to experience the thrill and satisfaction of working hard for an accomplishment.

L.A. Times sportswriter Eric Sondheimer called the Northern Division Championship one of the best he'd ever seen in his many, many years of covering CIF Southern Section high school football. Hollywood is about 35 miles away from the town of Westlake Village, but they may as well have been the same municipality during the game between archrivals Oaks Christian and Westlake. It was one for the ages.

I wish I could have seen it.

I, however, was left fogging the wrong side of the candy store window, so to speak. The game was sold out to the gills, and no amount of begging, pleading, or influence peddling worked. Trust me, I tried. I made promises that would make a U.S. Congressman blanch. After successfully worming my way into almost 80 consecutive events, who would've thought that the one that ended my streak would be a high school football game?

Thankfully, I had a Plan *B*. See, the California Interscholastic Federation conducts football championships in several different divisions, specifically to address situations like mine. OK, maybe not to help me personally, but their system did work in my favor. With a little luck, and traffic on my side, I figured I could make it to Gardena in time for the Western Division Championship kickoff. And miraculously, I did. I promise never to complain about L.A. traffic again. Wow, see what just *one* reference to politicians does for my tendency to play fast and loose with the truth?

Usually when sportswriters or other "experts" offer up pregame analyses and predicted scores, they tend to keep the margin within reason. So it was particularly telling when previews of the game between the Junipero Serra Cavaliers and the Arroyo Grande Eagles had Serra running off with the Western Division title by almost three touchdowns. Serra hadn't lost a game since Bush was in the White House—and only a handful of losses prohibited them from extending that unbeaten status to the White House days of the *first* Bush in residence. An L.A. dynasty, the Cavaliers were the defending Division II California state champions. And California is a big state.

In stark contrast, Arroyo Grande had snuck into the playoffs as a wild card, having finished third in its small Central Coast League. A monthlong Cinderella run through the playoffs had put them on a bus that afternoon for the 200-mile trip to L.A.'s south side, where they would take the field against a team that outweighed them by an average of more than 30 pounds per player.

I arrived pretty comfortably before kickoff and chose to sit in the visitors stands, from where I watched Serra crisply go through their practice drills. I never saw Arroyo Grande, though, until just before kickoff. They sent their captains out for the coin toss, but the rest of the team was sequestered elsewhere until it was go time. Perhaps a strategy to keep them from focusing on the disparity in player size?

From a support standpoint, Arroyo Grande brought the house. A fleet of creatively decorated buses had transported a good chunk of the town's population that didn't drive down on their own—and keep in mind this was a nearly four-hour ride. Orchestrating the crowd was a veritable army of cheerleaders. Eight of them occupied two-to-three-foot platforms, which were centrally grouped and flanked on each side by somewhere between 16 and 473 additional cheerleaders. The overall temperament of the crowd was a mix of bluster and hope; it was as if they thought that by simply ignoring their huge underdog status they could render it moot. Conversations around me were sprinkled with sentences that began with, "If we can just…"

As the minutes prior to kickoff dissipated, I became quite sure that I was the only gimlet-eyed realist on that side of the field—a status that I took no pleasure in occupying. After having listened to their unflaggingly upbeat banter, my heart went out to these folks. I really, really, *really* hoped I would prove to be wrong, but I wasn't exactly expecting a barn burner.

So I was pleasantly surprised when Arroyo Grande came out and waged a field-position battle in which they actually earned the upper hand in the early stages of the game. The Eagles boomed the opening kickoff deep into the end zone for a touchback, and the two teams proceeded to trade three-and-outs—with Arroyo Grande picking up ten yards in each exchange of punts. Inevitably, the Eagles penetrated into Cavaliers territory in this way and were in the process of attempting a short fourth-down conversion inside the Serra

30-yard line when they were flagged for a false start. The ball was moved back five yards, which changed the Arroyo Grande coach's plans. He sent out the kicker. Not the punter—the *kicker*. As in Garrett Owens, a high school junior who was about to attempt a 51-yard field goal on a chilly, damp night.

"OK, *this* is optimistic," I chuckled to myself. I stopped chuckling when the kick was good, with several yards to spare. The underdogs had bitten first, 3–0. Euphoria engulfed the visitors grandstand, as the requisitely perky cheerleaders whipped the Arroyo Grande faithful into a frenzy.

In retrospect, the Eagles should probably have called timeout and run over to the scoreboard to pose for photos in front of the display that showed the world that they were at one point actually *winning* this game. Because shortly thereafter, they weren't.

Serra was renowned for its nearly unstoppable passing game and its assembly line of talented receivers. The previous year's undefeated team featured Robert Woods, who went on to start as a true freshman for USC. Stepping right into the void that he left was George Farmer, who may have gone Woods one better with a senior year that made him one of the best college prospects in the country—and landed him at USC as well. And the talent pool at wideout wasn't limited to Farmer. Marqise Lee, who already had a CIF championship in track on his résumé, was the perfect complement on the other flank. And guess where he was headed to play his college ball?

So I was a little taken aback when the bulk of Serra's early play calling involved handing the ball off to tailback Shaquille Richard. That is, until I saw two things: (1) Arroyo Grande had loaded up the defensive backfield with everybody who could backpedal, and (2) Richard can apparently run the 100-yard dash in about three and a half seconds, give or take.

It was barely fair. After those first two possessions, Richard got it going, and in watching him in the open field one got the impression that he could score on any given play. Arroyo Grande noticed that as well and started to stack the defensive line to stop him. Serra didn't need an engraved invitation to go aerial.

If I was surprised by one thing, it was how good Cavaliers quarterback Conner Preston was. But then again, wide receivers don't gain national attention throwing to themselves, and the kid was 28–0 as a starter, after all. Preston didn't get much of the pregame ink, but all he did in the span of little more than 12 minutes in the first half was drop three feather-soft touchdown passes right into the barely outstretched arms of Lee, Farmer, and then Lee again—all when they were in full stride.

After this display of offensive shock and awe, there wasn't a sane person on the property who believed that Arroyo Grande had a prayer to win this game. It was 28–3 at the break, and it could have easily been much worse. A George Farmer touchdown on an electric punt return was called back on a penalty, and a Cavaliers' field-goal attempt from chip-shot range sailed wide in the waning seconds of the half.

By the time the two teams came back for the second half, the outcome had already been decided. It was really just a matter of how much the Cavaliers chose to win by. But this was high school and not a college game, in which running up the score on an outmanned opponent is called earning "style points"—and practiced religiously in order to get more votes in the popularity contest that the BCS conducts to decide our national champion. So Serra proceeded to "dial it back" in the second half. The offensive machine that had displayed the ability to score at will was stripped down to a mix of running plays up the middle and short passes in the flat. The only downfield pass came on a fourth-and-ten play when the Cavaliers were too close to punt and too far to try a field goal. When the play broke for a touchdown, Serra kept the celebration muted.

In other words, the whole thing showed class, dignity, and sportsmanship. And the Arroyo Grande crowd appreciated it. They appreciated their team too. Throughout the contest, the fans and cheerleaders never wavered from their initial vitality. They could no longer ignore the fact that their boys were outmanned by a larger, more talented team, so they focused on rewarding the team for its resolve. When the final gun had sounded and midfield congratulations had been extended to Serra on their 35–10 championship victory, the Eagles trudged over to their sideline—where they were met with a lengthy standing ovation. I'm not sure there was a dry eye in the visiting bleachers. I'd be lying if I said I didn't get a little misty myself.

Something important was gained, despite the lopsided loss. And during the Mingle, not a single Eagle head was hung.

* * *

The kindly, hyperfaithful fans of Arroyo Grande High School had adopted somewhat of a sports fan interloper when they welcomed me into their midst. Probably more accurate, though, is that I had adopted them. I loved their story and was prepared to commit SIOFFOLO allegiance if called upon. What can I say—I'm easy. Soon enough, though, events would unfold such that I no longer needed to shop my fandom around.

The California girls high school volleyball season had headed into the CIF playoffs, and I had been keeping a close eye on the tournament as it progressed, especially when it came to the Division I-AA draw. On one side of the brackets was a team that I was looking forward to watching in person, the Long Beach Polytechnic High School Jackrabbits. I prided myself on seeing the cream of the crop in every sport that I included in the IGTS Tour, and the Jackrabbits certainly filled the bill.

Long Beach Poly had spent a good bit of time during the season at #1 in the MaxPreps Freeman Rankings. Not #1 in SoCal. Not #1 in the state of California. No, we're talking #1 in the *entire U.S. of A.* When they secured their place in the CIF Southern Section Championship, it was not exactly breaking news in the volleyball world. In fact, they lost just *one game* in their combined playoff matches prior to the finals—and that by a score of 25–23. So they're fairly good.

But it was the other side of the bracket that had captured my attention. The side that included Redondo Union High School, a team that had one undeniable intangible going for it: they were from my town! From my *neighborhood*, in fact!! From the very first day of my walkabout, visitors to the IGTS Tour blog were greeted by a picture of yours truly, in happy repose in an otherwise empty grandstand. A grandstand that just happens to be the proud property of the Redondo Union Sea Hawks.

It was all so obvious. Before I had even coined the soon-to-be-world-famous acronym, I was destined to bring my full SIOFFOLO support to bear on behalf of my local team. Assuming they could get to the championship, that is. I was up early on the morning after Redondo Union's semifinal match, checking every online source I could think of. And about the time it occurred to me that it would probably be just as easy to walk over to the school and ask a passerby, the score appeared on the website of the local paper: Redondo over Lakewood: 25–13, 21–25, 25–18, 25–16. It hadn't even been close.

Needless to say, I was stoked. As for The Bird…well, she just rolled her eyes and suggested that I look into procuring a life. But come that Saturday, she didn't have to be asked twice to tag along to the CIF Southern Section Championships. Off we went to Don Johnson Court (or was it Sonny Crockett Court?), the centerpiece of the Cypress College Field House.

Earlier in the Tour we had been to the boys championships and learned the hard way that good seats are at a premium in volleyball-crazy Southern California. With the match between Redondo Union and heavily favored Long Beach Poly the capstone of the daylong volleyball championships extravaganza, we timed our arrival to coincide with the end of the previous match, so as to snag prime seats as they were vacated. Sure enough, the sizable gym quickly refilled to capacity with boisterous fans. I guess it's possible that the boys had attracted a slightly larger crowd for their championships—but then again, I didn't recall seeing the full Fox Sports West broadcast crew (including *three* analysts) that the ladies had drawn on this night.

There's something about girls high school athletics that mines the purity of sports. Everything's more casual, and nobody seems to take themselves overly seriously. For example, the Redondo Union coach, Tommy Chaffins, turned up in pink sneakers. Probably to match the pink Hawaiian shirts that the entire coaching staff wore. When it came to preparing for the game, though, it was all business. Chaffins ran his charges through an extensive series of pregame drills and maneuvers, ostensibly to hone their skills and intensity for the game. But I had to think it was partly to keep them from dwelling on the enormity of the task at hand.

While this was going on, the Jackrabbits of Long Beach Poly were engaged in their own routine. Lying face down in a circle at the end of the gym, they were…talking. Who knows about what. Maybe about being 35–2. Maybe about having dispatched Redondo Union once already that season, at the Sea Hawks' own invitational tournament, no less. "They're bonding" said The Bird. Oh.

Once they got down to it, the match was all execution for the Jackrabbits and all grit and desire for the decidedly smaller Redondo Union team. And the latter knew a little something about winning as an underdog. In 2006, the Sea Hawks had been in the same position against perennial volleyball powerhouse Mira Costa High School—and had improbably walked away with the title. A mainstay on that team was a senior named Devon Dykstra, who subsequently earned a scholarship to play for the University of Colorado. The senior leader of *this* Redondo Union team was Lara Dykstra—Devon's younger sister. In fact, the Sea Hawks were fielding a Dykstra "two-fer," which included sophomore sister Skylar.

Something potentially epic was brewing.

Long Beach Poly came out blazing, executing one perfect play after another, raining down kill shots on the heads of the outgunned Sea Hawks. In the first game, it seemed that any points that accrued to Redondo were the result of Jackrabbits mistakes borne of overaggression. After a while Redondo managed to stop the bleeding, but Game One was, as the saying goes, not as close as the 25–20 final score would indicate.

But Game Two…well, that was a different story.

Having learned that pretty much any standard offensive play that they ran would result in a block by Poly's formidable front line, the Sea Hawks started to focus on turning those unwanted second possessions into points. They dedicated themselves to relentless defensive play, digging at everything that came over the net and looking to place, rather than force return shots. And it worked.

Redondo jumped out to an early lead and knocked the Jackrabbits just enough off their game that they started to make mistakes. Down 13–6, Long Beach Poly called a timeout—but that didn't derail the Sea Hawks' momentum one bit. Game Two went to Redondo 25–16. It was the fewest points that Poly had scored in a game all year.

In addition to enjoying the strategic artistry that Redondo Union was using, I was mesmerized by the pure effusiveness that the Sea Hawks displayed. Each time they pulled off an improbable play—and especially when they engineered a successful block—their knees buckled and they fell upon each other, their animated faces registering sincere delight at what they'd just done. They were surprising even themselves and having the time of their lives doing it. By then, everyone in the place who wasn't a Jackrabbits fan had adopted these inspired underdogs.

Early in Game Three, an absolutely phenomenal point was played, during which each team rallied repeatedly to somehow save and return the ball against all odds. The digging and diving that took place during that rally seemed to suspend time—I really have no clue as to how long that point took to play. And that marked the entire third game. Redondo Union willed its way to a 21–19 lead, and Sea Hawks supporters—both old and brand new—could sense that something historic was in the air.

This is the point in the story at which I'd like to give you each and every detail about how this ring of destiny came full circle, about how my neighborhood team—coached by a guy in pink sneakers—knocked off one of the best volleyball teams in the country. After spotting them a game, no less!

That's what I'd *like* to do—but unfortunately I'd be lying.

Employing a power offense that was as relentless as the tide, Long Beach Poly came back to win that third game 25–23 and draw within one game of the title. Having come so close and fallen just short, it was almost inevitable that Redondo would suffer a letdown to begin Game Four. They fell behind early, and it soon became obvious that, heart and desire notwithstanding, their feet were no longer working quite fast enough to keep digging out the onslaught of Jackrabbits kill shots.

When it was all over, Redondo Union held their heads high and graciously congratulated their opponents. The expressions on the faces of the Sea Hawks throughout the trophy presentation and the Mingle didn't convey anything other than pride and satisfaction at having left all of themselves on the floor.

But the story didn't end there. Both teams wound up with invitations to the California State Championships and—wouldn't you know—faced each other again in the Division I semifinals. Once again Long Beach Poly prevailed, but their mystique had clearly been dispelled at the Southern Section title match that I had witnessed. The Jackrabbits had their hands full throughout and had to go to extra points in the fifth and deciding game before they could put Redondo away. The Sea Hawks had clearly come of age, and to a certain extent, right before my eyes.

When I began my walkabout, never in a million years would I have guessed that I would learn so much about my love of sports from the corners of the sports world farthest from the spotlight. I could barely conceive of how things had turned out, that I would be so much more enthralled by a girls high school volleyball championship than I would be by the Super Bowl. Then again, you don't tend to see the following kind of thing at the latter of those two…

Just prior to the pregame introductions that evening, the Redondo Union fans had started a recognizable call-and-response chant with a loud "We are…." But the response part of that cheer—something I expected to be "Sea Hawks!"—didn't materialize. Instead, the Long Beach Poly fans on the opposite side of the gym bellowed "Long Beach!"

My initial reaction was that the Sea Hawks fans were a little naïve, having just served up to the Jackrabbits fans the opportunity to steal some Redondo thunder. After the third or fourth rendition, though, it dawned on me: the Redondo fans were doing this on purpose—as an invitation to their opposite number to show support for their own team. And after they had gone through about a dozen back-and-forths on this, both sides of the gym stood and applauded each other.

At that moment I was proud of my community. I didn't know any of the Redondo Union players or their families. Prior to that evening, I'd never even met any of their fans. But I was proud to live among them, to be associated, however tangentially, with people who displayed that kind of sportsmanship. And then another thought came to me: it hadn't been so very long ago that I had witnessed fans literally assaulting each other in the stands for the unpardonable sin of mouthing support for their favorite team.

The Grateful Dead said it best—what a long, strange trip it's been.

EIGHTEEN

Communities of Sport

COMMUNITY.

When I think of a community, the default image that emerges is that of a group of people who live near each other and who get together periodically to...well...to commune. I realize that this limited interpretation stems from a Paleozoic frame of reference, given that the Internet now enables the creation of "communities" of people who may never actually meet face-to-face. Call me old-fashioned.

Within the strict sense of the word, I've never really been a community guy. I grew up in rural New England, which isn't exactly ground zero for warm and fuzzy. Not a lot of "joiners" out there in the countryside. Add to that the fact that I've got a substantial case of wanderlust (the word "vagabond" seems so judgmental), and it's easy to see why the whole topic of community never really occupied much frontal lobe space for me.

So for me to experience a sense of pride in community while observing the sportsmanship of the Redondo Union fan base...well, that was a bit of a watershed moment. Either I was finally growing up and putting down roots—an implausible long shot at best—or my insight into the whole topic had taken on an unexpected new depth.

Technically speaking, I fell under the umbrella of Redondo Union's physical community because I lived only a few blocks away. But the more I thought about it, the actual community that I'd felt gratified to be a part of was much more intangible. It was more an alliance of those who deeply appreciate sports for all of the positive things that they bring out in people—a community of athletic supporters, so to speak. Wait, that didn't come out right.

The point is this: No matter how clumsy my interpretation, my wanderings in the heretofore hidden world of sports had come upon a new frontier. Not only were there athletes out there in the sports hinterlands thriving without the visibility I had mistakenly considered essential to sustain them, but there were all kinds of kindred spirits out there with them! Entire communities exist that are based almost entirely upon a shared passion for a given sport, however invisible it may be to the rest of us.

That's not to say that the old-school type of community is gone; a community's zeal for its local team is the hallmark of sports, and not just at the high school level. The Cape Cod Baseball League comes to mind as a premier example of just how tightly a community can embrace athletes who may only be in their midst for a short time. This renowned amateur summer circuit in Massachusetts is populated by highly regarded college baseball players who actually move in with local host families for the season—and even work part-time jobs in town as part of the package.

For a sheer feel-good bear hug of a community embrace, though, *nothing* comes close to what I inadvertently stumbled onto in the hills of SoCal's Ventura County.

I had been in search of an opportunity to fold amateur tennis into the IGTS Tour schedule and had been therefore pleased to learn that the Pac-10 Conference Tennis Championships would be in Ojai, CA. Good fortune was smiling on me, I thought, because of all places in the roughly 6.4 gajillion square-mile region that the Pac-10 Conference covers, they chose to stage this championship in a place less than 100 miles away from my humble quarters. While hosting the event in a small town located a fair distance from any major metro area seemed a bit unusual, I wasn't about to complain.

OK, I just lied. I actually did start complaining—while trying to find the damn event. The town of Ojai is nestled in Ventura County, between Sulfer Mountain and the Topatopa Mountain Range. It's a long and winding (albeit scenic) drive inland from the coast, so it didn't surprise me that the town is populated by fewer than 9,000 people. From what little I knew of Ojai, I was aware that it was somewhat of a tourism destination, though, so it didn't seem totally out of the ordinary that it would host a major collegiate tennis tournament. What did seem unusual to me as I navigated California Route 150 into Ojai, however, was how little effort had gone into promoting the Pac-10 Championships. Not a single sign or banner.

As I got closer to the picturesque town center, it became obvious that something called "The Ojai" was a much bigger priority that weekend. The whole place looked like the Fourth of July, except that banners proclaiming support for The Ojai assumed the traditional role of flags and bunting. And *everybody* had turned out. There were lines to get into at least two celebratory pancake breakfasts that I passed, and parking was hard to come by.

While it was a winsome environment, I found myself becoming annoyed. All I wanted to do was find someplace called Libbey Park and watch some tennis. And this quaint local celebration was in the way. After three passes up and down Ojai Avenue, I finally found a parking spot on a shady side street and hoofed it back to the center of town.

I intercepted the first passer-by that glanced my way. "Excuse me—can you help me find Libbey Park? I'm here to see the Pac-10 Tennis Championships, but all I've been able to spot are signs for The Ojai."

He was a tanned, trim older gentleman, sporting a full head of slicked-back white hair, and he gave me a long look through eyes on loan from Clint Eastwood—as if trying to figure out whether I was putting him on. Finally he said simply, "Well, you're definitely not from around here. And I'm guessing you're not a tennis guy."

I came clean on both accounts, and his steely gaze relaxed. "The Pac-10s are a part of The Ojai. And you're standing in front of Libbey Park."

Oh.

And that was how I arrived at the pearly gates of tennis heaven. I thanked my personal St. Peter, crossed a small grassy quad, and entered a green thicket that stood as the entrance of the 110th presentation of The Ojai. That is not a typo. This grand dame of tennis tournaments has been in existence for longer than a century. To put this legacy in perspective, consider that when the first Ojai was conducted in 1895, *the state of California was only 45 years old.*

I thought I was coming to a collegiate tennis championship, but I wound up stumbling across a phenomenon of civic spirit. Purchasing my admission ticket opened the gates to an environment that was fantastic, idyllic, bucolic—pick any *ic* word you want (the good ones, I mean). And, oh yeah, the tennis was pretty good too.

The Ojai is a veritable smorgasbord of competitive tennis into which the Pac-10 Championships were neatly folded in 1954, when the men's championships were first conducted there. In 1987, the women joined the party. And it's a big party. In addition to hosting Open (i.e. purse-bearing) competitions for men's and women's singles and doubles, The Ojai currently conducts amateur men's and women's championships in the following categories: Independent College, NCAA Division III, Community College, California Interscholastic Federation, Juniors 18 & Under, Juniors 16 & Under, and Juniors 14 & Under.

The sheer number of matches contested over a four-day time period is mind-boggling, and during the initial rounds of the event, tennis courts all over the Ojai Valley are pressed into service. If you live there and have a decent-size property, there's a pretty good chance you'll awake on Thursday to a match being played in your backyard.

This town doesn't just embrace their signature event; it's lodged in their DNA. As sporting events go, The Ojai long ago reached critical mass, and the town could no sooner decide *not* to hold the event than could the All England Lawn Tennis and Croquet Club decide to take a year or two off from hosting the Wimbledon Championships. Past generations of tournament organizers would spin in their graves. And so tasked with keeping a tradition that dates back to the presidency of Grover Cleveland (his second one, for you history buffs), Ojai residents redefine the words *grace* and *hospitality.* In the morning, fresh Ojai Valley orange juice, served in unassuming white Dixie cups, is available to all takers. In the afternoon, a simple sign is placed outside a hospitality tent set up on a grassy lawn—PLEASE BE OUR GUEST FOR TEA FROM 1:00 TO 4:00. Organizers and volunteers wear badges of the "Hi, My Name Is" variety, with county fair-type ribbons descending below. And there is no question to which they won't fully invest in providing an answer.

While The Ojai has studiously avoided becoming an anachronism, it definitely memorializes its past—and in so doing puts its grass-roots charm on full display. The names of each of the 85 players who have competed in The Ojai and gone on to win one or more Grand Slam events appear on a modestly erected wall of fame. You may recognize some of them: Pete Sampras, Billie Jean King, Lindsay Davenport, Arthur Ashe, and local products Bob and Mike Bryan—the twin brothers who currently dominate men's doubles worldwide.

The shady path that wound from the front gate to the Libbey Park courts was lined with triangular stand-up displays, onto which were affixed pictures of both the winner and runner-up of every competition conducted each year since...well, I don't know exactly how far back they went. But as I browsed the collection during a break in tournament action, it struck me that I was literally walking through a home-Polaroid version of tennis history.

There was a picture taken in 1978 of Tracy Austin holding a trophy almost half her size for winning the Junior Girls division. Just over a year after that she was in the semifinals at Wimbledon—just prior to becoming the youngest-ever winner of the U.S. Open. Further down the line, another picture grabbed my eye—this one of a 12-year-old Michael Chang in 1984, hands thrust in his pockets and clearly chagrined at being the runner-up of the Under 14s. He would recover from that devastating blow, however, and go on to win the French Open at the age of 17.

This stuff is priceless, and each year a group of volunteers is entrusted with meticulously posting the pictures in just the right spots on the three-sided displays, only to take them down a few days later to be carefully filed away. The history of The Ojai is a public trust, passed down through generations of volunteers—as is the tournament itself.

* * *

While The Ojai as a cultural phenomenon long ago set the standard for consistency and stability among "build it and they will come" events (predating *Field of Dreams* by a mere 94 years), it now stands in loving testament to a time long past. In this day and age, sports communities have increasingly come to resemble movable feasts. Ironically, the very thing that insidiously works to isolate us from physical communities in the 21st century, the Internet, is the very tool leveraged to create and build today's communities of sport. The ability to mine the "long tail" of the Web enables people of similar yet esoteric interests to find each other. And in so doing, their sport becomes a wonderful vehicle for attaining what we as human beings are genetically programmed to seek: a sense of belonging.

It's easy to see how communities of sport get their start. Kids pick up a sport when they're growing up and, for a whole variety of reasons, wind up sticking with it. Sometimes for a few years and sometimes for the rest of their lives. Typically these sports are available through high school programs or via local sports clubs. Those who discover a passion and find a knack continue on through intercollegiate teams. The cream of that crop goes on to qualify for Team USA in their particular sport and competes internationally.

There are National Governing Bodies (NGBs) for 46 different sports under the umbrella of the U.S. Olympic Committee. Sumo wrestling, however, is not one of them. So without the nurturing ladder just described, how is it that the sumo community can grow to such a size as to culminate in the U.S. Sumo Open? Where did those ties that bind originate?

You've probably figured out by now that I'm incapable of simply asking rhetorical questions and then letting them float off. It's a curse. And it's why I wound up spending three hours of a Sunday afternoon watching very large men engage in a centuries-old tradition. In diapers. That is to say, *they* were in diapers, not I.

A sumo tournament is a treat for the attention-span-challenged, at least partly because of the rapid-fire nature of the competition. The vast majority of matches pack an inordinate amount of action into a time frame of less than a minute. And as soon as one match is done, the short ritual preceding the next match begins.

The reason for the brevity is twofold. First is the basic rule that a match ends when one competitor either touches the ground inside the ring with anything other than his feet or touches the ground outside the ring in any way. It's a basic one-throw-and-done sport. Second, this is an aggressive competition where both parties are usually on the offensive from the start. There is no "feeling out" stage of each match, and as a result the initial surge and accompanying strategy is usually a make-or-break one for each sumo.

See, here's the thing about sumo—it is a sport with all pretense stripped away. It's a one-on-one flashpoint collision with one sole objective: to overwhelm and physically dominate one's opponent. Testosterone on testosterone. And if you lose, it can often be in humiliating fashion. Yet over the course of the entire afternoon, I witnessed not a single display of anger or bitterness. Literally dozens of matches took place without incident. No taunting. Zero smack-talking. Not a trace of the intimidation techniques so common (and celebrated) across the pro sports ranks today.

These guys just lined up, looked each other in the eye, and had at it, with the best man winning that particular match. And after each match was done, both sumos stood to face each other across the ring and bowed. It was an environment of deep mutual respect and competitive humility. It was the anti-NFL. The NBA with a muzzle. It was dignified, diapers and all.

If the rise of the sumo community in the U.S. came as a surprise to me, what was there to make of the Derby Dolls? When I bought a ticket to see the San Diego Hard Corps host the L.A. Sirens in a roller derby bout (yes, they call it a "bout"), I didn't know if I was expecting classic Bay City Bombers mean-girl shtick, spacey Drew Barrymore characters à la the movie *Whip It*, or something in between. What I got was more like Halloween—the trick-or-treating kind, not the Michael Myers kind.

I never actually did figure out whether Derby Dolls is an official sanctioning body, a loosely affiliated collection of leagues around the country, or merely a state of mind. One thing is certain, though. At the local level it is a decidedly grass-roots endeavor, with a hefty dose of DIY event-management touches. Event organizers and producers wear a number of hats and enlist the volunteer services of anyone willing to help. For example, I bought a $5 string of Derby Dolls raffle tickets from an enterprising purple-haired girl—who was *maybe* ten years old. I'm going out on a limb here in guessing she was related to either an event organizer or a skater. And speaking of the latter, team members who weren't in uniform that night served as ushers, wearing Ask Me buttons that underscored their willingness to invest unlimited time in educating fans about roller derby.

This may come as a bombshell to you, but nobody's retiring from roller derby wealthy. For most skaters, in fact, the next game check they receive will be their first. They do this for fun, if flinging yourself with wild abandon around a banked track and bouncing off of nine other crazies can be considered "fun." And just in case you're wondering, this is all real-live contact; the sport has abandoned the staged mayhem of its roots and gone legit. Spectacular wipeouts were commonplace throughout the bout, as were multiplayer pile-ups.

Most of the skaters were younger than I had anticipated. In *Whip It* parlance, there were far more Ellen Page-style characters than the older, world-weary types that were her teammates in the movie. And they were nothing if not clever in creating their personas: Shiva Mi Timbers, Dash Assault, Anna Notherthing, Gnarly Simon, Roxy Cotton. And my personal favorite, Heidi Evidence.

Even the halftime air was sweet perfume, as Don McLean might say (well, OK, he actually *did* say that). A band that was set up behind the bleachers played a full set—including an encore. And it wasn't as if this was being done to allow the skaters to rest and strategize in the locker room. For the most part, they were mingling and dancing with friends in the SRO

General Admission area.

At the risk of getting elbowed in the solar plexus by a woman wearing fishnet stockings, I feel compelled to say it—roller derby is charming. Yes, charming. Borderline cute. *Definitely* endearing. Nothing about the entire spectacle made much sense, sports-wise. Unless you looked at it in terms of community and culture. Thankfully, I was getting used to doing just that. What was being presented to me with increasing regularity is that something in the human psyche compels people to get together and revel in the simple pleasures of competition. The specific mediums for doing so are almost irrelevant, the specific activities almost interchangeable.

Like the forest for the trees, I had witnessed this over and over—but only recently was I actually *seeing* it. And it became easy to identify the cast of common characters in any given sports community. Such as, for example, the Accidental Fans—those who started out as Little League dads, soccer moms, or softball sisters and then watched with wonder and admiration as their flesh and blood grew into masters of their chosen sports. These parents and siblings, along with the boyfriends and girlfriends of accomplished young athletes, exhibit unconditional support and become, by extension, part of that sport's community. And sometimes the whole dynamic is flipped; the parents are the dedicated athletes and their children grow up within the embrace of that particular community of sport.

Synchro Dad was one of my favorite Accidental Fans. During my visit to the Synchronized Swimming Nationals, I found myself characteristically short on information. In scanning the sparse audience for a prime source, I became uncomfortably aware that I was getting "looks" from the Synchro Moms, who no doubt perceived me as there to leer at all of the young girls prancing around in bathing suits. After all, I was clearly not a member of the community—so what exactly was I doing there?

Fortunately, Synchro Dad was a much more approachable target. And one that was easy to spot. Sitting among a bevy of anxious women, his eyes were glued to…the newspaper. A quick nudge to his ribs alerted him that his daughter was about to perform, thus snapping him to rapt attention. Her routine completed, it was back to his *USA Today* with his hotel's COMPLI-MENTS OF sticker on the front.

I figured he had some time on his hands.

Sure enough, he turned out to be a treasure trove of information on all things synchro. His daughter was a member of the Ohio State University team, and he shared with me that the Buckeyes are to synchronized swimming what John Wooden's UCLA teams once were to college basketball. In the 28 years that the sport had conducted an NCAA-sanctioned championship, OSU had captured 21 national titles—although he did ruefully admit that, of late, Stanford had worn the crown more often.

I started to ask him about his daughter's motivation for taking part in the sport, and he began nodding his head as if he'd entertained that conversation many times. "Well, I can tell you she's not doing it for economic reasons," he said, grinning ruefully. Although synchronized swimming is an NCAA-sanctioned sport, there are few, if any, free rides. Even as one of the elite programs in the country, Ohio State had the equivalent of five full athletic scholarships that could be parsed out among a team of ten or more synchronized swimmers. As for any kind of career path or next step, he explained that the ultimate goal was to make the national team, compete internationally, and hopefully experience the Olympics. Aside from that...not so much.

There are a few entertainment-oriented opportunities in shows that take place on high-end cruise ships and in Las Vegas hotels, but the vast majority of collegiate competitors simply hang up their nose plugs when they graduate. In sum, they take part in a physically grueling, virtually invisible sport simply because they love to do so. He shrugged and gave me a wry smile as if to say, "I don't really get it, but it makes her happy."

Now operating with the benefit of hindsight, I certainly got it. I remembered the outsized presence in and around the pool that the Ohio State University team had possessed. They carried themselves as champions, bearing T-shirts that read, LIFE. DEATH. TEAM. When one of their own was competing in the Solos or Duets, the entire team was visible and highly vocal in their support. And when they entered the pool for practice, they did so as a group—holding hands.

That feeling of solidarity achieved through shared sacrifice creates bonds that are hard to come by. Some people never get to experience them, and those who do tend never to forget them.

I had been able to lure my friend and weekend host Chrissie into tagging along for the evening session, and she'd told me of the requisite double takes that she'd received when she told people at work of her entertainment plans. But it was her mom's reaction that took her by surprise. Upon mentioning that she would be attending the Synchro Nationals, Chrissie was treated to a sepia-toned recollection of the golden era of water ballet—an era that her mom had participated in decades prior. It was a conversation that the two had never had before, and it obviously brought back a flood of fond memories. Chrissie's mom proudly recalled that, back in the day, people had paid 75 cents each to see her troupe perform. Not that she'd shared in any of that bounty—she did it because she loved it.

And apparently when it comes to water sports, that sense of belonging and community comes with an extra price for women. I recalled going to the NCAA Women's Water Polo National Championship and being surprised that so many of the players were of a "healthy" size, given the amount of calories that they must burn during a water polo practice or game. I fully anticipated slim, muscle-toned physiques. Hmmm…not the case. Fortunately I had brought along an expert source on the topic. The Bird explained to me that extended exercise in a pool causes the body's core temperature to *fall,* which then triggers protective mechanisms that cause women's bodies to slow down metabolism and store fat. Which is patently unfair.

I wondered, *How does a coach go about recruiting female water polo players?* "Ladies, we're going to spend hours of exhausting practice in a cold pool, and as a reward you're going to gain weight in places where you least want it. Now who's with me?"

They do it because they love it.

Six months after my first encampment in the synchro community, I returned—this time to attend the U.S. Masters Synchronized Swimming

Championships. And I thought immediately of my friend Synchro Dad. If he marveled at the dedication that his daughter had for her sport when there were NCAA championships and Team USA berths on the line, he would have been positively astounded by the spectacle of the Masters.

I'm not sure which delighted me more: the discovery that there was a division in the Free Duets competition composed solely of women who were 70–79 years of age or the fact that this division consisted of *six* different teams! Imagine my surprise when it turned out that these girls were relative youngsters in comparison to the next group of athletes—the 80-to-89-year-olds. This division featured just one team, the pride of San Rafael's Redwood Empire Synchro Club, Joy Dalgren and Barbara Brown. Which begged the obvious question: where were all of the other octogenarian synchronized swimmers? Slackers.

It wouldn't have amazed me in the least if the next group introduced was the Over 90 Division, but it turned out that the pool at that point was turned over to youngsters in both heart *and* chronology. The 20–29 age group started by taking the graceful water ballet origins of the sport, as displayed by the two previous divisions, and adding a healthy dose of sheer athleticism. And as the meet progressed, the thirty-somethings, forty-somethings, and each subsequent group of athletes put their own stamp on the proceedings.

The entire environment underscored perfectly the powerful draw of sports communities. Every athlete and coach involved was an amateur in the true sense of the word. They had managed to squeeze practice and training for this Team USA Synchro–sanctioned event into their busy lives—and then paid their own way to California to take part. But they hadn't immersed themselves in their team so much for the glory of victory. It had been done for the kinship and sense of belonging to a sports culture that had been in existence long before most of them had first jumped into a pool.

And in one particular case, it had been done to help heal.

For much of my day at the Masters, it was my pleasure to share a sunny spot in the bleachers with Deborah Van Dyne, who was there in her multifaceted role as competitor, recruiter, and part-time publicist for Breathless of Central Ohio, a club team from Columbus. By chance I had picked a seat next to hers, and as the Duet competition progressed, we conversed pleasantly. Eventually I asked her how she got involved with the team, and she said matter-of-factly, "After my husband died on our honeymoon, I needed to find something that would help my mind, body, and soul."

That was not exactly the answer I'd expected.

Theirs was a love story in its purest form. "If you knew me, you'd realize how unlike me this was," she said with hand over heart in the classic "honest to God" pose. "But I had only known Larry for six months before we were married." Twenty-three minutes into their very first date, Larry had pronounced, "We're going to go on a cruise for our honeymoon." Which they did. And it was while on that cruise that they booked an excursion for some snorkeling. An asthmatic attack set off a rapid-fire chain of horrific events, and Larry literally died "right there in the dinghy."

That would have shattered 999 out of 1,000 people. It shattered *me* just to hear her story. But by all appearances Deborah seemed to be truly at peace with her loss. She fixed me with one of those warm, sincere smiles that come as standard equipment with Midwesterners and said, "I was so lucky to have known him and to have had what we had. Not many people get that, you know."

Deborah had returned to Ohio from her honeymoon a widow, and she cast about for a way to keep herself occupied outside of the hours she spent managing a dental office. She had competed in synchro from her early teens all the way into college, so when she saw a newspaper article about the Breathless of Central Ohio team, she contacted the coach. It had been more than 35 years since her last team performance, but she felt inexorably drawn back to the pool. "Be here at 9:00 AM tomorrow," she was told. She's been there ever since. "It's hard to believe this is my *fifth* Masters competition," she radiated.

The team became her community. And it was clear from the charming stories she told about each competitor as they performed, that she had found a surrogate family. In addition to training and performing with the team, "I do whatever else I can to help out—sometimes it's not much," she laughed. She mentioned that she probably got more than she gave in the deal. But I'm guessing it's the other way around.

The dynamism of sports communities had bewildered me. Actually, let me clarify that. It was my previous cluelessness about their vitality that bewildered me. I was astounded at how long their pivotal role in sports had escaped me—and how in hindsight, how self-evident it all was. But *bam*—there it was again. The two-by-four between the eyes. All the really, really good stuff about sports communities had been there all along, seemingly just waiting for me to notice.

Notice taken.

NINETEEN

The Economics of Begetting

I'VE ALWAYS WANTED to be able to use the word *beget* in a sentence. I don't know why. It's just one of those words that tickle my ear. Like *shrubbery.* Or *kerfuffle.* Unless you want to come off as a character in a Charlton Heston movie, though, *beget* doesn't lend itself to casual conversation. But, at long last, here is my opportunity.

Because I've discovered that communities beget societies. There—another item checked off the bucket list.

Hear me out on this. My recent enlightenment about the wonder of sports communities had represented another milestone on my journey. Another affirmation that the love of sports was alive and kicking inside me, available at a moment's notice for a road trip to some unheralded sports event, where stories borne of the drama of competition would unfold before me. The solace and delight that I had experienced by immersing myself in sports at the second-tier level had undoubtedly talked my inner sports fan off the ledge. Never again would I be at a loss for finding a gratifying sports event to watch. This I knew for certain, and it gave me great comfort. But still…

My walkabout would inevitably come to an end, and it would be time to go back to the day-to-day task of earning a living in the business of sports. And I couldn't help but wonder: would doing the occasional drive-by through someone else's sports community be enough to offset the morale-squelching effects of the Monster? After all, a healthy majority of my time prior to this journey had been spent in the pursuit of collecting eyeballs to sell, and I couldn't see that changing after this sabbatical, reaffirming as it had been. It was what I knew best.

Fortunately, just as this line of thinking began to seriously concern me, the aforementioned begetting began.

* * *

Metaphorically speaking, I had for some time been leaving the door open behind me when I went out to revel in one sports community after another. And ironically enough, a sports community walked right in and took up residence while I was out. See, The Bird is not one to sit around with time heavy on her hands, and she was getting a wee bit tired of seeing more of my tail lights heading out of town than of me. So she ran.

Please don't be alarmed—she came back. What I mean is, The Bird *took up* running. But befitting her nature, semiregular jogging on the beach just to get the endorphins pumping wasn't going to cut it. From day one, she focused her sights on marathons. And although she's nuts ("Hello, pot? This is kettle..."), she's not crazy. She knew she needed help. So it wasn't long before she discovered her SOLE. Not "soul" but SOLE—otherwise known as Seeking Out Life Experiences, a running club based in L.A.'s South Bay region.

Founded by running gurus Steve Mackel and Gary Smith, SOLE Runners focuses a good deal of its energy on introducing beginners to both the physical and metaphysical benefits of long-distance running. Steve and Gary conduct step-by-step training programs designed to gradually prepare even the most novice of runners for conquering marathons and half-marathons, and the group training sessions that they conduct are the program's centerpiece. By the time a marathon for which the group is training takes place, each runner has been imbued with both a quiet confidence and a communal bond. As you can imagine, "first-timers" in particular flock to SOLE Runners.

In addition to following the independent portion of her training program religiously, each Saturday for several months The Bird rose at 5:00 AM and made the 30-minute drive to join her SOLE-mates for a crack-of-dawn group run. She would effervescently arrive home shortly before noon with warm stories about the people she had run with that day.

Even if that had been the extent of it, her experience as a member of this particular sports community would have been well worth the expenditure of time and money. But it was merely the opening act. For this particular band of SOLE Runners had been nurturing each other's aspirations in preparation for Southern California's winter marathon season—a series of major running events that begins with the Long Beach Marathon and climaxes with the Stadium to the Sea course of the Los Angeles Marathon. As the days grew progressively shorter, the training clock ticked down for this close-knit group of athletes. Soon enough, it was go time.

The city of Long Beach was *wide* awake by 5:30 on Marathon Sunday morning. One of the things that Steve had stressed during SOLE Runners' final preparation meeting was this: Whatever you do, stay off the 710 freeway! And sure enough, as early as 4:30 AM, this main artery leading down from L.A. and points north was backed up with sheer volume for further than a mile. Even with the benefit of local traffic-route knowledge, I absolutely crawled through city streets on my way to the smartest online buy I'd ever made—a personal prepurchased parking-lot space, a concept that lies somewhere between noise-cancelling headphones and fire in terms of ingenuity. I sincerely have no idea how those who had *not* prepurchased parking ever made it to the race.

Don't get me wrong—this pileup didn't take place for lack of event organization. It was just indicative of the number of people for whom it was vitally important to be in the Long Beach Marina area before sunrise.

The Long Beach Marathon field was estimated at 2,500 bicyclists, 11,500 half-marathoners, 6,500 marathoners, and untold numbers of people taking part in the Run Forrest Run 5K fun run/walk. Add to that the event organizers, volunteers, and spectators, and you had a self-contained, not-so-small city, fully open for business well before the sun rose. I had been invited as a guest of SOLE Runners to join them in the private runners club village area of the event's sprawling build-out, and from there I gazed out in wonder at the eerie predawn glow of my surroundings.

If you've ever played a team sport and experienced the unconditional support that envelops the locker room just before a game, fix that dynamic in your mind and multiply it by 20,000—because that's how many "teammates" there were on the premises. And that spirit was amplified even more on the small patch of lawn where Steve led the SOLE Runners through prerace stretching. They were primed.

The cyclists went off at 6:00 sharp, and for at least half the route, they rode only in the light cast by streetlamps and their own bike lights. They were followed at 6:15 by the marathon walkers. And then the sea of humanity began to swell toward the starting line in waves—literally and figuratively. There were far more people running than could be accommodated by a single starting command, so runners went off in waves—eight of them according to my count. Faster runners went out first, and slowest went last. With five-to-ten-minute breaks between wave starts (depending on the size of the wave), it took more than 45 minutes to get every competitor across the *starting* line.

As successive waves progressed toward their outset, the mood that accompanied each one evolved. The first two were quiet, focused, and goal-oriented—all business. The next few consisted of people who had run marathons before and who today were out simply to enjoy the event. High-spirited and vocal, they knew exactly what to expect, and the race emcee worked the crowd expertly to pass the time. The last two waves were heavily made up of "first-timers" taking part in their maiden distance-running event. They were lively as well, but a lot of it was nervous energy, because every last one of them was wondering, *Can I do this?*

What unified all of the waves was an atmosphere thick with pride. As you might expect, it was easily visible on the faces of the runners. But it was the friends and loved ones of the runners who were simply bursting with it. Everyone in attendance had a keen awareness of what it took for the runners to reach this stage of preparedness for tackling a personal challenge, whether that challenge was to qualify for the Boston Marathon—or simply to cross the finish line upright. Lined up three- and four-deep on the sidewalks, people strained to pick out the face of their favorite runner from the thousands that streamed by. When visual contact was made, both runner and onlooker glowed, buoyed by the unspoken bond. And all of this, mind you, was at the *beginning* of the race!

While I'm sure it was done to maximize the operational efficiency of the race, it was also great for the event's atmosphere that the marathoners and half-marathoners both started the race together and finished in the same spot. They ran the same course for roughly the first 11 miles, at which point the marathoners branched off onto an outer loop of 13.1 miles. This loop brought them back to rejoin the main course (and their half-marathon brethren) for the final few miles. Everyone crossed the same finish line, which, in a nod toward spotlighting the marathoners, had been divided into two separate final lanes and chutes. The whole thing was well thought out and well executed, without a trace of the potential chaos that always lurks when elite athletes and rookies compete shoulder to shoulder.

The first six miles of the course took everyone on a loop through the tourism and entertainment district of Long Beach, out to where the HMS Queen Mary is permanently docked. For what was a *very* diverse crowd of runners, everyone looked pretty much the same at the 10k mark (6.2 miles), coming back through the festival area. Nobody appeared to be struggling, and everyone's stride was still intact. Once again, onlookers craned their necks to pick out their favorite runner, and runners scanned the crowd to complete the connection. Humans are funny that way.

Enclosed by the immediate group by whom they were surrounded, the scale of the event was lost on the runners. Those of us in the crowd, however, had a much more astonishing view of the sheer amassing of people. As I stood at the 10k mark scanning the field for The Bird to pass by, I must have mentally processed more than 1,000 faces until hers appeared and lit up with a smile. So far, so good.

Climbing up to a hilltop vantage point, I watched the runners begin their trek along the coastal portion of the route. The field had spaced itself out naturally by then, creating what would literally be a continuous, hours-long river of runners, coursing along the paved pathway that split the sandy beach.

I headed on bike up to Ocean Drive, the main drag along which the runners would travel for their last few miles before turning a final corner and heading down the hill to the finish line. Away from the crush of the central festival area, things were much quieter. People lined the streets in small clusters, some armed with placards and shouts of encouragement. Most, though, just looked on in silent admiration at the early waves of half-marathoners already gliding toward the finish in still-perfect form—and in awe when a yellow-bibbed marathoner ran by, having already conquered the outer loop in an astonishingly short period of time.

Riding further out into the course, I reached the 11-mile split point and stationed myself where the half-marathoners were branching onto the homeward stretch of Ocean Drive. This was the intersection of pain and pride for the "halfers," especially those with minimal big-race experience to draw upon. For these late-wave starters, this was the hardest part of what for most was a personal quest. They'd been running up a long gradual hill from the beach for quite some time, and you could read it on their faces; they were thinking about the Wall. Many were alternating between running and walking—anything to keep moving forward—and normal running strides were in short supply. Thanks to some uncharacteristic humidity in the air, there were also more than a few cheeks bearing swaths of evidently nonwaterproof mascara.

At the top of the hill was a water station with a huge inflatable red arch symbolizing that the worst of the course was now behind the runners. A sizable group of vocal supporters had gathered to help will the athletes to the other side of that arch—and to the flat and eventually downhill ground that would greet them for the rest of the race. When The Bird came through she was obviously struggling. While she was glad to see me, she was in no mood to chat as I rode along beside her. We agreed it best that I meet her at the finish line, and I reluctantly rode away, glancing over my shoulder at her bobbing ponytail and bright orange Newton running shoes gamely soldiering on.

Back at the festival area the amplified voices of the race emcees reached out to pull people across the finish line. Their lightheartedness at the start had been the perfect antidote for nerves, and at the other end of the event, their sincere words of encouragement in greeting people coming down the final stretch created a soothing soundtrack voiceover—"Congratulations! Great Job! Welcome to Long Beach!" I'm positive it was appreciated.

Out of the thousands of personal victories that played themselves out, a few finishing snapshots stayed with me: Mycle Brandy, who had literally just that week completed a walk across America to raise awareness for the American Heart/Stroke Associations…A marathoner who had carried a sizable Marine Corps flag aloft for the entire 26.2-mile run…82-year-old Carlos Mora, completing his 26th Long Beach Marathon, one of 16 men who had successfully run every LBM since the inaugural race in 1982…And Steve Mackel, looking fresh as a daisy as he passed by and called out, "Where's the love, SOLE Runners?"

But I never saw The Bird cross the line. She had dug deep and picked up her pace, and in the time that it took for me to drop my bike off at the SOLE Runners tent and spawn my way over to the finish, she had already completed her first half-marathon. One step ahead of me, per her usual.

Back in the runners club village, where hours earlier Mackel's anxious disciples had assembled in the dark, a quietly euphoric vibe was in the air. The exhilaration of the finish had passed, as it had taken a good bit of time for each runner to cross the line, proceed into a long chute where they received a medal and a foil blanket to ward off the postrace chills, and then make their way back across the festival area to home base. By the time they arrived at the SOLE Runners tent—where loved ones, massage therapists, and a healthy spread of food awaited—"woo-hoos" had melted into proud, satisfied auras.

I have a picture of The Bird from that day, wearing her medal and surrounded by her SOLE Runners comrades. Hair and smile plastered to her face, I've never seen her happier. It was the personification of the power of a sports community, and its envelopment had taken her by sweet surprise.

As I surreptitiously watched The Bird bask, my mind drifted back to the visual of the river of humanity streaming up the beach pathway earlier in the day. And that's when the metaphor hit me. If that was indeed a river of runners, it had been fed by dozens and dozens of tributaries. I looked around the village and noticed for the first time just how many other groups of people were assembled—how many communities just like the SOLE Runners. Operating within their own spheres, they had created social environments framed by a common interest. Nothing new there. I had been seeing this over and over of late. But! Merged together, they formed an entire society—a society drawn from many different localities but sharing the same characteristics, traits, and rituals.

The Bird was a SOLE Runner in the immediate but a runner in the broader sense. She would tell me about other runners she would meet while traveling on business and how that common thread united them for the short period of time they spent together. They'd compare notes on training methods, commiserate about nagging injuries, share reviews of different equipment. She had joined the SOLE Runners community, and it had implicitly led her to citizenship in the entire running society. It was an organic process.

I know what you're thinking: *Community, culture, society…so what? Aren't we just talking semantics here?*

Well, yes—and no. True, these words all share their roots in people being drawn together, but where they differ is in scale. A society represents critical mass.

Almost by their very nature, sports communities are drawn inexorably toward a critical mass. One of the cornerstones of the competitive mind-set is the pursuit of progressively stronger fields against which to test one's self. Add to that the opportunity to congregate and commune with a large group of like-minded people, and you've got a sports society just begging to materialize. And here's the critical point: people will gladly part with some of their hard-earned disposable income to be a part of their chosen sports society.

Here's a perfect example: if our lives depended on it, neither The Bird nor I could tell you when exactly it was that we paid her Long Beach Marathon entry fee. Or, more to the point, how much it was. Unless it threatened to match the GDP of some small island nation, there was absolutely no way we would have engaged in a cost/benefit analysis of the fee. It was immaterial. And in looking around at a sea of happy faces sharing race experiences and reinforcing each other's sense of accomplishment, I sincerely doubted that financial considerations had impacted anyone else's decision to be there either.

I'll go one step further. Given the pull that a sports society can have on its members, I'd be willing to bet that if a hypothetical belt-tightening discussion were to occur within a household of runners, event entry fees would be one of the *last* budgetary line items to be impacted. And if you substituted *cyclists* or *archers* or *kayakers* or any one of dozens of different sports for the word *runners* in that last sentence, it would be just as true.

This may not strike you as particularly cutting-edge thinking, but consider my frame of reference. For years my vocational pursuits had centered around the following mantra: sponsors and advertisers pay the bills in sports, but only in exchange for eyeballs. No eyeballs = no money = no event. Nowhere in the daily conversation did the notion arise that perhaps there was money to be made by facilitating the *participation in,* as opposed to the *watching of* sports.

But, on that Sunday morning in Long Beach, I was surrounded by 17,000 reasons to seriously consider taking up that line of thought.

TWENTY

Paying to Play—Happenings and Destinations

NOT TOO LONG AFTER the Long Beach Marathon, I happened to begin my day by reading an online blurb about an upcoming Ironman Triathlon event having sold out in 11 minutes. Not sold out of sponsorships. Not sold out of advertising opportunities. Sold out of available competitive slots—at $575 a pop. In a recession.

Once again I had reason to be grateful for how much my walkabout had altered my perceptions, how many forests it had cleared so that I could view the trees. I recalled a presentation that I had done sometime not too long before the IGTS Tour had commenced. Something about the changing face of opportunity in sports management. Pretty sure that I'd be embarrassed by reading it, I still couldn't help myself. I booted up my computer and called up the file…

> *There is only so much that can be done to attract additional fans to any of the "lesser" sports, and it's quite likely that as many will simply go away as will grow. Most have been subsidized to a large extent by an NGB or parent organization, or more commonly by Corporate America, and with the economy stuck in the current malaise for what seems like some time to come, those subsidies are in the process of drying up.*

The result will most likely be a bifurcation of the sports world into the handful of well-known sports that are "safe" for corporate marketers to invest in, and those that exist almost exclusively to "do" rather than watch. Of course the removal of any fan-based spectator component of the latter will relegate that particular sport to bootstrap status and probably price many of its participants out if they have to assume all of the operating costs themselves via entry fees. In any case, sports as we know it today will suffer. Blah blah blah, blahblah blah...

Based on what I'd witnessed since I wrote that nonsense, someone has clearly forgotten to notify the...ahem..."lesser sports" that their prospects are pretty dismal. According to some idiot's white paper, the objects of these second-tier sports folks' passions are on the verge of dying. Wait a second...I was that "some idiot."

With the benefit of hindsight, I had started to comprehend how Ebenezer Scrooge must have felt, looking out his window on Christmas morning with a hard-won new perspective. One after another, I had stumbled into sports societies quietly thriving away without courtesy cars or Too Big to Fail Bank sponsorships. Imagine that.

At this point, let me reassure you that I know what you're thinking: *But what's in all of this for our faithful narrator?* OK, even if you weren't thinking that, it's about time you did. Let's get with the program here. How about I spell it out...

The athletes that populate sports societies thrive on the opportunity to compete while expanding their horizons, both athletically and personally. Their own local sports communities nurture that desire only to a certain extent, and therefore these athletes are drawn inexorably toward sports Happenings—toward *events*—some of which are nearby but many of which involve some subset of planes, trains, and automobiles.

I am, right down to my core, an events guy. Almost everything that I have done in my sports-business career has revolved around creating and producing events. But here's the thing: the very existence of those events had always been predicated largely upon how successful my colleagues and I were at convincing corporate entities that there was a benefit to sponsoring them. Now, much like a lifting fog can often reveal spectacular beauty in its wake, the concept introduced to me was that, instead of spending my time in the mind-numbing exercise of begging companies to help create events, real fulfillment in my work might just spring from switching to a world in which athletes are *craving* opportunities to spend their own money on well-run sports Happenings.

Would this switch be easy to pull off? I didn't know the answer to that. Was Rome built in a day? Well, I didn't know the answer to that one either—I wasn't there. But it does seem unlikely. I mean, the materials requisition process itself could drag on for weeks. But I'm getting off track here. The point is that an entirely new field of opportunities—*rewarding* opportunities—had presented itself within the business of play. And I was highly intrigued.

I started mentally connecting the dots. I recalled the U.S. Table Tennis Nationals. The Las Vegas Convention Center is not a small place. But two of its largest exhibition halls had to be conjoined to hold the nearly 100 tables used for competitive play. And that's not even counting the Center Court, which consisted of two tables surrounded by an amphitheatre of aluminum bleachers. I thought I was going to have to call a cab to get from one side of the venue to the other.

There were 843 registered competitors in those Nationals, coming from 41 states and territories and taking part in 63 different "Events"— table-tennis speak for divisions of competition. And trust me on this: You can't imagine what a huge room full of airborne ping-pong balls looks like until you've seen it for yourself. Picture an arsenal full of ripened dandelions exploding.

Was there corporate sponsorship signage plastered all over everything in sight? Not by a long shot. The vast majority of the freight for this particular event was paid by the participants.

A few weeks after that, there it was again. A whole bunch of people who had traveled a great distance just to have fun. The U.S. Synchronized Team Skating Championships unquestionably took the prize for "most ironic" of all the events on my walkabout. Given that we're talking about an ice-and-snow sport, two things about the event shouldn't come as a surprise to you. First, its date fell smack in the middle of the winter portion of the IGTS Tour. Second, it took place in Ontario.

But not *that* Ontario.

No, to reach the Championships of synchronized team skating, you had to travel to the winter wonderland of Ontario, *California,* where 80 degrees of sunshine bathed at least the outer confines of the host venue, Citizens Business Bank Arena. Granted, it felt a little odd wearing two layers of clothing (and carrying a third) as I crossed the parking lot, but at least I could be sure that here the ice and chill would be confined to the arena.

At that point in my walkabout, I liked to think of myself as a bit of an aficionado on the relative structure of second-tier sports—how successive levels of competition were interwoven among collegiate, amateur, and Team USA event sanctioning. So naturally I assumed that while the Adult, Master, and Senior Championships would be made up of "club" teams—unaffiliated self-funded groups—the Collegiate Nationals would include teams from colleges and universities that fund synchronized skating as a varsity sport.

And naturally I was wrong.

While synchronized skating is currently working on changing this, the sport does not carry NCAA status, even though it holds varsity status at a handful of universities. Therefore, the Collegiate Championships are also a club-level competition—it's just that the members of the "club" all happen to be enrolled at a given college or university. And while the sport does fall under the umbrella of U.S. Figure Skating, the national governing body that is part of the USOC consortium, it is not yet included in the Winter Olympics—and therefore not heavily funded.

Net/net—with few exceptions, the skaters on hand pay to play. And ice time is not cheap. Nor is coaching. Or equipment and apparel for both practice and competition. Or event entry fees. On top of the cost is the commitment of time required for the pursuit of excellence in skating, both individually *and* as part of a large choreographed team. It is impossible to oversell the importance of the latter, and not just from a purely competitive standpoint.

These women skate in tight formations, in both directions. Often, one athlete is skating backward, directly on course for a teammate who is also skating backward at her. It takes a lot of trust to know that your teammate isn't going to take that one extra disastrous step, and that kind of trust only comes from a lot of practice, during which more than a few unintentional body checks are no doubt delivered. Particularly chilling to consider as I watched was the potential consequence of one skater's face being in the wrong place at the wrong time when a teammate lifted her skate into the air.

Yet in spite of the expense, the sacrifice of time, the risk of injury, and the assumption of stepsister status within both the NCAA and the U.S. Figure Skating Association, these women were all clearly thrilled to be there. The looks on their faces at the completion of their performances were priceless, as were their reactions on the podium when their scores came in—no matter where in the standings those scores placed them.

It was authentic. And it was heart-warming to watch. Even though I had become a trained professional at ferreting out a story line that would generate a strong rooting interest in every event that I'd attended, it was really tough at this one. I really, truly wanted every team that performed to win. But all of that changed about an hour into the competition.

For the most part, the schools that had proceeded through regional qualification to earn a spot in the Collegiate Nationals were those that one might expect to see. The lineup was dominated by large universities from Frost Belt locations. But one qualifier drew more than its share of "Huh? Where's that?" from the crowd when they took to the rink—the Ice Effects from Oswego State.

Known more precisely as the State University of New York at Oswego, this small Upstate institution sits directly on the shore of Lake Ontario. And I mean *directly*. I have been to Oswego State. I have been to Oswego State during the winter. I still have nightmares about eight-foot walls of snow and winds so strong that sidewalks at the school are outfitted with rope handrails to help people remain upright while negotiating their way across campus. Needless to say, I started pulling hard for the Ice Effects. They were dressed in pink and black (actually *fuchsia* and black, The Bird corrected me), and much to my delight they performed to an upbeat mix of U2 songs, as opposed to the more theatrical musical fare of other squads.

Bless their hearts—in this strange foreign land of sunshine, warmth, and dry pavement, the Oswego State Ice Effects...well, they didn't finish last. But if you had just happened to wander into the arena at the moment that they were on the podium receiving their postroutine scores, you would have thought they'd just won gold. It was clear to me that they weren't celebrating their score as much as they were displaying a palpable love of competing and achieving as a team. This band of athletes from a college whose enrollment is a fraction of that of its major competitors had made it all the way to the U.S. Nationals. Together. And those bonds of affiliation were clearly worth every minute of practice and every cent it took for them to fund this trip.

* * *

There are understandably lots of happy campers in the humble corners of the Smaller Is Better sports universe. But I had come to recognize that true, rhapsodic bliss...well, that's the province of the destination event, the apogee of the sports Happening world.

Sports societies are nothing if not mobile. *Fan-based* communities have been traveling to popular sporting events for a long, long time, as evidenced by every host-city economic-impact study ever done. That much I knew. I was also coming up to speed rapidly on the willingness of *participant-based* sports communities to travel distances both great and small in order to meet and compete. For those who have a passion for their sport, it becomes their chosen pastime and inevitably the repository for a good chunk of their discretionary income.

So imagine the allure of an event that enables people to both participate in *and* watch their sport being played at elite levels of competition. Toss an attractive travel destination into the mix, and you've got something special. I've seen it with my own eyes.

What water polo and beach volleyball are to Southern California, lacrosse is to the Mid-Atlantic states—especially Maryland. As anyone who has spent some time in the state during warm-weather months can attest, lacrosse sticks are a *de rigueur* fashion accessory among teens of both genders, and lacrosse matches up minivan for minivan against soccer in terms of youth leagues. It is as embedded in the state's culture as are soft-shell crabs. So looking back on it now, it's with more than a little embarrassment that I admit to the following story.

When I first laid out the schedule for my walkabout, I only stumbled across the NCAA Women's Lacrosse Championship and included it because its date and location were convenient to that of the men's version of the same. On a side trip from the NCAA Men's Lacrosse Final Four in Baltimore, I had honestly expected to be able to roll onto the campus of Towson State University, choose from a wide assortment of parking spaces, and stroll leisurely across campus to find a humble field bracketed by a couple of sections of bleachers.

It actually turned out to be a little different than that.

The blinking EVENT PARKING highway signs on the interstate first tipped me off. Then there was the wait through three light cycles just to get onto the campus—on a Sunday that fell well after the completion of the school semester…followed by the ten-minute wait to *pay* for parking…and the line of ticket-seekers that stretched back more than 50 yards from the box office. The anticipated "humble field bracketed by a couple of sections of bleachers" was instead the football stadium at a midsized Division I school. A stadium that wound up being pretty much sold out. I had clearly underestimated the draw of women's lacrosse in the Mid-Atlantic.

But still…the attendance tally of 9,782 for the championship game (and 18,559 for the semifinals and finals combined) suggested to me that more than just the locals had shown up. And it turned out I was right.

It was 5:30 in the evening and the temperature was still well north of 80 degrees. Thrilled to be occupying seats removed from the glaring sun, The Bird and I were equally happy to make the acquaintance of one Steve Taylor, who, like us, was in the top row of the stadium and hugging the shade cast by the press box. I'd seen quite a bit of lacrosse over the years—certainly enough to watch the game knowledgeably. But there was much to be learned about the game as the women play it, and fortunately Steve has spent years on the front lines of coaching and teaching the game to women through his affiliation with the International Federation of Women's Lacrosse Associations. The game has taken him to 14 different countries, and what he shared with us could fill the pages of a manual on how to grow a second-tier sport.

Steve turned out to be a handy and valuable reference guide as the game progressed. But it was almost by accident that we learned that part of the reason for the huge influx of fans was the existence of an annual lacrosse conference and expo held in nearby Bel Air—evidently a huge lacrosse community, even by the lofty standards by which lacrosse addiction is measured in the area. Promising female players from all over the country had descended upon the rolling hills of northern Maryland, all with dreams of eventually qualifying for Team USA and the Women's Lacrosse World Cup. And they were there in full force on this warm Memorial Day weekend.

Coincidence? I think not.

Much more likely is that the organizers of the conference saw an opportunity to enhance the participant experience by scheduling it for the same weekend as the collegiate championship. I don't know this for a fact, but I would guess that they then reached out to the NCAA to create some synergistic programming. I know I would have. *Voila!* A bona fide women's lacrosse Happening.

I had occasion to reflect back on this as I sat bathed in the desert's winter sunshine at the USA Sevens Rugby Championship. It was still early in the final session of competition, but it had already been quite a day, what with the early morning drive to Las Vegas and…the Incident.

When I began this walkabout, it was not without careful consideration of the risks: Eye strain. Chapped hands from excessive applauding. Being trapped on a Delta Airlines middle seat between two 300-pounders. But I never contemplated the chances of being victimized by crime. Yet there I was, being robbed. In broad daylight, no less. She didn't fit the profile—they never do. She couldn't have been more than 25 years old. Pleasant looking. A little on the slight side. I don't know how tall she was, because she was sitting down at the time. I never saw it coming.

"Excuse me, sir—did you not hear me the first time? That will be 50 dollars."

I managed to pull myself together. "There must be some mistake. I just wanted to buy one single general-admission ticket to the rugby tournament."

That's when she brought out the big guns—the eye roll and exasperated sigh. "Sir, there are people waiting in line behind you." And just like that, I became another grisly statistic.

I had come to Las Vegas full of anticipation. I'd not seen rugby played before, at any level, and now I was going to witness the final day of competition in the lone North American stop in the IRB Sevens World Series circuit. This kind of experience was the hallmark of the IGTS Tour. Apparently the price of a hallmark—along with an unreserved spot on an aluminum bench in the upper deck—is at a premium here. When they say things "stay in Vegas," I didn't think they were talking about my life savings.

Rugby in the "union" form has been around for a long, long time. But the popularity of the full 15-a-side game has always been limited to certain parts of the world. Not so with rugby sevens, a shorter variant of the game, in which teams are made up of seven players. Sevens has grown steadily in popularity around the globe, to the extent that it will make its debut as an Olympic sport in the 2016 Summer Games.

Once I had settled in and absorbed the action in the first couple of matches, I could see how this abbreviated version of the game could catch on quickly. While the specific rules and regs differ somewhat, rugby sevens has so much in common with American football it's almost impossible not to pick up the essence of the game immediately. Which is important, because the games are incredibly quick. While a rugby union match lasts about an hour and a half, a normal sevens match consists of two seven-minute halves. Halftime lasts one minute. Yes, I said one minute.

I had read that sevens tournaments are known for having more of a relaxed "festival" atmosphere than 15-a-side games, and in a short time I knew exactly what was meant by that. It doesn't take too long to see the entire 16-team field in a rugby sevens tournament-slash-festival. Two teams take the field and then alternate between running around wildly and tag-team wrestling for about as long as it takes to figure out which color uniform belongs to which team. Then time runs out, the teams shake hands, and two more squads come in off the assembly line. The rapid-fire nature of the games made it such that you could go to the concession stand and the restroom and miss an entire match in the process. It's enough to make somebody with Attention Deficit Disorder complain, "That's it? Is that all there is? I wasn't done watching yet!"

Despite the cost of entry, the crowd was of pretty good size. I had an extra 26 seconds of down time between a couple of matches, so I began pondering the source of the healthy attendance. Las Vegas is perhaps the epicenter of the real-estate crash and consequent deep recession, so I couldn't imagine that residents of the city had snapped up overpriced tickets in great number. And Boyd Stadium wasn't exactly a short stroll from the Strip; even if those in town for traditional reasons had been inclined to do something a little different for a while, this wasn't a "drop-by" venue. To be sure, there were fans in attendance who had traveled from around the world with their teams, but far more spectators appeared to bear no specific allegiance.

Clues to the puzzle began to emerge. At some point, my section of the bleachers became quickly populated by a group wearing logoed apparel that bore the legend STONY BROOK COLLEGE RUGBY. Later, a fan from Buffalo was interviewed on Fan Cam after he won a prize-package drawing. And finally, when leafing through the event program, I found the key, in the following description:

> *Among the many things the USA Sevens has created is the massive satellite tournament, the Las Vegas Invitational. The LVI began when the USA Sevens was in San Diego. Former USA player Jon Hinkin brought together an amalgam of touch teams, college Sevens squads, masters outfits, and women's international Sevens teams to create a tournament around the Tournament.*

More than 100 sevens teams, along with more than 60 teams of 15s, had come to Las Vegas to play matches at venues in and around Sam Boyd stadium on Thursday, Friday, and Saturday. And of course, once here, it was unlikely that they'd pass up the chance to see the world's best compete, especially because a ticket to the event also secured admission to its companion festival. I'd even be willing to bet (I was, after all, in Vegas) that the tournament organizers had bundled all four days of activity into Play & Watch packages.

They had taken the formula that I'd seen work so successfully for women's lacrosse and gone it one better. For while the two halves of the destination event for lacrosse had been connected, they were separate entities. Not so with this one. The rugby organizers controlled all aspects of the entire Happening. They understood that the passion that the society of rugby players had for their sport would set the perfect stage for a communal event whose price was more or less inelastic, if I remember my economics terminology correctly. Even the merchandising take had to have been huge. Despite prices for event T-shirts and international team jerseys that started at "expensive" and ran to "Oh my God!" there was a constant buyer presence at each of the stands that I passed in the stadium concourse.

The pure economic power of a sports society was on full display, and it centered upon *affiliation*. And it focused my attention on the following lessons to be learned: (a) Participant affiliation has more staying power than spectator affiliation, and (b) Nothing can touch the combination of the two.

Sports communities beget sports societies, which beget sports

Happenings. And while sports watchers own the airwaves, sports doers are where the opportunity lies—at least for a certain rejuvenated sports-industry professional.

I resolved from that point on to dedicate my career to the creation of sports-society experiences. Granted, I was a little sketchy on the details. But not since The Deal, struck by The Bird and me almost 15 years prior, had something felt so right.

TWENTY-ONE

Requiem for a Game Junkie?

IT WAS THE DEAD OF WINTER, and my walkabout was headed into its final stages. I had been at this for almost a year. I was rounding third and heading for home on this magical mystery tour, but I still had the uneasy feeling that I still hadn't found what I was looking for. Which leads to the inevitable question. No, it's not "How many more musical references can be piled into one sentence?" But I'm happy you're paying attention.

The question is this: Would sports ever again be able to deliver to me that purity of appreciation that I had as a kid? That feeling of fun so palpable it almost made me giggle? That grip that guarantees a lack of comprehension of the time passing by?

It was almost too much to ask, and I almost felt guilty wishing for it. My walkabout had already given me a huge gift. Sports were once again a centerpiece of my life, and for all the right reasons. Much to my delight, I had rediscovered my ability to be an appreciative fan. Moreover, my sense of purpose within the sports industry had been redefined—and consequently rejuvenated. Wanting more at this point was like getting a fully loaded Ferrari as a present and grumbling that the seat warmers didn't radiate heat evenly enough. Besides, when looking to recapture purity of any kind, it's hard to ignore that a synonym for "pure" is "unadulterated," which pretty much says it all. To be able to experience sports like I did when I was a kid, I was going to have to "unadult" myself. Yes—*even more* than I ever had before. Which I wasn't sure was technically possible.

Don't get me wrong. I can do "childish" with the best of them. But I was going more for child*like* here. I'm not sure of the precise difference between the two, but I know when I've entered the realm of the former, because it never fails to draw the Look from The Bird.

Semantics aside, I got to thinking one day about the 2-1-2.

Back in my college days, I used to summer on Cape Cod. No, wait—I just reread that phrase and it made me feel as if I should be donning a smoking jacket and ascot. What I really mean is that I used to spend the summer on Cape Cod, living with a half-dozen (or so) buddies in a house whose lease agreement clearly specified a maximum of four occupants. We weren't real good on math back then.

We worked hard and we played hard, and at the end of the summer we went back to school with great tans, full bank accounts, and some measure of sleep deprivation. It was a priceless time, and anybody who was there in that era would trade anything to recherish the experience. So a few years back, a few of us decided to try and recapture at least a taste of it. Doc, my friend and former rental fraud co-conspirator, made the arrangements for us to return to the scene of the crime for a week in September, accompanied by our exceedingly tolerant wives. We even abided by the lease occupancy limits this time.

Just as I had done years earlier during a vacation on Nantucket, I brought along a small football. It didn't have quite the same legendary performance characteristics of that original throw-it-over-the-house ball, but then again…neither did we. And as luck would have it, this new ball was waterproof.

Doc and I were the only ones in the pond on that first day. The water was waist-deep in this particular sandy-bottomed Wellfleet treasure, so the environment was perfect for executing the diving catch. Literally. After a time, though, we abandoned the sprawling, splashing acrobatics and started simply tossing the ball back and forth, chatting and laughing, enjoying the day and the fluid feel of each pass. It was probably me that first started the counting.

"Doc, did you know that we've thrown 50 passes now without dropping the ball in the water once?" Whereupon the 51st pass went right through my hands and skipped across the pond's surface. So we had a record to break. Try as we might that day, however, we never again approached that threshold.

Murph showed up the next day. It didn't take long for him to start ridiculing Doc and me for the pursuit of our quest. It took even less time after that for him to join us in the pond. The three of us nudged the count up to 84 and deemed it the Official Pond Football Toss Consecutive Passing Record. The next day we steamed effortlessly past that total, crossing the century line on our way to what we thought was a newsworthy mark of 192. We envisioned Pond Football Toss teams springing up all over the country, in passionate pursuit of our record.

That weekend, Kels arrived, adding a fourth arm to the team. At first we thought this gave us an unfair advantage, but a quick review of the PFT Rulebook yielded no limits on the number of participants—as long as everyone was in the water throughout. After hours of trying in vain, though, the best number we'd posted was less than half of that needed to establish immortality. The next day it was the same. We began to view 192 consecutive dry passes as occupying the rarified territory of DiMaggio's 56-game hitting streak. Many would mount an impressive assault, but nobody would ever seriously come close.

On the last day of vacation we weren't even planning on a trip to the pond, let alone another attempt at the record. But it was a picture-perfect sunny day, and we'd otherwise been unable to pull together anything more ambitious. With no serious thought to competitive PFT that day, we were in the pond but back to simply tossing and talking, with the occasional theatrical catch mixed in. Nobody in the water was keeping track.

But The Bird was.

Unaware that it was an off day on the PFT schedule, The Bird had taken up her standard Stat Girl role. Bottle of Corona in hand, she lounged in a beach chair on the shore, idly counting our passes. Nobody processed it when she lazily called out "100." Or "125." But when the words "That's 150, guys" came languidly floating out to us, it got our attention. The unbreakable record—one we hadn't even been trying to break—was suddenly right there, like a deer jumping out of the brush into our headlights. Chatter subsided. Arms got shorter. Hands adopted the feel of granite.

Soon the only sound was Stat Girl's voice across the still water: "160"..."170"..."180." At 182, there was a bobble and recovery, followed by nervous laughter. At 189, a leaping catch of an errant toss. And at 193, jumping, arm-flailing spasms of joy. But we quickly recovered—we were seasoned pros with work still to do. "200"..."210"...and when on the 213th pass Murph couldn't quite get his hands underneath a low pass from yours truly, the first splash in more than an hour occurred. It was over. Pandemonium erupted as the stands (i.e. three beach chairs) emptied out to join the celebration in the water.

Back on shore enjoying victory beers, we reveled. We wallowed. We savored. We made up hand signals, flashing the 2-1-2 and posing for cell phone pictures. We *giggled*. I doubt any of us recall the specifics of anything else done on that vacation. But all I have to do is say "The 2-1-2" to Doc, Murph, or Kels, and the same Pavlovian giggles come back in response. Kels, who works in television, even took the opportunity to flash the 2-1-2 when he was on camera once. I have it on tape for posterity.

Childish? Of course! But also childlike, in all of its glory. In and amongst all of the tongue-in-cheek celebrating and clowning around, we were temporarily transported back to a point in our lives when the pursuit of something called the Official Pond Football Toss Consecutive Passing Record just might have been truly important to us. Time stood still in that pond, and all of the really good stuff about playing sports—even made-up ones—came back.

So I knew the Game Junkie was still in there somewhere.

✳ ✳ ✳

I love L.A. No, seriously, I do. I'm not trying to get all Randy Newman on you, but picture this...

I'm sprinting up and down a crowded Hollywood sidewalk on a Saturday afternoon in the middle of winter, dodging the likes of Marilyn Monroe, Captain Jack Sparrow, Darth Vader, and the Joker—as well as the phalanx of admirers that surround each of them. I've been doing this kind of thing all over the city for almost three hours, and I'm sure my heart rate is hovering in the "Maybe you should rethink this" zone. But I am lost in the hot pursuit of precious information that will lead to...well, I'm not exactly sure what. All I know is that I want to win whatever it is that's at stake. And I wonder, *Where else in the world would my current sweatball status and bizarre behavior raise not a single eyebrow among the people I'm trying desperately not to run over?* I love L.A.

My overall fondness for my adopted city aside, on this particular day I had a specific love for the Amazing L.A. Race, which had inspired 50 or so other maniacs to do what I was doing. So I wasn't alone in my lunacy. In fact, I had five teammates: a filmmaker, a professional golfer, an organizational-development guru, an action-sports event manager and, of course, The Bird. We ranged in age from 23 (the pro golfer) to 50...ish (yours truly) and were split evenly across gender lines. It shouldn't surprise you to learn that the name we chose for our team was the Mixed Bag. But let me go back to the beginning...

I don't know exactly how she does it, but if, during casual conversation with The Bird, you happen to mention something that piques your interest, within days she will provide you with a full color-coded, cross-tabbed dossier on that particular activity. Apparently in one of my more coherent musings, I had conveyed the great delight that the memory of the 2-1-2 had recently brought me. So in the spirit of scratching my itch for pseudoathletic competition, she introduced a short time later the idea of taking part in the Amazing L.A. Race.

Long before CBS struck ratings gold with *The Amazing Race*, there was BARF—the Bay Area Race Fantastique, which in turn can trace its genealogy to the mother of all urban scavenger hunt marathons, The Game. Begun in 1973, The Game became an underground legend as a mental and physical competition that, over the course of several days, covered hundreds of square miles of constant motion and puzzle solving. A slightly less apocalyptic version of The Game, the BARF was created in 1985 by a group of Stanford students. And through natural West Coast migratory patterns, some of them brought the concept with them to SoCal…just for a LARF. Sorry.

Larry Toffler and Bob Gloverman, the proprietors of Los Angeles Race Fantastique, shortened the contest a bit and added all of the elements that make it a blast for virtually any adult willing to spend half a day dashing around L.A. in search of successive clues that will unlock the mysteries of the city and lead to unnamed but presumably fabulous prizes for the first team to complete the puzzle. Thus was born the Amazing L.A. Race.

So it was that 12 teams of people of various walks of life gathered on a cool sun-splashed Saturday morning at the Hollywood Bowl. Since some members of our team were meeting for the first time, we felt the need for a quick round-robin cleansing session in which we revealed what we felt might be any weaknesses that the team would have to pull together to overcome. I copped to bad knees that precluded long-distance running, and The Bird admitted that she could get lost in a long hallway with no doors. Molly asked, "Is a hangover a weakness?" We mulled that over and, deciding that it wasn't, turned our attention to sizing up the competition.

Some teams had matching shirts or similar apparel—one charming woman named Robin had made sequined ball caps for her team. OK, so they had us on preparation. Some teams were made up primarily of young athletic types. Others bore boastful names like Defending Champs, even though they'd never taken part in the event. OK, so they had us on creativity.

At exactly 11:28 AM, following a thorough and humorous briefing from Larry on the rules and regulations (the "no sabotage" statute was particularly unpopular), Team Mixed Bag sprinted off toward our first destination—without the slightest hint of a plan of attack. Like a class full of overachieving kindergarteners let loose on an unsuspecting playground, we didn't know exactly what we were doing, but we were doing it with gusto.

It was then that a wonderful thing happened, brought out no doubt by the dynamics of a team-based competition. We just naturally meshed. Our communication patterns fell into automatic synch, with each of us subconsciously putting forth our particular strengths when called for and stepping back to let others lead when their respective strengths were in play. And we hustled. Nobody wanted to be the weak link in terms of keeping up. Remember my previous mention of knee problems and difficulty running? On this day I was magically cured (the *next* day…well, that's a different story).

We arrived at the finish line exactly 2 hours and 59 minutes after we had started. Bob was there to greet us—and while perhaps it was my imagination, he appeared startled to see us so soon. We were told that we had missed setting the course record by just 17 minutes, but that might have fallen under the category of "I bet you say that to all the winners." Multiple hugs and high fives ensued all around, followed by a beer (or two) to fuel the animated discussion of how we might conceivably have been able to shave 18 minutes off our time.

As each of the other teams finished, they were met with a rousing ovation from those who had preceded them, and classy displays of congratulations flowed freely throughout the awards ceremony. I won't reveal what our hard-won prize was; let's just say I didn't need to add a Personal Articles rider onto my property insurance policy. But it was precious just the same. In fact, it made my History Box.

I'm not exactly sure of the origins of the History Box, but for as long as I can remember, anything that had special meaning to me went into it. Little League trophies, ticket stubs, newspapers that marked the dates of major happenings, wedding invitations from close friends—all of that stuff. Not just anything goes into the History Box (which, truth be told, has grown over the years into a series of four boxes); it has to be representative of what is truly important to me. I think of it as a time capsule that, if unearthed a century from now, would provide its discoverers with everything needed for them to understand what made this "Tim person" tick. And my Amazing L.A. Race swag, however humble, was included as testament to the fact that even old guys can occasionally generate enough adrenaline to compete and win.

As I was packing my memento away in History Box #4, I was reminded of the Synchronized Team Skating Nationals and particularly about the awards presentation. I remembered being somewhat surprised that the fourth-place finishers had been added to the medal ceremony—and thinking in particular that there had to be something a little more...sparkly, perhaps, than a pewter medal. As I sat there sifting through the remnants of my recall of the Periodic Table of Elements for alternatives to pewter, it occurred to me that those medals—like the gold, silver, and bronze ones—were destined for their recipients' versions of the History Box. And in future generations, anyone who comes across them will know that their original owner had competed—that they may have lost more than they won, but that they competed.

It was one of those good news/bad news things. I had located my Game Junkie...but found him to be ethereal. Much like the 2-1-2 before it, the Amazing L.A. Race was a one-shot deal whose magic came out of nowhere. There and gone, it wasn't something that could be summoned up again at will. Which quite honestly irritated the crap out of me. Mostly because I had seen with my own eyes that others could do it with regularity.

I speak, of course, of kickball.

Yes, kickball. The red-rubber-balled hallmark of elementary school recess everywhere. They do still have recess in elementary school, don't they? Never mind...it would be too much for me to take if they don't. And besides, I'm talking about kickball for grown-ups. *Alleged* grown-ups, anyway.

I say this with authority: if you are young, socially inclined, and even marginally athletic, your life can be immeasurably enhanced simply by typing "kickball.com" into your Internet browser. This will introduce you to WAKA—the World Adult Kickball Association.

Then again, chances are that WAKA has already infiltrated your city and is hiding in plain sight while earnestly orchestrating Big Fun. Under their auspices, scores of adult kickball leagues have been formed, spreading across 32 (and counting) different states. There's even rumored to be a WAKA league cavorting about in London's Hyde Park. Literally thousands of grown men and women have given over to chasing that red rubber ball that you remember from childhood. Only, this time, the postgame spread is usually cold beer and wings instead of warm milk and graham crackers. In fact, each league (or division, in WAKA-speak) is strongly encouraged to secure a host bar when developing its charter.

A prototypical WAKA team consists of men and women in their twenties and thirties, possessed of wildly varied levels of athletic skill. The emphasis is on socializing and, shocking as this may seem, not everyone takes the winning and losing thing deadly seriously. What's really the most surprising thing about adult kickball is that it took so long for the idea to gain critical mass. The WAKA motto sums it up nicely: "Best Parties. Best Games. Best Friends." Note what gets top billing there.

At this point you may be thinking that all that's missing from this picture is a road trip. Funny you should say that. For as if competing and socializing with like-minded others on a weekly basis wasn't enough to entice people to sign up, there is the annual WAKA Founders Cup Weekend, a veritable kickball binge that culminates in the modestly titled World Kickball Championship Game. Now I ask you—what sports walkabout could possibly be considered complete without experiencing this?

And so it was that after a leisurely five-and-a-half-hour drive, I found myself unfolding from my car and stretching in the warm sunshine of Desert Breeze Park, on Las Vegas' west side. As I did so, it was impossible not to be at least somewhat awed by the spectacle that greeted me—once I got past the strange notion of "kickball" and "awe" occupying the same mind space. Acres and acres of open parkland stretched out before me, covered entirely by prefabricated kickball fields. And by "prefabricated" I mean somebody went out with a measuring tape, walked off distances, and plopped down rubber bases. *Poof*—instant kickball diamond.

Mind you, this was not my first rodeo in terms of sussing out the context and rules of engagement at a sporting event. But all around me, things were transpiring that needed some expertise in translation. Fortunately for me, there were ten full-time WAKA officials on-site for the event, and they were walking around bearing lanyard tags that displayed their names and the simple words, Ask Me. So I did. Repeatedly. I'm not positive, but toward the end of the day I thought I saw one of them attempting like mad to scratch those words off his name tag when he saw me approaching. Another had written an addendum in crayon: Unless you're that annoying walkabout guy.

At the cost of acquiring *persona non grata* status, though, I was eventually able to cobble together the following history of the event. Both WAKA and the Founders Cup were born in 1998. Since WAKA's original divisions were in the D.C. area, that inaugural Cup event was played there as well—with just four teams taking part (as opposed to the nearly 100 teams on hand for this rendition).

Recently, and much to their credit, the WAKA organizers took to heart feedback received from member teams who don't necessarily have the skill level or the inclination to play cutthroat kickball all day long—but who still want to experience Founders Cup Weekend. In response they created the Kickball Games, whose sole goal is to offer round-robin play between teams just looking to have some fun. While the Founders Cup is an often hyper-competitive tournament that ultimately crowns the World Kickball Champions, the Kickball Games are equal parts competition and costume ball.

Think of it this way: the Kickball Games are to the Founders Cup what beer pong is to table tennis and what keg ball is to softball. But with much more inventive uniforms.

Standing on the hill that bisected the north side of Desert Breeze Park, it was like watching the casts of dozens of different senior class plays as they cross-migrated lock, stock, and dugout from one diamond to another. And by "dugout," I mean pop-up tents supplied by the teams themselves. Once a particular game was over, four team members would each pick up a tent leg and lug the whole assemblage over to their next assigned field. As best as I can recall, we never had to carry around our own dugout at Windermere Elementary School, but hey—these are the sacrifices you make to play in the big time.

In case you were wondering…yes, the WAKA brand of kickball is pretty much like you remember it from your favorite schoolyard. There are a few pretty notable exceptions, though. First of all, instead of just rolling the ball benignly toward home plate, most pitchers use some combination of throwing and rolling the ball with a sidearm motion. As a result, the ball spins, curves, and bounces up to the plate, making it much harder to contact solidly. Balls and strikes are called, so you can theoretically walk or strike out, although to be honest I didn't see a single instance of either.

Second, the game is played more like baseball than I remembered. For example, securing an out by throwing the ball to the base ahead of a runner is far more common than throwing the ball *at* the runner, as we used to do. This makes perfect sense to me now, because missing the runner with the ball causes it to go bouncing off into the distance while everybody gleefully circles the bases. How did our razor-sharp eight-year-old minds not pick up on that subtle aspect of the game?

Last, and most important, there is actual *strategy* involved in kickball as it is played at this elite level. Merely running up and kicking the ball as hard as you can doesn't cut it here. I attribute this largely to the fact that there are 11 defensive players on the field—seven men and four women. And get this: *all of them are paying attention!* Billy and Sally are not running around in the outfield throwing stones at each other. Dusty has not become fascinated by the dandelions behind second base. Jennifer isn't screaming and fleeing across the infield to escape the butterflies in hot pursuit. This is a radical departure from the game I thought I knew.

During the early rounds of Founders Cup play, rubber balls were bouncing as far as the eye could see, making it reminiscent of the midweek day that I'd spent at the U.S. Open, where the sound of tennis balls being struck was all-encompassing. As the Open progresses, a tighter and tighter circle is drawn around the stadium courts until ultimately only Arthur Ashe Stadium is in use. And indeed at the Founders Cup, the equivalent of Arthur Ashe Stadium was Field #4, which drew its lofty standing due to the fact that it: (a) had actual foul lines drawn on it, (b) was well positioned under the park's best bank of light stands, and (c) required a very short walk to reach the beer garden.

About that beer garden…as best as I could tell, it wasn't open to fans. But then again, that might be because there weren't any fans. Well, any other than me, and I was more of an, umm…investigative journalist. Yeah, that's it—"investigative journalist." The reason for the lackluster turnout of spectators was simple. They would have been completely superfluous to the event. This was sport created of the kickballers, by the kickballers, and for the kickballers.

Make no mistake about it—after the initial novelty wore off, this was not a lot of fun to watch. But that's completely beside the point. It wasn't meant to be watched. It was meant simply to be played. And if you were there just watching (investigative journalism aside), well…what the hell's wrong with you? Why weren't you playing?

I got to thinking about this as the last strains of "The Star-Spangled Banner" trailed away prior to the World Kickball Championship Game (yes, the national anthem was sung—and sung extremely well—by a WAKA staffer, naturally). Not to get too Margaret Mead-y or anything, but there were societal forces at play. The generation of folks who were there enjoying the experience had grown up with far more recreational options than their forebears. So it stands to reason that they'll expect nothing less as they grow older—for themselves and their kids. Sports participation will, if it hasn't already, become a given.

This brought to mind a "special report" that I'd read in one business publication or another. The gist of it was that the sports industry would be wise to pay heed to the fact that kids coming of age now are far more interested in doing rather than watching—even if the "doing" is merely exercising their thumbs while playing video games. As I stood there watching the team captains for Panik Attack and the Other Shot Callers being briefed prior to the first pitch (roll?), that point became crystal clear to me. And I was envious. Scratch that—I was downright jealous.

See, WAKA doesn't work for me. The cold, hard reality is that I'm too old. There's probably not enough liability insurance in all of WAKA Nation to cover participation by geezers like me. Moreover, there's something undeniably creepy about a 50-year-old hanging out after the game in the team bar with a group of people young enough to be his children. There's no getting around it. My time has passed—consider this my *Requiem for a Kickballer*. If you can do so with a straight face, that is.

As the desert's evening chill descended, a small but shrill voice tried to make itself heard: *Maybe your Game Junkie is destined to live out his days in the comforts of your History Box.* Perhaps at one point earlier in the walkabout I would have shrugged my shoulders in silent agreement. But the new me was having a hard time surrendering.

TWENTY-TWO
Wouldn't It Be Ice If We Were Older…

IF I EVER GET A LITTLE FUZZY on the details of my motivation for leaving my native land of New England, all I have to do is travel there during the winter. Within moments after arrival I am reminded of two things: (1) It is dark and cold, and (2) I hate dark and cold.

Nonetheless, I had a walkabout to finish up, and it wouldn't be complete without the inclusion of a healthy dose of winter sports. I do have to admit that, once actually on-site at one of my Ice & Snow events, each was enjoyable in its own I-can-no-longer-feel-my-toes kind of way. It was the process of *getting to* each venue that provided a steady stream of…how do I put this?…opportunities to exhibit problem-solving skills. Two feet of opportunity one day. Negative-29 wind-chilled degrees of opportunity the next. Seventy miles of ice-encrusted pavement disguised as opportunity the next.

But like any good taxi driver, I considered that what was behind me was behind me. And the sun had risen brightly on the morning of the Connecticut Open short track speedskating event. The alternate title for this affair was the January Thaw, which turned out to be a blatant case of false advertising. Because when I arrived at Trinity College's Koeppel Center ice rink, the temperature was in the teens. In fairness, though, the January Thaw moniker was accurate on a strictly *technical* basis, but only because it had been about ten degrees colder than that throughout the previous week of the IGTS Tour's Great Northeast Winter Sports Swing.

This was one of those events that I was going into…well…cold. I didn't know the slightest thing about speedskating except that at last count, Apolo Ohno (or was it Apollo Creed?) had won somewhere around a million Olympic gold medals in the sport. How difficult could it be to pick it up, though? Everybody starts at the same time in the same place, and the first one to skate across the finish line wins. Right?

Well…yes. And no.

See, at the January Thaw, there were 13 different groups (i.e. competitive divisions), each skating in differing race distances. And frequently—but not always—there were multiple "heats" (a misnomer if there ever was one) for the same group and distance. So the first skater across the finish line in any given race may be that event's winner…or they may not be. It all depended upon whether that race was a heat or a final and how the skater's time stacked up against the best time in that group and distance in other heats. If there were any. Got it?

Fortunately for me, the event's unflappable organizer Lovey Russo nicely filled in some of the gaps in my knowledge by describing how this particular event had been structured. In order to make it the best possible competition for the elite skaters, they had chosen to use a hybrid system for assigning groups. Instead of simply clustering people together by age, they *began* with age-based assignments and then reassigned skaters who had earned good "seed times" in qualifying trials previously held. In this way, talented young competitors were able to transcend their age groups and test themselves against the overall best in the Open group. And I was told to be advised—there was a lot of "overall best" on hand.

While this was billed as the Connecticut Open, it was actually equal parts *Connecticut* and *Open*. The former confirmed that the event host was Lovey's own Connecticut Speedskating Club, and the latter highlighted the fact that there were skaters there from clubs all over the Northeast…and well beyond. Lovey rattled off some of the accomplishments previously posted by many of the athletes on-site—especially the rising stars. But it wasn't the youngsters' growing list of achievements that Lovey spoke the most glowingly about. That was reserved for her comments on the culture of speedskating and the social opportunities the sport offers. She pointed out with pride that these kids had grown up skating with a group of acquired friends from various other places, which proved to be invaluable in helping them broaden their horizons.

But it was what she said next that perked up my ears.

"And of course, those in the more mature divisions do it for the exercise and the camaraderie."

Say what?

Without the benefit of a program, I hadn't had much information about the skaters who I'd watched thus far that day. And with the helmets and suits they wore, it was hard to determine ages and even genders. From my viewpoint, each heat consisted of an androgynous group of individuals skating as quickly as they could around the track. Some skaters went fast and some…not so fast. Indeed, wide divergences of talent made it fairly common for the leaders in some heats to lap the stragglers.

As luck would have it, Lovey pointed out that at that very moment, a heat in the Masters group was about to begin. I quickly relocated to a spot on the boards where I could get the best close-up view of the skaters as they went by. And when they did, I saw some faces whose age bore a striking similarity to my own. As you might expect, most of those faces belonged to the bodies that wound up being lapped by the younger guns. But not always. I'll be damned.

I found out later that what I was witnessing was not an anomaly. In fact, most short-track speedskating clubs are populated by athletes of all ages and stripes who have chosen a nontraditional outlet for answering the inner call to compete—even if they are only competing against their own personal bests. And anyway, not all speedskating club competition is of the traditional variety. Lovey told me about two types of events that she would have loved to have included in the January Thaw, had there been time. Both would have had all the competitors in each group on the ice at the same time. One was a 3,000-meter race, in which everybody starts at the same time and those who are lapped must immediately leave the ice. The other was a relay race, which Lovey laughingly described as "simply wild."

Hmmmm…

* * *

Broomstones Curling Club is located in Wayland, a leafy western suburb of Boston. It's been around since 1968, and currently boasts an active membership of about 400, a number that pretty much pushes capacity. From October through March there are leagues almost every night of the week and special events and competitions on most weekends. And Broomstones is every bit as much a social club as it is a sporting club. These people *interact*. There's evidently something about ice that accentuates the unity gene.

I had become a wellspring of knowledge about Broomstones thanks to Sheila Hanley, whom I met in the parking lot as I was trying to figure out: (a) how a national championship competition came to be held at this somewhat tucked-away venue, and (b) how I could rush the door and get in without a ticket. As soon as I could find the door, that is.

"Come on in with me! *Of course* spectators are welcome." And she was right—an Amway convention has nothing on Broomstones when it comes to inclusiveness. Which was a fortunate twist of fate, for I had come a very long way to witness the U.S. Men's Senior Curling Nationals, the pinnacle of competition in this country for curlers 50 and older. My gracious host gave me a quick tour, offered me a refreshment, and then said cheerfully, "If you have any questions…" Poor, sweet Sheila. When she awoke that morning she had no idea. For in fact, I did have a few.

As it turned out, educating me became a team sport in and of itself, one that drew no shortage of participants. As I sat in the spectator gallery— the *warm, comfortable* spectator gallery, I might add—I learned pretty quickly that curling enthusiasts are knowledgeable and earnestly engaged in the action. Before and after every "throw," a running dialogue on strategy took place all around me. Of course I had nothing to add to the open-ended conversation, but with the help of Sheila and others who patiently answered my elementary questions, it wasn't long before I could piece together not only what had just happened but what I might expect next. Not necessarily well enough to weigh in on the dialogue, mind you, but certainly well enough to start enjoying the contest.

First things first—I learned that the big round stone that gathers all of the attention is called…a stone. And people "throw" the stone, although in truth the motion involved is more of a push—or for those with well-developed triceps, a back-then-forward motion more akin to rolling an object, as in bowling.

The target that curlers are fixated upon is called the "house." It is 12 feet wide, made up of multicolored concentric rings, and located about 100 feet down the ice "sheet" from the point at which one begins a throw. In the center of the house is a one-foot-wide yellow circle of promised land called the "button"—which I'm guessing clears up any mystery about the origins of the term "right on the button." Well, it was mysterious to me, anyway.

Matches are broken down into "ends," of which there are eight, each consisting of all four players on each team having two throws apiece—for a total of 16. The overall goal is to end each end, so to speak, with one of your team's stones in the house and closest to the button. That gives you one point and, more important, control of the score for that end—your opponent is shut out. Once you control the score, you add an additional point for each of your team's stones that rests closer to the button than the other team's best throw.

As you can imagine, playing the game is not solely about landing your throws near the button. Sometimes you are protecting a previous throw by setting up a shield. Sometimes you are trying to nudge a teammate's stone closer to the button. Sometimes you are trying to redirect an opponent's stone away from the button. And sometimes you are trying to blow the whole thing up by clearing the house. Trust me—I'm just skimming the surface here (curling humor) on how strategies change from throw to throw. I received perhaps the best, most succinct description of curling when I was told that it is often referred to as "chess on ice."

If there is one image that the average sports fan conjures up when the sport of curling is mentioned, it's that of the sweepers vigorously doing their thing to the ice that lies just ahead of the stone their teammate has just thrown. The ice on a dedicated curling surface is slightly pebbled, and the material on the pad at the business end of a curling "broom" is the somewhat abrasive texture of your average dishwashing Dobie. Rapidly scrubbing the ice creates enough friction to melt the tiny bumps in the surface, thus regulating the distance traveled by the stone. Well-executed sweeping can also cause slight curves in the overall arc of the throw. And when lines can curve, the strategic possibilities become endless.

Curling is a sport of honor, tradition, and respect, the depth of which I had only seen in sumo wrestling. You are about as likely to see a taunt during a match as you are to see somebody using an AutoLoc dual-exhaust flamethrower as a broom. In the traditional beginning to a championship match, both teams are "piped on" to the ice by an actual live piper who typically plays "Scotland the Brave." The teams then face each other and offer a toast of Drambuie (or ginger ale, where appropriate) and a simple but heartfelt, "Good curling." And when it's all over, the winning team buys a celebratory round of drinks for all concerned. Every time. No questions asked.

"So, do you want to give it a try?"

The question came from Jamie Hutchinson, a Broomstones member who had been one of those patiently fielding my questions. The second semifinal match of the Senior Nationals had just concluded, and there would be a break of some length before the championship match began. And the ice was just sitting there. I think that Jamie serves on the club's New Membership Committee—and if she doesn't, she should. For she actually made sliding around on ice in temperatures significantly below those found on the coldest of SoCal days sound…well, almost inviting.

Initially I tried faking an old war injury. But that required faking participation in an old war, and she wasn't buying it. She was a skilled curling pusher—"Here, Tim, the first one's free. I think you'll like it." And I had to admit that the washed-up jock in me was curious to see if I could perform the essentials of this complex new sport that I was growing fond of.

So I signed a waiver form (which actually contained the word "death" in it—and not merely in a "freezing to death" context), and minutes later I made my debut on the ice. Just to seal the deal, Jamie brought in the Big Gun to help with my tutorial: Greg Eisenhauer, who I understood to be a curling club's equivalent of a golf course's head pro and head greenskeeper all rolled into one.

The key thing that I learned right away about curling is that it requires balance. A *lot* of balance. You're propelling yourself forward on a sheet of ice while trying to maneuver a rock that's 40 pounds and a foot and half wide. There's a lot to think about. Like...*Did the waiver that I just signed* really *contain the word* death? for example. But not to worry. Between Jamie and Greg, I received very specific instructions, and when my big moment came, I was actually able to execute the push and glide without wiping out. Of course I forgot to actually throw the stone. Is the word "mulligan" somewhere in the curling lexicon?

"That was great!" Jamie and Greg lied in unison.

On the second and third tries I was able to actually thrust the stone in the general direction of the house, but the form I displayed in my first attempt had...*moderated*, shall we say. In other words, I barely avoided doing a full turtle. But in subsequent throws, as I flailed around the ice in full Zamboni mode, the only thing I was thinking about was that I was having fun! Seriously. I was actually laughing, even on the occasion on which my knee hit the ice with a resounding crack.

At one point in the day, somebody had shared with me that curling was "easy to learn but hard to master." Amen. My lesson taught me that in addition to balance and decent hand-eye coordination, flexible hips, glutes, and hamstrings are strongly recommended if one wants to maximize their skill level and enjoyment of the sport. I'm a little short on the "flexibility" thing—always have been. I was the only kid in my kindergarten class who couldn't successfully pull off the cross-legged style of floor sitting that was massively in vogue during story time.

There must be a lot of limber hips and legs out there, though, because in 2010 more than 40 new curling clubs were formed across the country. Most don't have the luxury of a curling-specific facility like Broomstones and thus have to make some accommodations to curl on a regulation hockey rink. The point is, however, that the sport is spreading inexorably—and the added visibility that a Winter Olympics provides every fourth year spikes the growth chart.

While I had seen that speedskating draws some older participants, the sport is still largely the province of the young when it comes to competition. With curling, however, it began to dawn on me that perhaps curlers are like a fine single-malt Scotch, getting better with age. Hear me out on this...

While in many amateur sports, those eligible to compete in the Senior division are welcome to try to qualify for the Open division championship, rarely do seniors seriously contend for a national Open title. Not so in curling. In fact, you could make the argument that the *better* curlers are the older ones (within chronological reason, of course), because experience and technique account for so much of what separates the elite from the rest. And indeed, the defending Open National Champions were on hand at Broomstones—a team of *seniors* from St. Paul, Minnesota. But their best-in-the-country-bar-none status did them little good here, as they were bounced out of these Senior Nationals in the semifinals.

I asked a fellow observer—and clearly knowledgeable curler—if, in fact, older is actually better in the sport. He gave some considerable thought to the proposition before granting that I might be on to something. Pointing out that the average number of years of competitive experience among the teams on hand that week was 20, he ventured that a curler's "prime years" might just be between 35 and 55; beyond that age the physical requirements of throwing the stone and spending so much time on your feet in a tournament are just enough of an additional consideration to tip the balance slightly in favor of a younger team. And then there's the eyesight thing. "You absolutely need to clearly see lines at this level of competition," my new friend offered. And by "lines" he meant those that are strategically conjured by compiling all of the tangible, visible clues.

Woohoo! I'm in my prime! Well, theoretically, anyway. Now I just need to retroactively add those 20 years of competitive experience.

The overall point, though, was this: twice in a span of a couple weeks I had stumbled onto people who had found a way to trot out their Game Junkie on a semiregular basis, despite having qualified for AARP's full frontal marketing assault. And I really had to hand it to them. Frankly, though, I couldn't see myself taking up either speedskating or curling.

On a bitterly cold Vermont day, I had previously attended the Winter Dew Tour's Killington Slopestyle Championship with my dear friend and ski diva, Dawn-Marie. It was a degree outside. Yup, just that single solitary one. "Not to worry," she said. "You never have to be cold as long as you dress for the weather." Sure enough, she showed up on event day with a small ski shop in the back of her SUV. Gloves the size of industrial oven mittens. Snow shoes (just in case). A ski jacket that a family of five tumbled out of when she pulled it from the car. And Dawn-Marie was right—once dressed for the occasion, I actually did survive. It's just that it's a whole lot easier to dress for the weather when it's 70 degrees and sunny. And truth be told, my particular Game Junkie would undoubtedly balk at being called out to play in conditions that required dressing in several layers.

TWENTY-THREE

Grass Roots

THANKFULLY, the Great Northeast Winter Sports Swing had ended without frostbite, and all that was left was another by-now patented grand migration back to L.A. True to my New England roots, I had fully anticipated the "You caahn't get the-yah from he-yah" nature of the trip and was well steeled for the trio of separate plane rides it would take to arrive home. In fact, it gave me a chance to put my Southwest Seating Strategy to the test. See, given the absence of assigned seating on Southwest Airlines, timing is everything if one has any hope for a quasi-comfortable flight. Unfortunately, my timing was bad. I had forgotten to check in online the previous evening and therefore found myself in the dreaded *B* group of boarders.

In my younger, more naïve days I would have scouted out one of the few remaining aisle seats at the back of the plane and hoped against hope that the center seat beside me would go unoccupied. But in these cost-conscious days, a Southwest flight is almost always completely full, thus prompting a strategy adjustment. Now I board with the *specific intention of sitting in a middle seat*—because that's the only way you can guarantee the identity of your neighbors. I simply look for the smallest two people I can find in any given row, give them my best "Aw, shucks" smile, and ask if that seat in between them is taken. And that is exactly how I came to make the acquaintance of Danette Kelley Smith.

She too was on her way to the West Coast, to scout out a potential college with her daughter. And to play in a professional poker tournament. For virtually anyone else, this was an unlikely combination of activities. But as I learned, Danette's entire family is not well versed in being conventional.

We got to chatting, and when I explained to her what exactly had brought me to the Northeast, Danette replied without missing a beat, "So I assume you're covering paintball at some point?"

Blink, blink.

I wasn't aware that anyone actually "covered" paintball, but then again there were a lot of things I didn't know about what I had previously assumed to be the province of corporate team-building outings. Like, for example, that there are *multiple* professional paintball leagues in North America alone. And how did this effervescent mom/Mary Kay independent sales director/aspiring poker superstar know this? Because her son Ryan played in three such leagues (PSP, NPPL, and CXBL, for those of you scoring at home).

Of course he did.

Over the course of the next hour, I learned more about paintball than I could ever have imagined. I listened intently as Danette described how her husband, Randy, had taken Ryan to join him at one of those previously mentioned company outings. Instantly hooked, they both embraced the game and its culture of ultimate teamwork completely.

In a pattern that had come to play itself out repeatedly for me, I experienced vicariously the unbridled passion for a sport that can only come from giving one's self over to it in both mind and body. I was fascinated by the dedication that Ryan and his teammates had for a game that is contested waaaaay outside the mainstream of well-known sports—and that offers next to nothing in the way of remuneration for even the best players in the world. Pro paintballers are commonly known to practice for six, seven, even eight hours at a stretch on weekend days in between competitions. And for Ryan's Chicago-based team, Distortion, it had recently paid off with a second-place finish in Division 2 X-ball at the 2010 PSP World Cup.

Danette brimmed with enthusiasm as she described the upcoming season and the aggressive schedule on the docket, finishing with, "And of course in April you'll be at the NPPL tournament in Huntington Beach, won't you?"

Of course. And since I got the strong impression that Danette Kelley Smith doesn't forget promises made, I knew that my list of 50 different sports to witness in person had just grown by one, IGTS Tour or no Tour. When we deplaned and headed for our respective connecting flights, I knew I'd see this particular sports fan again.

On the final leg of my day in the friendly skies I had another déjà vu experience. It wasn't fully Blair Dunlap-ian in import, but then again, what could possibly be? No, this was a little easier to connect the dots on. I was reflecting back upon my day at Broomstones Curling Club and wondering why the rules and strategies—even the nuanced ones—for a game that I had never seen played before had seemed so familiar to me. Then it hit me. And I was mentally transported back to a summer day at the Newport Harbor Lawn Bowling Club.

The Lawn Bowls U.S. Open had taken place during the most painful portion of my walkabout. It had fallen smack in the middle of a rapid-fire string of events that helped give rise to the distressing disillusionment with the Big-Time Sports that I've previously shared. At the time, it had been a "checklist" event—something to attend and catalog while focused on the theoretically more important sporting events to come.

Now, with plenty of airborne time on my hands, I dug out my notes on that "lost" event, looking forward to reliving it with a different perspective. Wouldn't you know—the first note scrawled at the top of the initial page of those event notes said it all: "*I don't get it. How can lawn bowls not be one of the most popular games played in the country?*" Maybe I wasn't as clueless at the time as I thought…

The very first thing I noticed about the Lawn Bowls U.S. Open was the smell. It smelled like golf—more specifically, like a putting green. And to put a finer point on it, like a putting green first thing in the morning. Which was really no coincidence, because the Newport Harbor Lawn Bowling Club's entire playing area was one big painstakingly manicured putting green equivalent. As soon as I opened my car door in the parking lot, the life-affirming scent wafted out to greet me.

I don't know why, but when I set out to attend the Open, I had expected to find a pretty tense environment. Certainly I thought the word "shush" would come into play with regularity, delivered with a harsh stare and pursed lips. I also assumed that Newport Harbor Bowling Club would be private. Maybe it had something to do with the word *Club* in the name. But when it took me more or less 20 uninterrupted steps to go from my car to a prime viewing seat on a greenside bench, it gave me pause. No admission fee. No ID check. No jacketed personnel eyeing me suspiciously. No full-cavity body search in pursuit of a camera or cell phone. Hmmmm... *What kind of exclusive, snooty sports environment is this?* I wondered.

The short answer is that it was the kind of "snooty" environment that appears dying to be infiltrated. One in which everyone with whom I made eye contact smiled warmly and asked if they could answer any questions for me. Not to be too harsh, but these people are in serious need of snooty lessons. And on top of it all, Newport Harbor Lawn Bowling Club was *not*, in fact, a private facility. It is part of a larger, meticulously maintained public recreation facility in Corona del Mar, California. Open to anyone who wants to learn the game. It didn't take long for me to conclude that this entire sport is hopelessly *inclusive*.

I'll grant you—the name is kind of quirky. Why not call it lawn bowling instead of lawn bowls? At the very least, that might cut down on any confusion created by the fact that "bowls" is the name of the game, the equipment, *and* the action taken. As in, "He bowls with his lawn bowls in lawn bowls."

Perhaps the repetition is part of an overall scheme to make absolutely, positively sure that lawn bowls is *not* mistaken for bocce. Yes, the two bear a family resemblance. But lumping them together is like saying that the Soapbox Derby and NASCAR racing are the same thing because both involve four tires and a steering wheel. Bocce is typically played at picnics by people holding a beer in one hand and winging the ball as hard as they can with the other (being careful not to spill, of course). Like bocce, the game of lawn bowls is very simple to learn. Unlike bocce, though, it is maddeningly difficult to perfect. Why? One word—*curve.*

The lawn bowls used in lawn bowls…oh, the hell with it—the lawn bowling balls—are not exactly round. They are perfectly smooth and circular around the middle circumference, but astride that middle band are two dissimilarly weighted sides, making the ball not quite spheroid. When bowlers roll the ball along that smooth circumference, the structurally uneven distribution of weight (its "bias," in lawn bowls lingo) causes it to curve. Exactly how much it curves depends upon how the bowler incorporates its overall heft and bias into the speed and aim of any given roll. And that's where the kinship with curling begins to emerge.

What separates the sports of lawn bowls and curling from their less cerebral cousins is that angles and trajectories come into play, as opposed to the simple aiming and propelling of something from point *A* to point *B.* When it's feasible to pull off a shot that can actually circle around behind your opponent's position, you've got yourself an entirely new game dimension.

Scoring in lawn bowls and curling is remarkably similar. In both sports, there is a target that the competitors are trying to cozy up to—curling's "button" is lawn bowl's "jack." And in both sports, only the team that winds up closest to the target can score points in any given "end." So the key to success lies in how skillfully you can negotiate your rolls through and around the scrum of stones or bowls.

As related as curling and lawn bowls are, however, there are two major differences between the two. One is the severity of the curves. While in curling the curvilinear lines are subtle, given the amount of sweeping work needed to affect a curve, in lawn bowls it is not uncommon to see wide, generous arcs. If you are a fan of angles, lines, and parabolas (and who among us isn't?), you'll love lawn bowls. This sport possesses the constantly shifting geometry of soccer or basketball, the linear imagination of golf, and the carom angles of pool, all wrapped up into one—and coming into play on almost every shot.

The second major difference is temperature. If curling is chess on ice, then lawn bowls is chess on grass. Which, I couldn't help but notice, is a lot warmer. And I'm a sucker for "warmer."

Neither curling nor lawn bowls lacks for advocates. In each of the venues that I visited, that came blindingly through in the way that folks who love and support their sport talked about it. And with lawn bowls in particular, they were anxious to both trumpet its merits and overcome stereotypes about their sport being musty and outdated. One of the tournament officials whom I had the pleasure of chatting with told me that lawn bowls suffers from the perception that it is played by "people primarily dressed in white suits sporting primarily white hair."

Truth be told, the competitors spread out over the Newport Harbor Lawn Bowling Club's 15 or so playing lanes (or "rinks") did trend older. At first glance. But as I began to watch more closely, I couldn't help notice that many were much closer to my own age—which is to say they were wicked young. Or so. And upon further inspection, I realized that, especially in the case of the teams that had traveled there from elsewhere in the world, many of the bowlers were not only still attached to their original hair, but it was still its original color. Some bowlers, in fact, were young enough to be on the *listening* end of stories that began with, "When I was your age…"

As I became absorbed in the tournament action, I found myself almost involuntarily moving closer and closer to it. Seen from close range in this way, the bowlers' affection for the game oozed from every match. In a display of fan-friendliness that set an absolutely unattainable bar, I found that the competitors were happy to answer questions and interact in between ends. And sometimes in between shots! With a smile, no less, as well as a sincere, "If you have any other questions, please don't hesitate to ask."

Time passed quickly. One match after another reached its conclusion, and the bowlers repaired to the clubhouse patio for drinks and laughs. Eventually, just one match was left unsettled. The team of Ed Quo and Dan

Christensen was locked in a tightly contested battle with Aaron Zangl and Tony Baer, who, it turned out, happened to be representing Hermosa Beach Lawn Bowling Club. Yes, the very same Hermosa Beach Lawn Bowling Club that is literally just down the road from my home. Upon making this discovery, my biased rooting interest kicked in. Team Hermosa had been down big early but had been gradually closing the gap coming down the stretch. Entering the 18th and final end, they were down four points—a tough number to make up in one end but certainly not impossible. The match began to draw a lot of attention from the terrace, as each bowl became a potential make-or-break one.

One intrigued onlooker was bowler Chris Davis who, after taking a close-up look at the match firsthand, walked my way smiling and shaking his head. I asked for an impromptu analysis, and he was more than happy to provide it. In fact, he took a seat on the bench next to me and supplied nothing less than a strategic play-by-play for the remainder of the contest.

Chris had been bitten by the bug seven years earlier. At the time, he had been vaguely aware of the existence of a lawn bowls club near his home in Seattle and was listening to an NPR segment on a completely different topic when it was mentioned on the air that the club was holding an open house. He decided to check it out. A sports addiction was born.

I had taken my conversation with Chris at face value at the time; he was yet another earnest proponent of his particular sport with whom I'd shared an enjoyable conversation. But now, almost a half year and several dozen sports events later, I started to think more seriously about that whole day and the sport that had been on display. And I went back to the original note that I'd scrawled—indeed, why isn't lawn bowls one of the most popular games in the country?

Without question, the lawn bowls environment is friendly, inclusive, and very social in a relaxed, low-key way. In other words, the kind of atmosphere that I had witnessed Americans seeking out in droves to satisfy their recreational urges. More than 25 million people play golf in the U.S., and only slightly fewer play tennis—and virtually all of them do so at least in part for the communal aspects of each game. So why is it that lawn bowls garners a tiny fraction of the attention in America that it does in Australia, for example—where there are professional leagues and television coverage? Many teams had in fact traveled to the Lawn Bowls U.S. Open from places like New Zealand, Northern Ireland, Wales, and Canada, in addition to Australia. And in all of those countries, it's not unusual for people to take up the game and fall in love with it when they are as young as eight or nine years of age.

I started to think about it on a broader scale. Lawn bowls originated in England. Curling is widely thought to have been born in Scotland. As was golf. Three of the world's greatest social sports, all from the same relatively small geographical area—an area that just happens to be the land of origin of our own country. All three stress widespread participation, competition, and camaraderie in equal parts.

Here in America, we have a proud heritage of inventing sports as well. Many of which have since evolved to a current state which celebrates in equal parts: passive spectating, trash-talking or otherwise demeaning your competitors, flamboyant narcissism, and the naked pursuit of obscene amounts of money.

Apparently something didn't translate on the voyage over from the U.K.

"What's wrong with Americans?" I mumbled. "Why don't they see lawn bowls for all of its benefits and charm and turn out *en masse* to play it? What does a sport have to do to…?"

Wait a second.

I turned to the 800-pound gorilla seated next to me and asked, "Why don't *I* play lawn bowls?" As gorillas tend to do on airplanes, he ignored me. But after a while he turned and said simply, "Why don't you just *play*—period? Pick a sport and just play." Then he went back to his *National Geographic* and banana daiquiri.

He was absolutely right. Badly dressed and generally unhygienic, but right. I had been on a grand tour of the entire sports world, immersed in the games that people play. But it had been almost anthropological. I had been an observer of other people at play. I tried to remember when it was that I had last played a real sport. I couldn't—unless client golf counted. Which, trust me, it doesn't.

That realization got me to thinking. As my walkabout had gathered momentum throughout the year, the number of people following my journey through my blog had increased as well. By this time patterns had emerged, one of which was that my field reports on the second-tier sports spawned exponentially more responses than did blog posts about more mainstream sports. Weeks and weeks after some of those original second-tier event posts had appeared, I would still receive emails and comments posted to the website, all of which were drenched in enthusiasm about that particular sport. Many included invitations to attend subsequent events. Some even offered lessons or similar free instruction—all in the same spirit displayed by Jamie Hutchinson at Broomstones Curling Club.

As I sat considering all of this, my recognition of the bigger picture came clearly into focus: people who *just play* (in the words of my favorite gorilla) are the happiest sports fans in America. And they are wildly interested in sharing their ardor with others. Zealously. Their approach is not unlike that of the puppies at a pet store's Adoption Day—*Come play with us, pleeeeease!* It is sincere, authentic, and representative of everything good about sports.

Meanwhile, yours truly had been, if I may mix my mammalian metaphors, living a sports version of *Goldilocks and the Three Bears*. Kickball was too young; curling and speedskating were too cold. But lawn bowls…

Lawn bowls appears to have all of the elements of sport that are precious to me. It is played outside, in warm weather. It's skill-based but doesn't require years of practice to achieve a level of proficiency at which semiserious competition becomes a plausible option. It doesn't require exceptional strength or agility in order to fully enjoy the benefits of playing. And here's the really good part: the Hermosa Beach Lawn Bowling Club is just 3.9 miles from the palatial world headquarters of the It's Game Time Somewhere Tour.

The first call I made the next day was to schedule a lawn bowls lesson. It was time to *just play*.

* * *

Unbeknownst to me at the time, the direction of my walkabout had been altered before I'd left the driveway on the way to my first event. I know now that for it to have been as meaningful as it was, I had to let go and take things at face value.

For sure I had tried to force things early on. I think the military calls it "mandatory fun." I was determined to right the ship on what was left of my existing sports fandom—repair the decks, sand down the hull, mend the sails. Do a thorough reconditioning. But not actually change course. Little did I know that, like Quint in *Jaws*, I needed a bigger boat. Or at the very least a different one.

Once I backed off and let the current take me, all kinds of wonderful things happened. I'd actually been given a three-for-one deal. My walkabout had indeed awakened my sports fan, but it had also refashioned my sports artisan and ultimately revived the Game Junkie in me. For probably the first time in my life I can now say that I truly love the impact of sports on my life as a spectator, a professional, and a participant. What more could I possibly have asked for?

How about this for a fringe benefit? As the years go by and I come across coverage of the latest rendition of an annual event that I attended during my walkabout, I will no doubt be able to transport myself mentally right back to that event, to that venue. How do I know this? Well, as I write this, it's already happened on multiple occasions. Simply driving by a Little League baseball game in progress, for example, brings all of the sights, sounds, and smells of Lamade Stadium in Williamsport right back to me. I have no reason to believe that this won't always be the case. It's the gift that keeps on giving.

Here's the thing, though: only when I allowed sports to come to me on its own terms did I reap the full benefits. The truly valuable experiences were those that were the most unexpected. Who knew that some of the most interesting athletes I'd meet would be those who had little chance of gaining elite status and no designs on fame or fortune? But they taught me the best lesson of all: to regain *and maintain* the love of sport that I had as I child, all I had to do was *just play*. For to fully appreciate athletic endeavors from any angle or perspective, you must be an athlete, however humble. Once I'd embraced that notion, I had come full circle. I can now relate again to the ball-chasing ten-year-old I used to be—riding my bike down to Windermere School for a pickup game of whatever was in season. I now consider my walk-about to have been the definitive sports do-over.

But there was one more thing left to do. I had to reconcile with an old friend.

Part of what had drawn me inexorably to the sport of lawn bowls was its familiarity to me. In addition to the attractive attributes previously mentioned, it is a game that you can play your whole life—one that always holds out the potential for improvement. It is cerebral in character, involving a strategic plan for play instead of merely athletic reaction. It is a celebration of nature, contested on some of the greenest (and best-smelling) grass to be found. And it is played in an environment of cordiality and mutual respect.

It kinda, sorta sounds like golf.

Taking up lawn bowls was unquestionably enjoyable, but it was more than a little bit like being dropped by a longtime girlfriend and then dating someone who looks just like her. It may or may not have been done out of spite, but there were no doubt some unresolved issues lurking. Who better to consult than the world's best golf therapist/teaching professional, Cindy Miller? I hadn't spoken with Cindy since the great Tour de Golf Tours, when we'd shared both enthusiasm and concern over the fate of the professionals who play on the LPGA Tour. But I certainly needed her now.

Whatever it once had been, I had let my golf game go completely. Other than the 14 holes at the Futures Tour Pro-Am that I shared previously with you, I hadn't played a round that didn't involve directing most of my attention toward an accompanying client or prospect in…well, it might as well have been forever. And practice? Alan Iverson famously exhibited more fondness for practice than had yours truly of late, even though I used to *love* my time at the range. At this point, I was capable of discerning which end of the club to hold, but that was about it. I needed a golf boot camp, and coincidentally enough, the Miller Golf Group offers a program of that very name.

In a feat of favor asking that was positively Olympian, I called Cindy one Sunday morning and bore my soul. I explained to her that I missed golf but knew that if I tried to pick it up again cold turkey, I would be so frustrated I might be tempted to pack it in on the sport for good. Was there perhaps a small chance that I could slip into the back row, so to speak, of one of her Boot Camps? I promised I wouldn't make any noise or do anything to bother the paying customers. I begged. I pleaded. But I was basically wasting my time at that point—I had her at "I want to play golf again."

In full wounded-soul-patrol mode, Cindy was happy to host this reclamation project. I breathed a huge sigh of relief and thanked her profusely. I also felt compelled to warn her about exactly how badly my game had deteriorated. In the spirit of full disclosure, I asked, "Do you know what you're signing up for?" There was a pregnant pause, during which I was certain I'd undone all of my successful panhandling.

But she was merely pausing for effect. "Do you *really* think you can scare me?" she asked.

Mutual paroxysms of laughter followed. I was all the way back.

EPILOGUE

TRUTH BE TOLD, I had received all of the benefits—all of the gifts—that my walkabout could have possibly delivered before it was even over. But I am a goal-oriented creature (the terms "anal retentive" and "obsessive compulsive" are a bit too clinical for me), and I had committed to 100 sports events and 50 different sports. And I was no longer alone in that pursuit.

When I posted the very first entry on the It's Game Time Somewhere blog site, I was pretty confident that only members of my immediate family would read it. I was wrong. Even *they* took a pass. As time went by, though, a funny thing happened. Somehow or another people found me. And they told other people. Google eventually got into the act, and dozens of site visits became hundreds of site visits, which gave way to thousands. I heard from people all over the world, many of whom posed variations on the same two questions: (1) "Is there something seriously wrong with you?" and (2) "Does The Bird have a sister?"

The answers: I still don't quite know, and no, they broke the mold when they made her.

The point, however, is that people were tracking my progress, urging me on and otherwise acting like they'd be less than pleased if I aborted the IGTS Tour on account of prematurely fulfilled expectations. Plus, with the absence of pressure to hunt down and liberate my inner sports fan, the last few weeks consisted of simply a wicked lot of fun. So I "persevered" until the end. Which went something like this...

***

March 20th is just another day—equinox, schmequinox. And Punxsutawney Phil? He's a groundhog, for God's sake! Just another figurehead with no real authority. Ask any sports fan when spring *really* begins, and they'll reply without hesitation, "The day that pitchers and catchers report for spring training." No matter where you live, from the snowiest of Frost Belt towns to the warmest Sun Belt city, the day that baseball's preseason camps open is always the most reliable harbinger of hope. And what is spring, anyway, if not the Official Sponsor of Hope? When spring training begins, every team is a potential World Series champ. Yes, even the Pittsburgh Pirates! OK, that's patently ridiculous, but see how easily the concept can sweep you away? With that in mind, what better place to end my journey than at the home office of renewal?

I bounced that very concept off of my buddy Kels, and he was completely on board with it. Quite literally, in fact—as in on board USAirways flight #245 from Newark to Phoenix. And as luck would have it, his beloved San Francisco Giants were scheduled to play (warning...BIRG alert) *my* Los Angeles Angels of Anaheim in a "pivotal" Cactus League contest. On St. Patrick's Day. Which also happened to be the first day of the NCAA basketball tournament. That flash you may have just seen was that of stars aligning themselves perfectly.

The 100th and final event of the It's Game Time Somewhere Tour positively dictated that I go the extra mile in preparation. I'm sure you'll agree that I couldn't just blindly wander into such a momentous occasion. I needed a dress rehearsal. So on the day before *the day*, I rose at 4:30 AM and poured myself into the car for the six-and-a-half-hour drive to Phoenix's Sky Harbor Airport, where I was to collect the equally sleep-deprived and giddy Kels.

From there it was a short drive to Glendale, to the spring-training complex shared by the L.A. Dodgers and the Chicago White Sox, the latter of whom were hosting Kels' Giants that afternoon.

The game had already started by the time we entered the center-field gate, and even from a distance it was easy to see that San Francisco's star pitcher and cult hero Tim "the Freak" Lincecum was pitching. Much to the delight of Giants fans, he remained there longer than expected. After completing the fifth inning, he left the mound to a standing ovation of appreciation for his day's work. Except that his day wasn't exactly done, for when the bottom of the sixth inning began, he was out there again. Oops. Hey, it was spring training for the fans too.

There's a unique strand in the male DNA that researchers have found responsible for the irresistible road-trip urge. Curiously enough, it's right near the strand labeled simply BEER. The Bird has found the whole topic to be fascinating. "What do you guys actually *do* on road trips?" she once asked. The answer is simple: (a) play games, (b) watch games, and (c) make fun of each other. Is there anything else?

Sure enough, like moths to a flame, Kels and I soon made the acquaintance of three fellow grandstand residents who had come down from North Dakota for some desert biking and some baseball. It was the last day of their trip, and they were in need of some visual keepsakes. Naturally we were happy to help out with the camera work, as were they to reciprocate.

Over the course of the next 48 hours, that scenario replayed itself repeatedly. "Where are you in from? How long you here for?" And of course, "How's your team looking this year?" Everywhere we went, we were greeted by a bright visual mix of shirts and hats bearing the logos of the Cubs, the Reds, the A's, and pretty much every one of the 15 teams that call Arizona their spring-training home. It was like a political convention—minus the nasty name-calling.

The batting heroics of the Giants' rookie first baseman Brandon Belt and Lincecum's seven-strikeout performance combined to serve as catalysts for a 5–3 San Francisco win, which put a warm smile on the faces of Giants fans. The game had clocked in at 2 hours and 28 minutes, and we were left wanting more. We hadn't even finished our bag of peanuts when the final out was recorded. So we lingered in our seats for a few minutes before slowly meandering toward the exit. And that bit of loitering exposed us to an extra bit of entertainment: the Senior Stroll.

If there is one single thing I would pick to personify the difference between spring training and the regular season, it would be the Senior Stroll. At major and minor league ballparks across the country, it's become a universal promotion to offer kids the chance to line up and run around the bases after the pro game is over—and there is never a shortage of takers. Here in Glendale there was a new twist on the concept.

The line of men and women "of a certain age" waiting their turn to stroll began at first base and snaked off the field and all the way up the grandstand aisle, spilling out onto the concourse above. And the event was every bit as festive and euphoric as those involving their grandchildren. As they toured the base paths, the seniors laughed and joked, hamming it up for pictures that documented this distinctively American activity. The musical accompaniment wafting through the PA system? A Sinatra medley, followed by Wayne Newton singing "Danke Schoen" ("Bueller?...Bueller?"). There was just one posted rule: No SLIDING.

It had been a worthy dry run, but the next day was the Big One. So there was no such thing as being too early for the game. As enjoyable as watching opening-round coverage of the NCAA Tournament was, Kels and I had no remorse about leaving March Madness behind in Scottsdale's Fox Sports Grill at 3:45 PM for the 7:05 PM first pitch that would begin Event #100—the game between the Angels and the Giants. After all, we had almost ten miles to travel.

Some 20 minutes later we pulled into a *free* parking lot adjacent to Scottsdale Stadium—an absolute gem of an old-school downtown ballpark. We were by no means alone in our eagerness. It would be another 45 minutes until the gates would open, but already there were hundreds of people milling around, despite the fact that all 11,622 tickets had long since been sold. These people, like us, just wanted to get inside and drink up the atmosphere as soon as possible.

Scottsdale Stadium is one of the original Cactus League venues, serving since 1992 as the spring-training home of the Giants. It's an environment that already screams authenticity, but this year it was augmented by the unmistakable swagger that goes with being the reigning World Series champions. It wasn't a puffed chest "Yes, we're all that" bluster, though; it was more an air of quiet confidence. Giants fans greeted each other as if they were part of an ancient secret society. I wouldn't have been surprised in the least to learn that a special handshake or code word was being exchanged surreptitiously all around me. If that was the case, Kels was dialed in to it. As the undisputed biggest Giants fan in New York's Upper Hudson Valley, he had earned his stripes.

When the gates opened, Kels peeled off to join the full-scale assault on the team merchandise store. I took the opportunity to peruse the starting lineups that had been posted on a humble erasable whiteboard on the concourse—and quickly became confused. Under the heading of VISITORS was a long list of names that I didn't recognize. I initially thought that a mistake had been made. Maybe nobody had updated the board from the previous day's game? But then I saw ANGELS written at the top and Haren in the starting pitcher's spot, and I knew that for whatever reason, the team had chosen to field a squad of rookies and minor-leaguers—including four guys whom I'd never even *heard of*—for this momentous game. Evidently manager Mike Scioscia hadn't been tracking the online IGTS Tour itinerary.

It was a fairly rare spring-training night game, and when combined with St. Patrick's Day, a unique vibe was in the air. You got the feeling that you might see just about anything. And sure enough, as we rounded the concourse onto the third-base side of the stadium, "just about anything" took the form of Bill Buckner, who was there as part of a group of retired baseball stars who were populating an autograph-signing booth.

There is probably no baseball player in history whose name is more closely linked to disaster and heartbreak than Bill Buckner. Every man, woman, and child remotely familiar with baseball has seen the replay of the ground ball skittering through his legs in the 1986 World Series. The man was hounded out of New England, and only two World Series titles in four years softened hardcore Red Sox fans enough to "forgive" him. Buckner has experienced the absolute worst side of baseball, yet there he was, relaxed and engaging as he chatted with fans and contemporaries, such as Rollie Fingers and Gaylord Perry. Have I mentioned that spring training is all about renewal?

As for the game itself…well, I'd love to tell you all about how a scrappy bunch of Angels unknowns came out and blistered the pitching of the World Series champs—I really would. But a smart reader like yourself would uncover that lie soon enough. The game was every bit as devoid of offense from the Halos as I had anticipated. But while the prospects for an Angels win (or even an extra-base hit) became more remote with each inning, the social situation in Section 213 was hitting full stride. It was like the neighborhoods depicted in beer commercials—full of smart, witty people watching sports together. And friendly? I've seen *Up With People* productions that were more standoffish. Had it been a doubleheader, Kels might have wound up on the ballot for San Francisco's next Board of Supervisors election.

As informal group conversation began to reveal to others the IGTS quest—and the place that this game occupied within the Tour—new friends began to offer congratulations, share similar stories, and provide suggestions for future endeavors. I had gone to a baseball game and a focus group had sprung up.

Spring-training uniform numbers exhibit a basic pecking order—the higher the number, the less likely it is that the player wearing it will be plying his trade in the major leagues come Opening Day. Thus, in the bottom of the eighth inning when the Angels sent out a trio of outfielders whose uniform numbers averaged 83.3, any hope I had of a spirited comeback quickly deflated.

At 9:14 PM an anonymous Angel wearing number 81 flied out to center field, and it was official—the It's Game Time Somewhere Tour was over. The Halos had mustered just two measly hits in a 4–0 loss. On the bright side, however, Kels and I had received invitations to two weddings, a bar mitzvah celebration, and a half-dozen backyard barbeques.

To pin the Surreal-O-Meter firmly in the red, in the street outside the stadium I ran into Ashley Kettmann (née Gomes), a professional golfer with whom I'd had the pleasure of working for three tour seasons. "What are you doing *here?*" she asked innocently. So I told her. I think she was still struggling to process my answer when the taxi carrying her and her new husband pulled away.

As the cab's tail lights receded down the street, it occurred to me that fresh reminders of all three of my reframed relationships with sports had popped up at various times that evening.

Like this, for example: Ashley was no longer a tour pro, having decided to direct her energy instead into founding a series of golf camps for women that would help them to…well…to just play. Evidently she too had discovered that golf is best when done for fun and, like me, felt a desire to create the opportunity for a sports community to blossom.

Then there was the elephant in the room—my presence at the game itself. Major League Baseball had been the only Big-Time Sport that I'd been hesitant to write off attending. I had been concerned that my embrace of the Smaller Is Better philosophy might, as an unintended consequence, sour me forever on the very first pro sport I'd ever given my heart to. And while that evening's MLB contest wasn't an actual full-fledged regular-season contest, I knew it would be a good proxy. To my immense relief, the game had come through with flying colors. Whether it was the low-key atmosphere, the camaraderie of my fellow fans, or my recent coming to terms with the sports world at large, I was able to sit back and enjoy having the entire event wash warmly over me.

Maybe it had something to do with this: not a minute had gone by that evening without my wanting to climb down onto the field and (a) play catch with anyone who appeared willing; (b) take over infield practice, rapping out sharp ground balls while barking out things like, "Let's get two!"; and (c) conduct my own Not-Quite Senior, Not-Quite Stroll around the bases—completely ignoring the No SLIDING rule in the process. This gut-level connection with my Game Junkie hadn't appeared at a baseball game in a long, long time.

Ironic, I thought, *how my new focus on playing sports has enhanced my experience of watching sports.* In fact, irony lay almost everywhere I'd turned that evening. Prior to the start of the game, when Kels and I were wandering the concourse soaking it all in, we came upon a little oasis that offered us a great view of right field, where players were stretching out and warming up just a few yards away. There we met Pam, who was in her second night of staffing a standalone beer concession. Pam had recently relocated from Spokane to Phoenix in search of—what else—a fresh start, and she knew her sports. She asked if we had any scores for the late-afternoon NCAA games, and a lively discussion about college basketball ensued. It turned out that she was wearing her team allegiance on her sleeve—or something akin to that. She took off a sneaker, revealing, to my startled amazement, Gonzaga University socks. The very same Gonzaga University whose upset loss to Loyola Marymount more than a year earlier had started the ball rolling on this whole crazy walkabout!

Part of the beginning was there to greet me at the end.

A few days later, at 12:37 PDT on March 31st, I hit the PUBLISH button on my Wordpress screen, and the final blog post about the final event of the IGTS Tour had been completed. Exactly 33 minutes later, third baseman Maicer Izturis stepped into the batter's box in Kansas City to face the Royals' Luke Hochevar and start the 2011 Los Angeles Angels season.

End and beginning. A new cycle had started.

ACKNOWLEDGMENTS

THIS JUST IN——you need a lot of support, encouragement, and assistance to write a book, especially one that entails traveling some 40,000 miles in the air and another 16,000 on the ground. So for starters, I'd like to thank everyone I know and anyone I encountered along the way who thought to themselves, *This guy is out of his mind*...but never said it to me out loud.

In addition to a certain amount of lunacy, you also need a lot of passion for a project like this. For me, that was instilled many moons ago, when my dad shared with me his love of sports and my mom passed along to me her love of books. Both were gifts for a lifetime.

And while we're on the topic of family members, I want to express my appreciation to my cousins Ginny Lehman and Dick Grider for introducing me to the extraordinary author Steven Pressfield, whose novel *The Legend of Bagger Vance* has long been a favorite of mine. Another of Pressfield's books, *The War of Art*, is required reading for anyone who has ever seriously considered becoming a writer, and I consider myself fortunate to have had the opportunity to discuss with him several of the topics in that book. I want to thank Steve both for his words of encouragement and for treating me from the beginning like a colleague instead of the fledgling writer that I was at the time.

The UCLA Extension Writers' Program features a number of top-notch teachers, and Lisa Cron is among the best. She played a major role in the development of this book, as it was in her classroom that I began to wrap my arms around the not-so-simple task of crafting an actual *story* out of the marginally connected hundreds of thousands of written words that I had accumulated during the It's Game Time Somewhere Tour. Lisa's simple but essential question, "And so…?" has been with me every time I've put fingers to keyboard since then.

In the area of unselfish assistance I want to recognize Eric Beck, Jerry Huffman, and Ken Kottke for agreeing to serve as advance readers (aka, guinea pigs) for the first incarnation of this book, and I *especially* want to thank the supremely talented writer Megan Floyd for her tremendously honest, supportive, and thought-provoking feedback as she labored word-by-word through my initial manuscript. Somehow Megan always managed to make me feel upbeat about my writing at the same time she was saying, "Tim, you need major surgery on this section—it doesn't work."

In today's brave new world of publishing, an author needs to be more than just a writer to make a book a viable commercial endeavor, and I want to thank those who shared their expertise with me toward that end. Christine Mercer and Debbie Slutsky put me on the right track by introducing me to the wonderful, indispensable world of blogging and social media. Jeff Coon, Brian Brinkman, and everyone at Stream Creative (simply the best boutique inbound marketing agency in America) enabled me to not only attract thousands of visitors to the IGTS website and YouTube channel but also to toss off acronyms like SEO in casual conversation. Jerry Huffman at Go2Guy Communications has been just that—my go-to guy for all things related to media, public relations, and promotion. His expertise and years of experience, coupled with his heartfelt desire to see me succeed, have been invaluable. And of course I would be remiss if I didn't mention entrepreneur extraordinaire Tamar Vezirian, who on a Cape Cod beach first uttered to me the magic word: Kickstarter.

I also want to express my sincere gratitude to all of those brave souls who ventured into the grandstands or bleachers with me at one or another of the events that made up this crazy venture. Trust me on this—even though you're constantly surrounded by people, a sports walkabout can get pretty lonely at times. Just when I needed company the most, one or more of the project's "unindicted co-conspirators" would volunteer to come along. Serial offenders included John Cook, Ken Fisher, Rick Guerreri, Chris Kelly, Chris Schlacter, and the tireless Chris Osche, who was present at the very beginning and, still undaunted, came back several times for more.

And finally...The Bird. My wife Cheryl is the quintessential partner in all of life's challenging journeys, self-imposed or otherwise. Her understanding and tolerance for a husband who can be counted on for at least one totally off-the-wall idea per decade is immeasurable. As well as barely conceivable. Hey, even *I* couldn't imagine being married to me—and I'm certifiably nuts! There's only one thing that I can count on in life more than Cheryl's love and support, and that is her upcoming annoyance with me for singling her out for recognition in this manner. Am I the luckiest guy in the world, or what?

Tim Forbes
Redondo Beach, California
June 5, 2012